The Polka Dot File

on the Robert F. Kennedy Killing

— PARIS PEACE TALKS CONNECTION —

FERNANDO FAURA

Published by:
Trine Day LLC
PO Box 577
Walterville, OR 97489
1-800-556-2012
www.TrineDay.com
publisher@TrineDay.net

Library of Congress Control Number: 2016935447

Faura, Fernando.
—1st ed.
p. cm.
Includes references and index.
Epud (ISBN-13) 978-1-63424-060-4
Mobi (ISBN-13) 978-1-63424-061-1
Print (ISBN-13) 978-1-63424-059-8
1. Kennedy, Robert F., -- (Robert Francis). 2. Sirhan, Sirhan Bishara, -- 1944-.
3. Conspiracies -- United States -- History -- 20th century. 1925-1968 -- Assassination. I. Faura, Fernando. II. Title

PHOTO CREDITS: PAGE IV-PUBLIC DOMAIN; PAGE 4 © BILL EPPRIDGE, GETTY IMAGES; PAGE 8 © POPPERFOTO/BORIS YARO, GETTY IMAGES.

FIRST EDITION
10 9 8 7 6 5 4 3 2 1

Printed in the USA
Distribution to the Trade by:
Independent Publishers Group (IPG)
814 North Franklin Street
Chicago, Illinois 60610
312.337.0747
www.ipgbook.com

There are those that look at things the way they are, and ask why? I dream of things that never were, and ask why not.

It is from numberless diverse acts of courage and belief that human history is shaped. Each time a man stands up for an ideal, or acts to improve the lot of others, or strikes out against injustice, he sends forth a tiny ripple of hope, and crossing each other from a million different centers of energy and daring those ripples build a current which can sweep down the mightiest walls of oppression and injustice.

What is objectionable, what is dangerous, about extremists is not that they are extreme, but that they are intolerant. The evil is not what they say about their cause, but what they say about their opponents.

Few will have the greatness to bend history itself; but each of us can work to change a small portion of events, and in the total; of all those acts will be written the history of this generation.

– Robert Francis Kennedy
11/20/25 – 6/6/68

To my children: Keli Jacobson, my gentle, loving eldest with a heart of gold for humanity; Carlos Faura, the most courageous, determined person I have ever met; Denise Bohdan, my talented and devoted daughter, a crusading lawyer for human rights; and Adam Faura, an adventurous, businessman risk-taker who never met a mountain he could not climb.

C 6- 5 -68 LOS ANGELES POLICE
J -68
BK 495 139

4204DEF94

PREFACE

In the first few minutes of June 6, 1968, Sirhan Sirhan, a Palestinian youth, shot at Sen. Robert F. Kennedy as he passed through the kitchen of the Ambassador Hotel in Los Angeles. There is credible evidence that there was a second gun firing, raising doubts about who killed the Senator.

Seconds after the shooting stopped, a young woman in a polka-dot dress ran out of the kitchen, past Sandra Serrano, a Kennedy campaign worker. The woman shouted, "We shot him, we shot him." Asked who they shot, the woman replied, "Kennedy," and she ran into the morning darkness and history, never to be found.

Early in the investigation, witnesses reported having seen her in several places inside the hotel, accompanied by Sirhan and two other men.

Today Sirhan, in his appeal for a re-trial, claims to have been a "Manchurian Candidate" and the "Girl in the Polka-Dot Dress" his trigger – a "Manchurian Candidate" being a person induced to commit murder while under hypnosis.

This book concerns itself only with my first-person experience. I was then a reporter with the *Hollywood Citizen News*, and I spent many hours hunting for the mysterious "polka-dot girl" – long after the police lied about her existence, saying there was no such person, because they had failed to find her.

Here is the day-to-day account of my hunt for the mystery woman. The story here is a firsthand narrative of my personal, detailed investigation, recorded as it happened. It includes actual, accurate transcripts of interviews I conducted before the police or the FBI intimidated the witnesses into changing their stories. FBI and Los Angeles police records clearly show that my investigation was more advanced than theirs.

"The girl in the polka-dot dress" remains a mystery today. Yet many know she is the key to solving the Robert F. Kennedy killing.

Who was she? What was her role in the assassination?

Other than Sandra Serrano, did anyone else link her to the assassination? Will she ever be identified or found? Or is the truth gone with her, lost forever?

Robert A. Houghton, Chief of Detectives of the Los Angeles Police Department stated: "That woman will haunt me for the rest of my life," an assertion he would likely deny ever making in the wake of the cover-up.

It is a sentiment many of us live with. What is notable about Houghton's remark is not that he is puzzled about that woman, but that the declaration was made weeks after the Los Angeles District Attorney and the LAPD had publicly denied the existence of "that woman."

Who was this mysterious lady, capable of haunting a hard-nosed police official and driving a host of no-nonsense investigative reporters and FBI agents to the heights of frustration?

The "Girl in the Polka-dot Dress."

Was she part of a conspiracy? It is not known who she was working with when she shouted, "We shot him, we shot him." But my firsthand account of the first days of the investigation will provide insights to the intriguing circumstances that led to a multi-agency manhunt for the "girl in the polka-dot dress."

My investigation began with a piece I wrote shortly after the assassination that placed Sirhan and the "girl in the polka-dot dress" at another political party at the Ambassador Hotel earlier in the evening, before the shooting. That spurred a full-blown worldwide search, and the involvement of the highest levels of our government, to find the mystery woman.

For more than forty-five years my children have urged me to write a book chronicling my investigation. At the time risks to my family were too high to bring the story public. I was pursuing very powerful people who did not want me nosing around.

I was followed, spied on and harassed. Manny Pena, the detective in charge of the investigation, was a CIA front and falsified records regarding my involvement in the investigation. Because my children were so young and precious to me, I decided to stop pursuing the story after *Life* magazine, with whom I had been collaborating, killed the investigation because of a call from White House officials, who asked that it be stopped due to "national security reasons" – or so *Life*'s bureau chief in Los Angeles told me.

I did share me information freely with other researchers – Robert Kaiser, John Christian, William Turner and Theodore "Teddy" Charach, to name a few. Most of the information I shared was eventually published in various books on the subject, and some authors have done an outstanding job exposing details of the coverup. But never has the story been told firsthand from the man who did the most important interviews and uncovered what is known of the "girl in the polka-dot dress."

The story of many witnesses never made it into the pages of the other books, because the LAPD did not reveal their existence and never recorded their interviews. Those witnesses whose stories gave life to the existence of the "girl in the polka-dot dress," and her declaration. "We shot him, we shot him," were bullied and pressured into changing their statements as police records revealed twenty years later when they were ordered released to the public.

This book will give you the evidence straight from my investigation, and from the police and FBI records. All of the books, and two documentaries on the assassination feature my work with John Fahey, an important witness who spent the day before the assassination with the "girl in the polka-dot dress."

Fahey told his story first to the FBI and then to me. I arranged for him to tell the LAPD. Initially a star witness, he was later – without explanation – bullied, pressured and discredited by the LAPD. Why do that to such an important witness? If they had given his testimony the importance it deserved, they would have discovered the link between the "girl in the polka-dot dress" and the Nixon conspiracy to scuttle the Paris Peace Talks.

After *Life* magazine shut down the investigation, I put it all behind me, until recently, when in 2013 I saw an article about Sirhan's new defense on appeal, asserting he was a "Manchurian Candidate." That got my attention.

The same day, and by coincidence, surfing the Internet I ran into mentions of several books written about Richard Nixon's conspiracy to scuttle the Paris Peace Talks. When I read the names of the Nixon co-conspirators, I was shocked and stunned to recognize one of them as a person the "girl in the polka-dot dress" had mentioned as having met in New York, just three days before the assassination. That spurred me to renew my investigation. I reviewed my notes and tapes and decided to publish this firsthand account.

The time has finally arrived for me. I feel responsibility to complete the record of such a seminal moment in American political history. In doing so I want to thank Lisa Pease and Shane O'Sullivan, fearless investigators, for their encouragement.

My children finally get their wish, and this book is dedicated to them.

PROLOGUE

Within minutes of Senator Robert F. Kennedy being shot, witnesses' statements to reporters at the scene indicated there had been a conspiracy.

Sandra Serrano, a young Kennedy worker, focused on "a woman in a polka-dot dress" and a "Latin looking" companion.

A "second gun" theory, with physical evidence to add credibility to it, has also emerged.

Some of the answers have been found, while others are still elusive.

A clear pattern has taken shape. Many sober and clear-thinking investigators have sadly concluded and agreed on the meaning of some of their independent findings.

For the next few weeks, interest in the mysterious woman heightened. Police forces in the United States presumably launched an international search for the woman, as other witnesses came forward to confirm her existence.

On June 21, Evelle Younger, District Attorney for Los Angeles County, issued a statement that the "girl in the polka-dot dress" was a figment of Sandra Serrano's imagination. So, long before the investigation of the assassination would be over, the authorities attempted to squash speculation of a possible conspiracy. The existence of the girl was denied in spite of the fact that numerous other witnesses had seen her and some claimed she was in the company of Sirhan Sirhan, the accused assassin, early in the evening.

More significantly, the Special Unit Senator (SUS), an elite group of investigators assembled from all police specialties to investigate the killing, already had transcripts, tapes, and personal interviews of a local salesman who alleged to have spent June 4 with a woman who allegedly had prior knowledge of the killing about to take place. Eventually, another witness identified this woman as "the girl in the polka-dot dress."

FBI agents, displaying somewhat more talent than the SUS unit, maintained a feverish search for the girl even after the statements by police and district attorney investigators had branded her a figment of someone's imagination.

Private investigations by local news reporters and a national magazine managed to uncover reliable witnesses and more clues which strengthened the theory of the "polka-dot girl's" involvement in the assassination before police deliberately and methodically throttled those investigations and attempted to prevent the dissemination of those findings to the public. As the SUS unit and other authorities recovered from the original disarray and shock, considerable time was spent in discrediting legitimate witnesses, pressuring others to change their testimony, suppressing information that pointed to a conspiracy and introducing into the record unverified and fabricated information that would discredit the findings of the independent investigators. Expediency, or perhaps lack of talent, caused much of the bungled police attempt at "covering up" this huge fraud being perpetrated on the American people for a second time, the first being the sham investigation of the assassination of President John F. Kennedy.

Typical of such researchers are Robert Kaiser and Michael McCowan.

Kaiser secured the rights to publish the biography of Sirhan Sirhan, convicted assassin of the senator, shortly after the killing. His privileged position as an investigator for the defense gave him access to Sirhan in prison and to most of the investigative documents and information collected by the FBI and the LAPD.

Because of this vantage point, Kaiser has become one of the few men familiar with all the aspects of the case. Most other investigators, at one time exceeding 1,000, never learned as much about the case as Kaiser.

This young writer's position as part of the defense team and Sirhan's official biographer, in the long run led to a conflict in his conscience.

Evidence accumulated that his subject was not telling all, and that the police hid, disguised and fabricated information that went into the official record. A religious man of principles, Kaiser chose to tell the true story.

In his book, *RFK Must Die: The Assassination of Bobby Kennedy*, Kaiser raises the first serious on-the-record challenge to the police farce that passed for a thorough investigation.

Michael McCowan, possibly the only man with more knowledge of the assassination and its subsequent investigation than Kaiser, now finds himself in the same quandary. Chosen as an "investigator-attorney" for the defense team, McCowan not only had access to all the material Kaiser did, but also drew the task of correcting the daily transcripts of the trial.

McCowan was, for a while, the investigator of record during Sirhan's appeal motions. McCowan insists there is no solid evidence that Sirhan was involved in a conspiracy. He also admits that Sirhan appears to be holding back information and that there are wide gaps in the investigation which still "are driving the police mad." He claims to maintain an open mind to the theory of a conspiracy.

More importantly, McCowan claims the defense team discovered important evidence that the police had suppressed and not made available to the defense. He claims Sirhan's defense had to sue for such evidence allegedly denied by the police in violation of court instructions during discovery proceedings.

McCowan supports Kaiser's contention that the police acted most irregularly, to say the least, and that the investigation was a sorry performance by a reputedly efficient police department.

It is of more than passing interest that the assassinations of John and Robert Kennedy and the ensuing investigations are uncannily familiar. After the assassination, the script followed by the investigating agencies in charge is very similar. It can be easily proven not only that leads existed that pointed towards a conspiracy, but also that the police and the District Attorney's office, with all due deliberation, steered away from them and, when necessary, suppressed or distorted such evidence. In other instances, police inserted into the record information which was clearly erroneous, if not fabricated outright.

The main thrust of this line of inquiry is better appreciated when one realizes that both assassinations occurred in cities whose police forces bask in the adulation and strong support of a large right-wing constituency.

In fact, sufficient evidence exists that Sirhan Sirhan was tracking Senator Kennedy and that the killing could have occurred in San Diego, another bastion of conservatism. It is generally held that the police forces in Dallas, Los Angeles and San Diego are fairly well infiltrated by ultra-conservative elements.

Other witnesses and clues that support a conspiracy theory weave and blend in an obvious pattern from which no reasonable person can turn away.

Here then is the fascinating factual story, never told before, of the chase for the elusive, mysterious "girl in the polka-dot dress." For readability, the story is told in the third person.

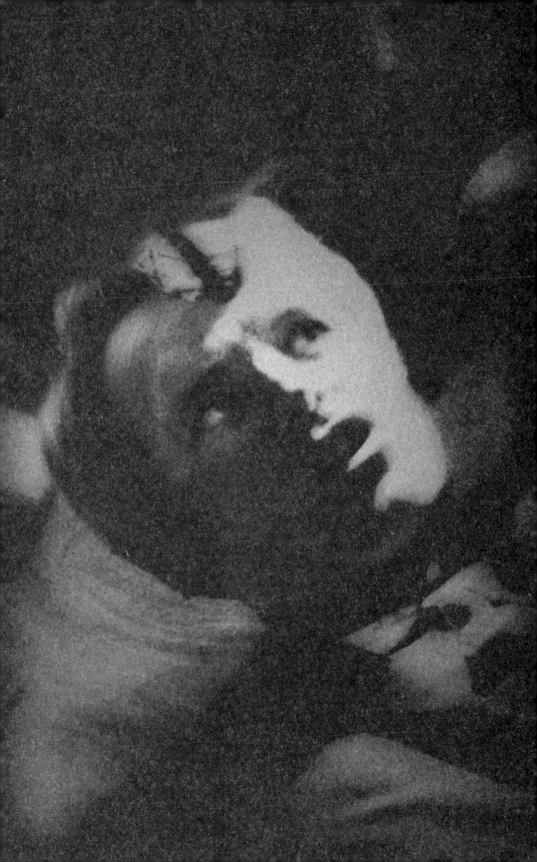

Chapter 1

Seen running away from the scene of the assassination of Senator Robert F. Kennedy, she reportedly cried, "We shot him. We shot him."

Sandra (Sandy) Serrano, a young Kennedy campaign worker from Pasadena, asked the mysterious woman as she ran by, "Who did you shoot?"

"Senator Kennedy," was the reply.

With that, the woman and a male companion ran out into the early morning darkness and into the same cloak that envelopes other clues that could provide answers to other modern American assassinations.

"That woman will haunt me for the rest of my life," said Robert Houghton, LAPD chief of detectives, in an unguarded statement to a respected member of the press not long after the assassination of Robert F. Kennedy. At that time a handful of tenacious newsmen were still looking for "the girl in the polka-dot dress."

They were not alone. The FBI, close-mouthed and single-minded as ever, also was frantically looking for the girl, perhaps as much to solve the mystery as to make up for amateurish and careless mistakes made early in the investigation.

But where does the "girl in the polka-dot dress" fit in the assassination puzzle?

To answer that question, we must go back to the first few minutes of June 5, 1968, at the Ambassador Hotel, 3400 Wilshire Blvd., Los Angeles – the tragic time and place when an assassin's bullet slammed into the brain of Senator Robert F. Kennedy.

Shortly after midnight, after Kennedy's brief victory speech to supporters gathered in the Embassy Room of the hotel, his staff spontaneously changed plans and led the victorious senator through the hotel's kitchen, instead of along a different prearranged route.

There, lurking in the shadows of his own aberrations, a small man with big ideas reached out and shot at the Senator.

Just outside the hotel where the shots were fired, a young Mexican-American Kennedy worker had been taking some fresh air, looking for relief from the heat inside and the throng of people bulging out of the doors of the Embassy Room.

Sandy Serrano was just coming back inside when she heard what she thought were car backfires. Seconds later, a young woman wearing a polka-dot dress rushed by crying, "We shot him."

Startled, Serrano asked, "Who did you shoot?" The fleeing girls answered: "Senator Kennedy."

Serrano noticed a man running out with the girl, a man she described as "Latin looking."

This was the story Serrano told before television cameras shortly after the shooting. It was the story heard by millions of viewers as they watched in stunned disbelief at the realization that the "City of Angels" had become another Dallas.

In the kitchen, the assailant had been pummeled, subdued and disarmed while police cars raced to the Ambassador Hotel.

Confusion was the order of the day. Shocked, emotional Kennedy followers became immobilized by the impact of the news. One such person was Serrano.

Instead of following the fleeing couple or calling for help to stop them, she rushed to where the action was, and "the girl in the polka-dot dress" vanished into the darkness.

Two-and-a-half hours after the shooting, a police all-points bulletin was broadcast for "the girl in the polka-dot dress."

The search was on.

Chapter 2

A s most newsmen know, there are certain stories which, in spite of the newsman's determined efforts to shy away from them, seem to search them out, unyielding in their persistence.

It is as if the story goes to rest at night in the same bed where the newsman goes to rest his nosy bones.

The "girl in the polka dot dress" was such a case for Fernando Faura, investigative reporter for the *Hollywood Citizen News*, the second oldest newspaper in Los Angeles at the time.

Faura had not cherished working the evening of June 4th, 1968. In charge of the news bureau for the *Hollywood Citizen News/Valley Times*, his assignment was to cover the race for the California Assembly 41st District seat between incumbent David Negri and Henry "Hank" Arklin.

The silliness, noise and pompous, sometimes vulgar, behavior of precinct workers and parasitic "free booze" seekers were enough to make any serious man cringe.

The evening was being made bearable for Faura by a young man who had been actively engaged in the Kennedy campaign and whose brother was making prodigious research efforts to prove that their family was related to the Kennedys.

Full of energy, innocence and extraordinary ambition, Luke Perry of San Fernando had done an outstanding job of getting out the Mexican-American vote for Kennedy, and he had teamed up with Faura for the evening to visit the Negri and Arklin headquarters – Perry to participate in the excitement, Faura to suffer through the ritual necessary to file his stories.

During the campaign, Faura had used Perry's contact with the Kennedy advance team to relay word of a brewing and potentially embarrassing situation for the senator, which was bubbling out of a cesspool of political skulduggery by some black politicians in South East Los Angeles.

Flushed with his new found importance, and justifiably proud of the job he had done for the man he believed to be his "cousin," Luke Perry was in a mood for celebration.

Being the owner of the most comfortable car, Perry became the driver for the long evening. After a brief visit with Arklin, clearly the winner of the race by this time, the two headed for "Negri's wake."

Cruising on Sepulveda Boulevard in Mission Hills, in the North San Fernando Valley, home of the historical Mission of San Fernando, Perry turned on the car radio.

The news of Senator's Kennedy shooting hit their brains like bullets coming through the windshield.

"Oh, god damn it; not again, not again; not him," Perry's heartbreaking cry was as heart rending as the news itself. The on-the-spot broadcast, with its background pandemonium and the unaccustomed, unprofessional excitement in the newscaster's voice, gave the shocking news a B-movie quality.

As they raced to Negri's headquarters, twenty miles away, the Senator was rushed to Central Receiving Hospital in Los Angeles, his life running out of a head wound.

At 12:30 A.M., an aluminum table in Room 2 received the body of the dying senator, nearly pulseless, blood pressure dangerously low.

Dr. V. F. Bazilauskas immediately began his futile attempt to save the senator. Having raised his blood pressure through emergency procedures, Dr. Bazilauskas determined that brain surgery was required. With no blood bank and inadequate X-ray facilities, Central Receiving was out of the question for the operation needed.

At 12:50 Dr. Bazilauskas prepared the patient for the trip to Good Samaritan Hospital – "Good Sam" – a short distance away.

At Negri's headquarters, it appeared that everybody was or had been crying. Faura's hurried phone call to his city desk determined that Gay Scott, then political editor for the *Hollywood Citizen News,* was at the Ambassador. Another reporter for the newspaper was at Good Samaritan Hospital.

Without a specific assignment for Faura, he and Perry went to "Good Sam" where security was very tight. Police, news media and scores of citizens had started a vigil and anxiously waited for news of the senator's condition.

Perry and Faura left the crowd and headed for Police LAPD headquarters, a few miles to the east, where Chief of Police, Thomas Reddin, would be holding a press conference around 3 A.M. It was 20 minutes to three at the time.

Security at police headquarters was also very tight. Newsmen were frisked before being allowed to enter the building. Press credentials were carefully checked, flashlights going from the photograph enclosed in press credentials on the ID to the face. Briefcases and even tape recorders were inspected.

Not having press credentials, Perry had to stay outside with the crowd. Chief Reddin went through what was already known and revealed that the assailant had no identification on him and refused to identify himself.

He described the accused assassin as small, Latin-looking and of unknown racial extraction. He said there was not much more information at the time. He did not reveal that the LAPD was well on the way to identifying the assailant through the weapon he had used. The chief also claimed that he had personally spoken with the assailant – the first lie of many more to come.

At "Good Sam," Dr. Henry M. Cuneo, assisted by Dr. Maxwell M. Andler both of the University of California, Los Angeles (UCLA) were removing a two-inch section of the bone adjacent to the gunshot wound.

Perry, in his own personal anguish and vigil, placed himself close to the policemen guarding the entrance to police headquarters, so that he could obtain as much information as possible, under the circumstances. This later proved to be an excellent strategy on his part and a stroke of luck for the press.

As soon as he had questioned Faura about what went on at the press conference, Perry told Faura the following story:

"There were people trying to get into the building with all kinds of stories, but I think one of them might be important. See what you think.

"A young guy, college type, came to the policeman at the door and said he had some information that might be important and that he wanted to talk about it. The officer asked what it was, and the youth said that he had seen a minor incident that occurred at the Rafferty rally upstairs at the Ambassador. He observed that a man who appeared to be Latin- looking, or foreign-looking, and who looked rather suspicious, had an altercation at the hotel and was possibly frisked by one of the security guards.

"He (the youth) thought it was significant that the same man who was turned away up there was also seen at the Kennedy party downstairs by himself.

"The policemen at the door didn't think it was important and said that they would take care of it and turned the youth away.

"He was a young man, between 20 and 23 years old," Perry concluded; as it turned out, it was the lead to an important witness.

CHAPTER 3

The North Valley Bureau of the *Hollywood Citizen News/Valley Times* was housed in the police station in the small community of San Fernando. Around 8 A.M. on the morning of June 5, an anonymous call was received at the station.

The caller, a woman, had claimed that the man involved in the Kennedy shooting was a fry cook named Jesse and that this man worked at Tony's Drive In, which at one time had been called Truman's Drive In." She said, "It is located at Westwood and Wilshire Boulevard in West Los Angeles."

About 11:30 A.M., a police officer, who shall remain anonymous, for obvious reasons, informed Faura that he had been calling Faura's office to tip him off to the call.

Faura made a note of the information with little interest, since the same officer told him that the suspect had already been identified as Sirhan Bishara Sirhan, a native of Jordan.

A short drive took Faura to the Highlander Sanatorium in the course of his regular duties. A somber mood prevailed there, and conversation quickly turned to the events of the previous night.

Robert Christopher, administrator of the sanatorium, had been watching television the night before, and he told of seeing a Mexican-American girl on the news immediately after the shooting, telling "about a woman in a white dress and a man who was Latin-looking running through one of the hallways when she had gone out to get some air, because it was hot inside."

This was the first time Faura had heard this story, since he had not had any opportunity to watch television the night before, and the June 5 morning papers did not carry the story of the "girl in the polka-dot dress."

Christopher's story was somewhat more interesting since it provided a Latin-looking man running in the corridor with the woman, at the same time that the assailant was being subdued.

Faura returned to his office at the San Fernando Police station and called a friend at the Intelligence Division of the LAPD to tell him about the anonymous call.

His friend was not in and would not be returning for the next few days, so arrangements were made to meet with another member of the Intelligence Division. Since they did not know each other, the officer suggested, and Faura agreed, to some cloak and dagger procedures so they would recognize each other at the time of the meeting, which was to be in front of the NBC television studios in Burbank. Faura felt rather silly and a little embarrassed about the James Bond ritual, but later on learned to live with it and accepted the need for extreme security.

More details on Sirhan and the assassination were coming to light. Los Angeles Mayor Sam Yorty had visited the Ramparts police station and told the press of reading a notebook in which Sirhan had written, "Kennedy must be assassinated before June 5th, 1968." The newspapers noted that this was the anniversary of the Six-Day War, in which Israel had humiliated three Arab neighbors. Friends and acquaintances of Sirhan described him as "a nice boy" with rabid, fanatical anti-Israel feelings.

Chief Reddin declared that he saw no indications of a conspiracy: A strange statement to make, since he must have been aware of the report of the "girl in the polka-dot dress" and Sirhan's notebook.

The notebook, according to Yorty, contained "many statements about assassinating Senator Kennedy" as well as notes that showed the suspect to be pro-Nasser and pro-communist.

Police revealed that, at the time of the arrest, Sirhan had in his possession four one-hundred-dollar bills, one five and four singles, as well as two newspaper clippings and Kennedy's traveling schedule in California.

At Good Sam, the senator's condition was listed as extremely critical. By 6:30 P.M. his brain cells would begin to die.

At 1:44 the next morning, the promising presidential candidate died. Dr. Thomas Noguchi, Los Angeles County Medical Examiner, prepared for a meticulous autopsy.

The fatal bullet had struck the mastoid bone behind his right ear at a 45-degree angle and entered the rear portion of his skull. The amazing thing," said Dr. Noguchi, "is that he lived as long as he did."

The gun used by Sirhan and the bullets fired from it were later to become the subject of a controversy and a grand jury investigation.

Noguchi failed to say that Evelle Younger, the Los Angeles District Attorney, had called him to say that a thorough autopsy was not necessary. Younger did not say why he made such a strange request.

Perry went to the San Fernando Bureau on the morning of June 6. He told of seeing two men on a local television show talking about the shooting, and he recounted the story of the young man he had seen at police headquarters telling about the incident at the Rafferty party. In circulating among his political friends, Perry had also learned that the decision to move Kennedy through the kitchen had been spontaneous.

At exactly three minutes past 2 o'clock that afternoon, a young man waited for the traffic light to change at Olive Street in Burbank in front of the NBC-TV studios. A black briefcase sat on the sidewalk next to him.

When the light changed, he did not cross, but smoothed back his hair, letting Faura know he was the police intelligence contact. A few moments later they were sitting together at a nearby restaurant. He was told about Perry's story and the anonymous call to the San Fernando Police Department.

They decided to call "the man in charge of the investigation" so Faura could talk to him immediately.

They left Burbank and drove immediately within two blocks of the Ramparts police station, where the investigation was headquartered. They parked Faura's car and proceeded to the station in the officer's car.

Since the station was teeming with reporters and many other people, he told Faura to wait in the men's room. He soon returned and told Faura it would be impossible to meet with "the man" in his office, and Faura was directed to the parking lot. Faura complied, recognizing the need for security and a burning desire for an exclusive.

"The man" was waiting in his car when Faura got there. He took notes of the conversation and said that they had "many similar leads to check."

Tony's Drive In being on the way back to San Fernando, Faura informed him that he was going to check out the anonymous call lead.

"I can't stop you," he remarked. "Just be careful."

Journalistic instinct forced the reporter to gamble a question: "Why haven't you released a description of the man you are looking for?"

"What makes you think we are looking for a man?" he asked, mildly surprised.

"It is obvious. It's almost a matter of record after radio and television have been blaring the story about a woman crying 'We shot him' as she fled with a man."

"The man" sort of smiled as he said, "Well, we do not want to let it out."

Indications that Sirhan had possibly discussed the assassination with somebody prior to committing the act and that police might know the identity of the assassin's confidant was also learned from the discussion. There were also hints that the police might be close to apprehending him.

As they parted, "the man" reminded Faura to make sure he was not followed after checking the lead. The thought of a conspiracy fueled Faura forward.

CHAPTER 4

The intersection of Wilshire and Westwood Boulevards is west Los Angeles' version of Hollywood's famed Sunset and Vine.

A few blocks to the north, the University of California, Los Angeles reigns like a fat monarch holding court among the many businesses and manicured apartment houses in an area called Westwood.

Tony's Drive In, nestling on the southeast corner, was already a fading queen that had not kept up with the times. A modern coffee shop across the street lured away many of its customers and new high-rise office buildings frowned down upon it. The drive-in side of the operation had already succumbed to the competition and only the cocktail lounge and restaurant were left when Faura went to check out the tip by the anonymous caller.

Visitors for the manager were directed through the semi-darkness of the cocktail lounge and the short corridors that led to his office in the far northeast corner of the building.

After taking the security measures recommended by the police, it was chilling to realize that it could be difficult to get out of there should there be any substance to the telephone call. This was dangerous business. Was the story worth it? But it was too late for that kind of question. The point of no return had been crossed.

At the dish-washing area, a young Mexican, of light complexion, about five-feet eight inches in height and 150 pounds, was surrounded by what appeared to be all the dishes in the world.

Once more a shot in the dark was in order.

"Hi, Jesse," Faura said, casually approaching.

"Hi," he responded, turning to face the visitor.

"You are Jesse," Faura tried to confirm.

"Yes, I am."

Was this the man involved in the assassination? It was difficult to believe it. He seemed normal, relaxed. Besides he had been too easy to find.

Asking Jesse to wait a minute, Faura proceeded to the manager's office. Telling the manager he was a newsman working on an immigration story, he asked permission to talk to Jesse. He asked the manager how long Jesse had worked for him, and the manager told him Jesse had worked there since February of that year and that Jesse was a "good worker and a good kid."

Back in the kitchen, speaking in Spanish, Jesse confirmed the information the manager gave and other questions after being told the same immigration cover story.

"Have you any foreign friends, Jesse," he was asked. "No, just Mexicans," he replied. In his innocence and ignorance he did not think of Mexicans as foreigners.

"Have you got any Middle Eastern friends, perhaps from Jordan, Jerusalem, Egypt or any other country from that part of the world," he was pressed.

"No," he said with a sad expression. "I only have two or three friends. They are Mexicans. I don't associate with many people," he added after a brief pause.

"Have you got a girlfriend," He was asked.

"I did," he replied without hesitation.

"Is she mad at you? I mean mad enough to want to wish you harm?"

"No. There are no hard feelings," he said with sadness. "She had to leave town and go to live in San Francisco. There are no hard feelings."

All his replies had been straightforward, without hesitation and with a touch of sadness. His demeanor and the overall impression he gave was one of meekness and vulnerability, that of a very quiet humble soul with years of suffering, hard work and deprivation to call a childhood. From Faura's Jewish wife, he had learned a word that described Jesse. "A Neb." No way could he be involved in the assassination, Faura concluded.

Disappointed that this could not be the Jesse who "might be involved in the shooting" and somewhat relieved that there was no danger because of it, the reporter pressed for something to explain the anonymous phone call.

"Do you know of anyone that might wish you harm? Someone who might be the kind of person to make an anonymous call to cause you trouble?"

"No," he answered, and as if trying to be helpful suggested that a man who had been working there as a fry-cook was also named Jesse.

Having finished his day, Jesse was changing his shirt during the last few minutes of the conversation, and they walked outside together. Faura felt better under the glare of the late afternoon sun.

Jesse gave the reporter the name of the fry-cook: "Jesus."

It dawned on the reporter that his companion's name was in fact Jesus also, not Jesse. In the old American custom to "Anglicize" foreign names, they had changed Jesus to Jesse. The shy Mexican gave Faura the other Jesse's description and that of two brothers living with him. The trail cooled off again. They were two fat, too old and none of the information provided anything to warrant an effort to locate them.

Standing at the bus stop where Jesse was to board his bus home, they said good-bye, and Faura started to walk to his car. He noticed a car on the same side of the street with two men watching them.

CHAPTER 5

The two men sat in a small, blue car of 1963 or '64 vintage in a "no parking zone" in front of his own car. As he approached, there was a spontaneous, unexplainable exchange of looks between all three of them. Later, Faura could not explain to himself the strangeness of the three of them looking at each other in such a manner. Their lines of sight seemed to converge in a triangular manner.

Faura peered into the car as he walked past. The height of the sidewalk offered the advantage of looking into the car without fear of them seeing his face.

The man in the front passenger seat held a walkie-talkie on his lap, the antenna fully extended. His left hand moved to cover it, but it was too long. It appeared to be slightly smaller than those used by police but larger and more solid than those sold to the public.

Having covered the police beat for a few years, the reporter recognized it as a professional type.

Inside his car, the motions of getting a cigarette provided the opportunity to take note of the license plate.

Making sure he was not followed, he drove a few blocks to his sister-in-law's apartment and telephoned a source in the police department, explaining his need for a run-down on a license plate number fast.

Within minutes, the report was called back. No record of the license plate, noting that it could be a police car or a fake plate.

Faura considered the possibility that his friend at Police Intelligence had provided cover to make sure he came out of the restaurant safely. But in the light of the turmoil and monumental amount of work the police had at that point, it seemed silly they would allow a reporter to check out a lead and then give him protection. If they could spare the personnel, they surely would have checked the lead themselves.

The same train of thought brought other things into focus. The two reedy looking men in the car were a far cry from police types. The driver, a Caucasian, appeared to be about 5'8," heavy, thick, muscular neck, with that redness of skin associated with excessive drinking.

His walkie-talkie-carrying passenger appeared somewhat shorter and slimmer. Both wore opened neck sports shirts with suit or sport coats, crumpled and unkempt. The pair belonged more at the two-dollar betting window at the race track than any police agency. Their car was old, dirty and dented on the left rear fender. The more Faura dwelt on it, the more inconceivable it became that they were connected to the police. If they were checking anything it was not for the LAPD.[1]

Arriving at the San Fernando news bureau at about 9:30 A.M., Faura called his editor, Abe Greenberg, and asked him to make a note of the mysterious license plate number and related the events of the previous afternoon.

Then he went to the home of a police friend. They discussed the meaning of the "no record" license plate, and he advised caution. If it was a conspiracy, the reporter could stumble into serious trouble, he said. Then he dropped a shocker.

He had been in court that day, attending the trial of a man he had arrested. By coincidence, he said, the defense attorney in that case had at one time represented Sirhan Sirhan, the accused assassin. The reporter reminded him that Sirhan did not have a police record, but that his brother, Saidallah, had a narcotics record.

"Well, he showed me a jacket (file), and I saw the name Sirhan," he insisted. He admitted the possibility of being mistaken on the first name, but he was positive the last name was Sirhan.

He went on to say that a man and a woman had come to this attorney's office after the senator's shooting looking to be represented "in case they were picked up and ran into trouble." The attorney had advised them to go to the FBI with their story and come back, if they needed him. They had not come back.

Since a man and a woman were the objects of a police search at the time, the story held high interest. Who were they? What story did they have to tell?

Once again, things were being offered in a case the reporter could not ignore, drawing him further into the investigation. They agreed to meet in the courtroom the next day, and he would introduce Faura to the attorney, so they could attempt to get what they could from him. Obviously, the attorney could not give them the names and addresses of his clients, and whatever they had told him would be privileged communication, which he would not reveal.

But if it was true that he had represented Sirhan's brother, what could he tell about that? Could he arrange for Faura to meet with the family? If so, would the family be willing to meet with him?

Fired by the need to find answers and excited over the lucky breaks he'd been having, one thing was sure: he had to be at the courtroom the next morning and take his chances.

As it turns out, he was not only to get some of the answers, he was also to meet the Sirhan family, which in turn opened doors to more startling revelations.

---

1. Author's note: Faura could not believe official investigators would have that appearance, which was uncommon at the time.

There would be no word of the "polka-dot girl" in the newspapers until June 7, the day Faura was scheduled to meet with the Sirhan family lawyer at a courtroom in downtown Los Angeles.

Faura had always considered downtown depressing and ugly, as the buildings appeared to melt into smoggy ooze. The people who had to go there were so often lawyers, businessmen, politicians, criminals or those who needed to go to court to solve their troubles. He had never seen any room for joy in any of those categories. But downtown Los Angeles was where the story waited, and he took his place in the endless chain of freeway slaves and headed for his rendezvous.

Dave Marcus, the attorney, was a man of remarkable ability. In his early 60s, Marcus kept a gargantuan calendar that would send many younger men running for cover. A "bum" heart made his schedule twice as taxing. Pills for his condition where more common in his office than the traditional cocktails usually found in other offices.

Marcus appeared, at first glance, to have walked out of a television late show, an appearance accentuated by a felt hat haphazardly perched on his head and resembling those fashionable in the 1920s.

His soft speech and salt-and-pepper hair concealed an uncannily sharp mind. Slow walker, fast thinker. The law books he had read and used to the advantage of his clients probably were arranged neatly in the corridors of his mind. Frail in appearance, Marcus could easily lure an adversary into his den and then have him for lunch. How to approach a man like that to ask for the impossible?

Faura chose his favorite approach: straightforward honesty, with a gentle, humble demeanor to project that his target had the upper hand. An "I am not a threat, I just need a favor" kind of thing.

During a recess in the trial, they were introduced. Asked if he had ever defended Sirhan Sirhan, Marcus squinted and looked as if he were measuring Faura for a casket or trying to figure out if he could be trusted.

"No. It was not Sirhan Sirhan. It was one of his brothers." He spoke softly while he fumbled for a cigarette. "As a matter of fact," he went on, "I have represented two of them."

He explained that he was now representing Munir Sirhan, Sirhan's 21-year-old brother, during immigration proceedings.

"It is kind of ironic," Marcus continued, "that Munir should be getting ready to be sworn in and receive his citizenship papers at the same time that his brother is being indicted by the grand jury." He looked at the reporter as he said this. "Just one block away from each other," he added with measured deliberation.

His look and remarks indicated the Faura had passed his appraisal. He was offering a story. It was a little after noon when Marcus and Faura headed across the street for the Immigration Building. At the appropriate office, Marcus asked the woman at the desk for the list of the people who were scheduled to be sworn in as citizens of the United States that day. After some hesitation, followed by consulting with another woman, she handed him the list.

Munir's name had been ruled out in red pencil, and a notation next to it read: "Papers returned to INS." The date the papers were returned was noted next to it.

Not wishing to look obvious by taking notes, Faura tried to memorize the notation, only to forget the date later on. Overhearing the conversation, a man rushed to the counter and hastily took away the papers.

"That is wrong," he said testily, as he tore off the page they had been reading. "This is the official list."

He gave Marcus another list, neatly typed, on which there was no mention of Munir.

Downstairs, at a public telephone, Marcus called an Immigration official to inquire about the reasons for the withdrawal of Munir's papers.

"I am told that the papers have been withdrawn until this whole thing is over."

Leaving the building, Marcus asked Faura if he wanted to go to the bank with him. Not wishing to lose Marcus, Faura agreed, and they took a taxi to Fourth and Main Street.

While waiting in the taxi with Marcus' satchel, it occurred to the reporter that he had drawn the detail of carrying the dilapidated heavy thing for the day and imagined a servant from the Middle Ages trotting behind his master and carrying the luggage, not without some degree of embarrassment.

There was some consolation and justification in the fact that the satchel was heavy and Marcus' heart could collapse under the strain. In retrospect, it became clear that he had been thoroughly "conned" by a master: After all, Marcus had been toting that satchel around long before that day and would, no doubt, carry it around long after. No matter, the damned satchel strengthened the bond between them.

The taxi driver was the gabby kind. He was studying for his bar exam and, not surprisingly, commented on the propriety of Mayor Sam Yorty revealing the contents of Sirhan's notebooks to the press.

Back at the Hall of Justice which houses some Los Angeles courtrooms, Marcus gave Faura his telephone number and asked him to call him at 5:30 that evening. During the course of the day, it had been determined that he had been neither approached nor retained by the Sirhan family in the matter of Sirhan's defense. He had explained that even if Sirhan wanted his services he could not take the case because he had been sick during the prior three weeks and could not handle a case of that scope in his condition. He looked as if should actually be in bed instead of in a courtroom.

With that no-nonsense look, he had made it clear: "I could not comment on the case if I had it."

Faura had asked Marcus point blank:

"Has anybody come to you to represent them in relation to anything that might have happened in connection with the assassination?"

"Have been approached or retained?" Marcus asked.

"Approached," Faura said, with the idea he should give Marcus more room to maneuver if he wanted to help.

"No, I have not been approached," he answered curtly.

The line of questioning was dropped, since it was obvious it would lead nowhere; for whatever reasons he did not want to talk about "a man and a woman" coming to his office to retain him in relation with the Kennedy killing. And he never did.

Now Marcus knew what Faura's real interest was. If he was to help, he would tolerate the questioning. If he was to refuse, he would send Faura away. He chose to tolerate, which was a good sign. It was on that premise that Faura had trotted around town with him. Back at the building where they had met, the trial would be resuming soon. They took the elevator up to the courtroom, and Faura got his next break.

In the elevator Marcus struck up a conversation with a deputy district attorney. The conversation drifted to the Kennedy shooting, which seemed to be the only topic in Los Angeles those days. On the next floor the elevator took a new load, forcing Faura against Marcus and his D.A. friend. The deputy D.A. did not know who Faura was, and Marcus did not notice that they were back to back.

Unbelievably, the story of the two people Faura was looking for unfolded right there, in the Hall of Justice elevator, people pressing against each other completely tuned out by custom or need from the other human flesh that threatened to choke them. All but one, and Faura was so close he could not help but hear the conversation. He tried to block out all other sounds and not lose a word of what was being said.

"…one is a Mexican-American, the other Portuguese. They claim to have been at the Rafferty party. Just as they were coming in, Sirhan was having a scene with a waitress. Obviously the waitress did not want to serve him for some reason and he took the drink and threw a twenty-dollar bill down and said: 'Here is your money and keep the change.' He was pretty mad, and these two men said he made some very nasty remarks about Robert Kennedy – that Kennedy was a millionaire, a very rich man, that he did not need a job and many strong and insulting things about Kennedy."

All good things come to an end and so did the elevator ride. In his car, having left Marcus, the pieces starting to fall into place for the reporter.

CHAPTER 6

The story Luke Perry had picked up outside police headquarters appeared to have substance. Sirhan apparently had been at the Rafferty party earlier in the evening. While there he had been involved in an incident with a girl or waitress. The argument had been witnessed by the Mexican-American and the "Portuguese." Sirhan stopped to talk to them and unloaded some of his anger on them by insulting Kennedy. They were all seen talking together, and the men were being sought by the police for questioning. Two men were being sought, not a man and a woman as reported earlier.

It all fit rather nicely, but was Faura's reconstruction correct? It was still too weak to file a story. The men had to be found to confirm the story. If it was true, they were not implicated in the crime and they might be willing to talk.

Not wanting to be accused of withholding information from the police, Faura made two telephone calls: one to the Police Intelligence friend asking to check the license plate he had noted during his visit to Tony's Drive In and the other to Ramparts police.

"The man" at Ramparts was told of the new lead about the two men at the Rafferty party and the dead end in Westwood. They discussed the mystery car and the fact that only three people had known where Faura was going: himself, the Intelligence friend and "the man." It was suggested that perhaps the anonymous call was relayed to some other agency.

"The man" found the story of the two men at the Rafferty party most interesting, particularly the description – Mexican-American and Portuguese – and indicated that he would be very interested in finding the men and obtaining their statements.

The possibility that the information had already come to the attention of his department was discussed, since the pair had been sent to the FBI by Marcus when they originally went to him.

"No, I did not have the information," he said, "I would very much like to hear what these men have to say."

"You mean the FBI is holding back on you again," Faura joked.

"They never stopped," he quipped, joining in the joke. Faura was promised that he would be notified immediately if the police search was successful.

At this juncture, some clarification of Faura's relationship to the police is in order. It is not meant to imply that his friend or "the man" accepted him as part of the investigation or in a quasi-official position by the slightest thread of imagination.

Faura's was a position of advantage. The investigation was quite fluid at the time. There was no possible excuse for them to refuse to talk to the reporter or anyone, or ignore any information the *Citizen News* was willing to give them. There was no way they could discourage the press from undertaking their own investigations. Anything uncovered and offered was certainly welcome. There was no harm in listening.

While information was voluntarily offered, care was taken not to reveal sources or lose the story. Faura believed that members of the press had a responsibility to their employers, and it was a matter of balancing the job needs with those of their conscience and those of the police.

With the FBI withholding the story of the two men from the LAPD, the reporter saw a position of advantage in getting to the men first. There was no question about bringing them to the police after confirming their story. But his relationship to the police was to change considerably as they became more organized.

After calling Intelligence and Ramparts, Faura drove to his news bureau, where he made another call to Intelligence to get the results of the check on the license plate. This third check of the license plate also turned up "no record." There was no chance now of anybody having made an error in searching for it at the Department of Motor Vehicles.

Another source working on the license plate said that, while he could not provide license numbers for Intelligence and FBI cars, he could assure me that the one given to him did not belong to LAPD Intelligence or the FBI.

"It is much higher than either one of them – or it is the other side, if there is one. Just be very careful," he added.

Marcus was called fifteen minutes after the agreed time of 5:30 P.M. He was not feeling well and asked to be called back the next day. By this time, a girl claiming to be the "polka-dot girl" had come forward and been cleared by the Sheriff's department.

CHAPTER 7

On Monday, June 10th, somewhat ahead of the game but feeling the urgency to get much further ahead before some unknown competitor or the police would get his story, Faura brought to bear every resource he had to get the address and identity of at least one of the men. Late that afternoon, after hours on the phone, he had an identification; one man, not Mexican-American, but Puerto Rican. But it was definitely the man who had talked to Sirhan at the Rafferty party after Sirhan's incident with the waitress. Needing corroboration, Faura went to confront Marcus with the information.

Around six o'clock that evening, Marcus' reception room was full of people. The first two men to the left of the entry door did not seem to fit somehow.

They were young, smart looking, well dressed and they were obviously together. The tape recorder hanging from Faura's shoulder marked him as a reporter.

"Who are you with?" one of the young men asked.

"No one," Faura lied, and added, "I have to see Mr. Marcus on a personal matter." They did not buy it.

"I thought you were a reporter, tape recorder and all," he teased.

Faura though they might be police and hated himself for bringing such an obvious thing as a tape recorder to Marcus's office.

He chose to make a joke out of the situation. "It's a new kind of radio" he said. One of the young men courteously nodded, not believing. His companion had a hearty laugh.

Not wanting to stand around like a wooden Indian, embarrassed, he decided to do his own questioning.

"Who are *you* with?" The one who had laughed appeared to be younger and more jovial than his interrogator. He licked his lips, in a gesture, that said he wished Faura had not asked the question. "*Life* magazine," he answered and proceeded to introduce himself and his companion: Jordan Bonfante and Robert Kaiser.

The thought of losing his advantage and having to compete with *Life* and its resources soured what had been a good day.

Bonfante, Kaiser and Faura were called to Marcus's office

Not much could be ascertained since everyone present was trying to be as careful as possible. There was no way of knowing if Bonfante and Kaiser were onto the story of the two men at the Rafferty party.

Bonfante was the Los Angeles bureau chief for *Life*. Kaiser was working the story for *Life* as a writer, after a stint as a Time-Life bureau correspondent in Rome. Between the two of them and *Life*'s resources, the story would probably be pieced together in no time.

How had *Life* entered the picture at such a crucial time?

According to Bonfante, he had asked the New York bureau for the name of the top immigration lawyer in the country. Happily for him, it turned out to be Dave Marcus, in Los Angeles. A bonus to that coincidence was the fact that Marcus had represented the Sirhan family for some time. *Life,* being a picture magazine, needed all the photos it could get of the family. Marcus, being a man the family trusted, represented a bonanza as a line of communication and negotiation. This explained the stampede to his office.

Not having been assigned to the story placed Faura at a distinct disadvantage. With no resources other than his own, and having to cover other stories out of his news bureau, even time was at a premium.

Marcus, aloof and difficult in his own way, had taken a liking to Faura and continued to help him. He asked all three of them to have dinner at his house and said that Saidallah Sirhan was to meet us there.

That evening with Bonfante, Kaiser and Saidallah Sirhan at Marcus's estate in Pasadena rescued the remainder of the day.

A kind and loyal man, Marcus in his own peculiar style of caginess and concern for Faura's disadvantage, made sure that he would have more contact with Sirhan's family and drew him as close as he could to *Life* magazine's interests.

Always making sure that professional ethics would not be violated, he usually spoke without secrecy with the family and *Life*'s representatives so that Faura participated in whatever information could be shared.

The assassination was not discussed during the evening.

Bonfante briefly explored the possibility of obtaining family photos from Said, as Saidallah was commonly called.

Said was a cagey fox. Built as slender and frail as his brother Sirhan, he appeared nervous and complained of his inability to find a job. When the conversation turned to photos, he said he had no objections but that he had to consult with his brother Sharif. He was not sure what the others would say, but he would see what he could do.

He also angrily related how two men had come into the house around 2 A.M. and roughly and violently removed a number of photographs from the premises.

According to Said, they had claimed to be from *Life* magazine. Bonfante denied his organization would use such methods. We did not dwell too long on the subject since everyone present doubted *Life* was involved, and there was no way of knowing who the men were.

Leaving the dining room, they went downstairs to the den for a cocktail.

Genuinely feeling sorry for the pitiful man of no job and no income, and believing that he should not be held accountable for his brother's crime, Faura offered to help him find a job.

They exchanged telephone numbers for this purpose and joined the conversation of the others in the den.

Before the night was over, Marcus told Faura he (Marcus) could get him the rights for a book on Sirhan. Faura turned him down saying that anyone who took that chore would be taking on a nightmare. A few weeks later Faura learned that Kaiser had chosen the nightmare.

By the end of the evening Faura had surmised that *Life* did not have the name of the man at the Rafferty party.

The next day, June 11, Faura finished his work at his news bureau and waited until dark. It was the night he had chosen to go to the house of the mystery man who could corroborate that Sirhan had been drinking at the Rafferty party.

The address was in Orange County, a right-wing stronghold in the west. Somewhat apprehensive of getting involved with police in such a place, should anything go wrong, he made plans to go in and out as early in the evening as possible.

CHAPTER 8

The address and the man were found without any difficulty. The modest home in which he lived was set back from the dark street in a quiet, residential neighborhood.

Enrique Rabago came to the door and cautiously inquired who wanted him. Shown press credentials he was invited to come out and talk about his encounter with Sirhan.

Hurriedly he closed the door, and he and Faura walked out to the sidewalk. Reluctant to talk, Rabago claimed to have told his story to the FBI and said they had asked him not to talk to anybody.

"Have you talked to the Los Angeles police" he was asked.

"No, not yet," he answered without hesitation.

"Didn't the FBI tell you to go to them and tell your story?" he was asked.

"No, but I think they will take care of that," he said.

"Tell me the story," Faura insisted.

"I can't," Rabago protested, "the FBI said not to talk to anyone, and they could make trouble for me."

"How?"

"Well, you know, you can't fool around with those guys."

Faura reminded him that we were not living in a police state and promised to keep his name out of the story.

He refused and again asked who Faura was. He was getting nervous and defensive. He did not like the idea of standing on the open sidewalk feeling exposed.

"OK, then," Faura said, "I will tell you this. I already know the story. You have no reason to fear anyone. I just want you to corroborate it. You have not told the story to the police, and you refuse to talk to the press. There is no reason in the world any of us would want to protect you later on if you got into trouble."

"Don't put my name in the paper," he pleaded, interpreting the remark as a threat. Faura meant no such thing but took advantage of the opportunity.

"What did Sirhan say when you bumped into him at the Rafferty party?" Faura pressed, assuming Rabago was ready to talk. The question was posed to elicit an admission that he had been there and that he was the man who had witnessed the scene between Sirhan and the waitress.

"I don't remember exactly," Rabago started. "He called the senator a lot of things, bad names."

"Was he drinking?"

"I saw him with a drink in his hand. He had been drinking."

"Was he drunk?"

"I would not call him drunk, but he looked like he had been drinking."

"Who was there with you?"

"I'd rather not say."

Rabago started moving towards his house. Another couple of quick questions, and the story had been confirmed.

Back in Los Angeles and looking for further confirmation and strengthening of the story, Faura called the security chief for the Ambassador Hotel, Bill Gardner, and told him Rabago's story, while not revealing Rabago's identity.

"The police already know that, Gardner replied dryly, giving Faura unofficial confirmation.

An attempt to contact the District Attorney's chief investigator George Stoner met with an arrogant "don't call us, we'll call you" attitude in spite of the fact they still did not know the identity of the man.

It was then that doubts about attempting to help the authorities flooded Faura.

It was obvious that finding and questioning the men seen talking to Sirhan was important. It was also obvious that Rabago's story would help trace the other man and Sirhan's movements the night of the shooting and that, whether Sirhan had been drunk or not, could play and important part in the trial.

Yet the authorities had begun to treat people coming forth with information as if they were not interested. The pattern was to reveal itself many times before the investigation would be over.

Faura wrote the Rabago story and sent it to his editor.

CHAPTER 9

Gay Scott, political editor at the *Hollywood Citizen News*, almost killed the story, calling it a "nonstory" because of Faura's refusal to use Rabago' name. He could not do it in good conscience. In the end, the story ran the next day as a front-page headline. By the late afternoon every media outlet in Los Angeles was featuring the story of Sirhan drinking at the Rafferty party before the shooting. The police then got interested, and Faura reluctantly gave them Rabago's name and address.

Jordan Bonfante read the story and called Faura to confirm that Faura had talked to Rabago in person and that the story was true. Assured that it was true, Bonfante asked Faura to join the *Life* magazine investigation. Faura agreed, welcoming the association.

Shortly after the story on Rabago hit the streets, Faura, City Editor Mary K. Quinn, and Managing Editor Harold Hubbard stood around Hubbard's desk discussing the story. Quinn and Hubbard had lingering doubts about its importance (after everybody else had picked it up). Faura coasted on that, and on the fact that *Life* magazine had also picked it up and was running with it in its spread of the events that had taken place the night of the shooting. They then discussed other possible stories around Sirhan and the Sirhan family. They speculated about how long it would take the police to read the newspapers and come around to find out how much more they had, if anything.

As they huddled in animated conversation, Faura noticed a Caucasian man, sandy-haired, about six feet tall, well groomed, stop and talk to the receptionist. She looked in their direction and pointed towards him. The man had obviously asked for one of them and started walking in their direction.

"Speak of the devil, here he comes," said Quinn, hurrying back to her desk. Hubbard busied himself, and Faura headed for the stranger, thinking it might be LAPD.

"Did you write this story," the stranger asked without identifying himself and pointing to the large red headline.

"Yes, I did," Faura answered, not knowing what to expect. The man was frowning and could not be described as having a friendly attitude.

"I must talk to you," he said nervously.

"Who are you, are you with some official agency?"

"No," he replied looking around with suspicion, "but I cannot talk to you here."

He then said that he had important information about a girl he had been with the day of the assassination.

"I am afraid," he added. "Can you give me protection?"

The question caught Faura by surprise. The man was obviously agitated. He spoke softly, as if afraid that somebody might overhear and continuously scanned the surroundings with darting eyes.

"I don't know what kind of protection you need, but I will do the best I can. Sometimes the best protection is bringing things out in the open." Faura was trying not to mislead him by offering protection. "Have you been to the police yet?" he added, implying they would be the ones to ask for protection.

"No, no, I don't want to go to them alone. I'll trust you to make the arrangements." He seemed alarmed at the thought of going to the police alone. Not wanting to pass on any story that had to do with the assassination, Faura agreed to meet with him.

Since he was a stranger and not wanting to take any chances, Faura suggested that they meet at the San Fernando Police station where he had his news bureau. The place would provide privacy and protection. They met there early that evening.

The story the stranger told is one of the most important, fascinating and mystery-ridden of all of those that would come to light.

CHAPTER 10

Faura turned on his tape recorder.

The man's name was John Fahey. He spoke about a girl he had spent the day with on June 4, and who had knowledge of the assassination that was to be committed that night.

A transcript of the interrogation was made immediately. Fahey's story would soon involve the FBI, LAPD, *Life* magazine and Faura in a web of intrigue that is still unresolved. To this day the mystery is not solved, in spite of FBI and police denials. Fahey is the most important witness in the story of the "girl in the polka-dot dress." Because of its contents and implications the tale is best told by the man himself. In the interest of accuracy and to prevent conjecture and misinterpretation, here is the complete, verbatim transcript of the interview with John Fahey and his amazing story recorded on tape June 12, 1968. No attempt has been made to edit this transcript in any way or correct grammatical or syntax errors.

Faura: I would like your full name, please.

Fahey: John Henry Fahey.

Faura: Now, Mr. Fahey, where do you work?

Fahey: I work for Cal-Tech. It's a chemical company.

Faura: Mr. Fahey, were you at the Ambassador Hotel on the day – the night that the shooting occurred? Which would be the fourth?

Fahey: Yes, sir, I was there.

Faura: About what time were you there?

Fahey: I was there at 9:15.

Faura: In the morning or the evening?

Fahey: A.M.

Faura: Okay, now from 9:15 in the morning, tell me exactly what happened, who you met. Tell me in your own words the story as to how it went.

Fahey: Well, I had pre-arranged the prior day to meet another salesman of my company there. His name is Mid– (unintelligible) White. I can give you his phone number to verify this.

Faura: Put the phone number on the tape.

Fahey: I don't have it with me. It is at home. I was to meet him at 8:30 in the morning at the Ambassador Hotel and as it turned out I got there late because of heavy traffic and I left the house late. I took my wife to work.

Faura: At what time did you get there?

Fahey: I got there about 9:15. And so I parked in back of the hotel, which would be Eighth Street. Where it has one-hour parking or two-hour parking, I forgot which. I proceeded up the back stairs of this hotel, which has many stairs as you go up, and as I was walking ahead of me were a couple of fellows that were, I thought perhaps, at the time Spanish. And with my casual glance at them I thought perhaps they worked there. I paid no attention to them, but they were walking ahead of me. I got to the top of the stairs and started to walk down the side of – I guess you would call it the pool wall or something of this nature – toward the hotel, and there was a small entrance going elsewhere other than going into the hotel. They had stopped there and they were talking, but I could not make out anything they were saying.

Faura: Were they talking in a strange language?

Fahey: In a strange language.

Faura: Did it sound Spanish? Are you familiar with Spanish?

Fahey: I am familiar with Spanish. It was not Spanish. It was too fast and close so I didn't pay any attention. I still felt that they possibly worked there, maybe as porters. I didn't know what they were doing there – maybe kitchen workers. I proceeded down under the hotel, as the stairs go down, and I was proceeding to the coffee shop. You go down this long corridor, along where there, there's all this shops in there, and there is the coffee shop, etc. I went into the coffee shop to look for my man, thinking maybe he was still there, and I didn't find him. So I stepped back out of the coffee shop and waited in the hallway, which I guess you would call it a concourse or something of that nature. I was looking into this drug store window, like. There was two shops there. One was a clothing store, one was a drug store and I looked this lady in the eye. She was working in the drug store at the time. She seemed to be the only one there and I made sort of – window shopping there, thinking the he might come along because he did have an appointment with the housekeeper Mrs. Paul, because (unintelligible) ... this account.

But apparently he had made his appointment and left. In so doing I was unaware of this, thinking he would, maybe, still come along so I was looking in this window and this lady came along in this window, and I as a man – with ladies, with women, you see a pretty lady you pick one out they are all good dances, and this is what I said to the lady and she smiled and said, "Yes." Then all of a sudden she turned to me and said, "Do you know where the post office is?" and I said, "My goodness this is a hotel. I didn't realize there was a post office in the hotel."

So she stepped forward and went up about maybe 15 feet toward the stairs as you go up into the lobby, and there was a little sign there that says about something – Kennedy Reception – and gave the room or whatever it was – I forget that. Anyway, she asked some gentleman there a question – I guess it was the same question she asked me – where the post office was. So with that I decided to go into the coffee shop and have myself a cup of coffee and I was down at the bar there, the coffee bar. And I was all alone and there was finally a gentleman came up on my left and he was an elderly gentleman, and said, "good morning." Finally the lady came back – oh, I would say about 10 minutes later, and she sat down at the side of me, and here I am drinking my coffee. She proceeds to start talking to me about asking me asking her if there was a lot of good dances in the window. She made a remark and I can't remember that remark.

Faura: Did she speak good English?

Fahey: She spoke very good English.

Faura: Did she have any accent at all?

Fahey: Er... when she wanted to, yes sir. She did have a slight accent. It was hard to make it out. It was hard to say what nationality it was. So we started to talk, and I asked her if she was in the hotel and she said "no." So it kind of threw me off. I thought maybe she works around here or something. I said, "Do you work around here," and she says "no." And then she says, "I haven't been but three days here," she says. I said, "Oh, where are you from?" and she said, "well, I am from Virginia."

Well, it kind of struck a coincidence with me because my mother was born in Virginia, and I proceeded to tell her this, that she was from Richmond, and I gave her the street and the address. Then she said that she did not know anything about Richmond. She said that she was from New York. So, finally I said, "Well, how are things in New York?" and we got talking about New York, she had just come from ... (unclear, sounded like, Elock? Iran? Iraq?), and she named another – I don't know if you would call it a township or a country or a small something like Beirut or something like this – is there a Beirut?

Faura: There is a Beirut, but that is a city.

Fahey: So, anyway, she mentioned Akaba – she had traveled all over through the countries over there and she had come into New York and I proceeded to ask her name and she gave me her name as Alice. She wanted my name and I told her my full name and she asked me where I worked and I told her what I did for a living. I told her.

And then she told me, she says, I was asking her what she was doing here. She says, "Well, I don't want to get you involved," says. At that time I thought it was a casual statement so I let it go. She says, "I don't want to get you involved." So I says, "Who, what do you mean, you don't want to get me involved?"

"Well, she says; if I tell you too much they are liable to be watching me." And I says, "Well, who?" And then she said, "Well, I don't want to get you involved." Uh, rather than say involved she said, "I don't know if I can trust you," this was it. And she proceeded to tell me that she needed some help. Then she became very nervous her hands were shaking. She was wet on her hands because I did feel her hand and she was moist. And I asked her, "Is there something you can tell me?" and she says, "I don't know if I can trust you." So we get talking and I say, "Well, how about moving to a table?" By this time the counter's filled up, with all people drinking coffee and I say, "How about moving to a table?" She said she wanted to eat some breakfast.

So "fine" she says, and we moved to a table, so with this we moved – there is a cashier as you go in the door. We went up by the cashier and the hostess took us to a table which it was on the right hand side. This was a booth, and a blond waitress came over to wait on us. I didn't order any breakfast. I ordered toast and coffee. She ordered scrambled eggs and sausage, I believe, and toast and coffee. We stayed there quite – we were there at that booth about an hour and fifteen minutes and we talked. At that time she told me that she did not know again whether she could trust me and I told her that I was a salesman on the road and that I had run into people before with problems and I figured this was something small. And she said – that's when she said, "My name isn't Alice, my name is Jean. And I says, "Well" and she say, "There's reasons why I had to give you different names." She says, "I can't go by my real name." And I asked her why and she says, "Well, I don't want to get you involved, I don't know if I can tell you the whole thing."

So then by this time, she says, "I think we are being watched." And she looked out the door – straight ahead. And as she looked out the door I looked out the door. And here is where I saw this gentleman. He was I thought perhaps at the time, a Greek fellow, or a Spanish fellow, I couldn't put my finger on it. But it was one of the fellows that I had seen as I came through the rear entrance. It was taller than the gentleman – the assassin – I mean he was taller than him. His hair was straight back, little sideburns – down here, and as I looked at him – from what I have seen (sounded like "in the past") – why I have a feeling it's one of the brothers. I think I could recognize him.

"So I immediately came back to her and says, "Well, what are they gonna do?" and she says, "Well, I don't want to get you involved."

Always throwing this at me. "I don't want to get you involved." And I said, "Well, you can trust me." I says, "Is there something I can help you with?" and she was real nervous and sweaty. So she is eating her breakfast, and she proceeds to tell me she has to go away to Australia, that she wants to get away from this people, that she has to go to Australia, and that she needed a passport. And she asked me if I knew how she could get a passport.

"So, I says just like this – it kind of shook me up a little bit – I says, I don't have any experience with passports." She said, "Did you ever have one?" I said, "No, I never had one." So she says, "Well, I know how to get a passport," and she proceeds to tell me that she could take a deceased person's name, use his social security number, write to wherever he was born and get his birth certificate and get a passport made under these circumstances.

So I (sounds like "threw it out") because I thought maybe the girl – at first I thought she was a prostitute, but sex was out of the question. This girl was shook up, she was in trouble, her hands were moist and wet and her attitude was she needed some help.

And this is the way she asked me. She really wanted to – for someone to help her but she didn't know if she could trust me. So as it went on, she told me that she wanted me to come that night to the "winning reception" and watch them get Mr. Kennedy, and I says, "What do you mean?" She says, "I don't want to get you involved." And I says, "Well, you can trust me. Tell me. I am for McCarthy." And just like that I threw it off. And she says, "Well, they are going to take care of Mr. McCarthy tonight" – excuse me Kennedy – take care of Mr. Kennedy tonight."

"So, I says, "well, who?" and she says, – I don't know if I can trust you." She always cut me off with this. "I don't know if I can trust you."

So I tried to make her relax and she says, "Well, I'll tell you later on." She gave me this bit. So the circumstances went on to – at this time I was making up my mind – I wanted to leave really but being a gentleman, we were having breakfast, and I didn't want to cut it off and dump her. And she told me that we were being watched, and I did see this guy watching us.

"So then she said that she did not know what she was going to be doing that day but she had to be back at the hotel and she asked me what I was doing. I said, "Well, I am a salesman on the road" again, "and I'm going to toward Oxnard and Ventura. I've got some accounts up there that I want to call on." So she invited herself along, and I said, "Good enough." I said, "If this will help you, fine. Come along with me and be company for me." So she agreed, and she finished her breakfast and she wanted to leave, and in doing so, the chap that was watching us moved over closer to the door, and he looked right down on us and he realized that we were making a move. So, I asked the waitress for the bill, and she says, "No, I'll pay for it." And she brings out her wallet out of her purse, which was a foreign looking purse. She had fine clothes on and she had a foreign looking purse and she brought out this wallet and she had a fistful of money in it.

And this was big stuff – fifty dollar bills, hundred dollar bills, and I says, "No, no, I'll take care of it, I invited you here at the booth, so it is my responsibility. As I gentleman I will pay for the breakfast." So, I paid for the breakfast, and we went up and went to the cashier, paid the cashier. And that blonde, I am sure, wherever she is, she'll recognize that we sat there, because we sat there an hour and fifteen minutes.

So, I paid the bill, and went out, and we went to the right and we went all the way down the concourse as I got down the middle of the concourse I turned around to see if this chap was still watching us and he had disappeared. So, there was a stairway, she took me up. She said she knew a way to get upstairs, rather than go out all the way and go up. She cut a sharp right – or something like this – we went up a stairway and there we were in the lobby.

I said, "Oh, you have been here before." I says, "You say you are not staying in the hotel?" She says, "No, I've been here a short time," she says. "I have to go to Australia," she says. I said, "Well, come on, let's get in my car and we'll leave."

"So, we proceeded to go out the back way. And we go out the back way and get – we get in my car. There was no one out there at the time. We got in the car and we headed – I got over on Wilshire Boulevard and went all the way up Wilshire Boulevard and we were talking all the time and she thanked me for offering her along or bringing her along because she wanted to someone she could talk to and – I told her I had to call on some accounts up in Oxnard.

So, anyway we got on the Santa Monica Boulevard off-ramp of Wilshire and headed off towards Santa Monica. We dropped down under – we went up the Coast Highway 1. We were going along on the Coast Highway 1 when I picked up a blue Ford.

I guess this was a '67 or a '66, had a flat front to it. There was a slim man driving it, and he was right on my tail because I speeded up and he speeded up, I slowed up, and he slowed up.

It was a surging affair as we went along. When we got above Malibu –

Faura: Did you take a look at the man? Other than he was thin, could you tell if he was dark? Caucasian, or –?

Fahey: "This man was a light Caucasian. He had gray hair. So we got above Malibu. So anyway, as this man was following me in a surging affair, the lady in the car acknowledged to me that we were being tailed. She said that if they found out that she was to get me involved, they would take care of me, let alone her.

Incidentally, her – description is – she looks Caucasian, but she has an Arabic complexion, very light. She speaks very good English, she has a little accent when she wants to put it on. She admits being from that country. She's – her age is around 27, 28.

She has dirty blond hair – the color of the hair is dirty blond. She has it in such a way – it's not made up with a wig – it's not curled or anything-it's straight back in a bun and it comes down around here when she wants to put it down here or she can put it put it up on her head.

Faura: Like a pony tail over the side?

Fahey: Right, right. So her clothes were tan color, her shoes were tan color – a light tan – her purse was tan color – it was a foreign make.

"You could tell the stockings on her feet were not of the nylon the girls wear here in America. She even had an aroma about her. She was nervous, sort of halitosis smell, an odor. She wore lipstick – er, she was a very pretty girl. Her nose was of – on the hooked fashion where you can realize that she was from the Arabic world.

Faura: Was it a prominent nose – a larger nose than usual?

Fahey: Yes.

Faura: Hooked?

Fahey: Hooked, yes. And – uh – as she has acknowledged to me that we were being tailed –

Faura: What was her weight, more or less?

Fahey: I would say about 127, 125, 127.

Faura: Shapely?

Fahey: Uh – she had a framed body. She wasn't heavy set, she wasn't too thin but there was a frame there. And the style of dress she wears wasn't a mini or anything like this, it was a regular A-style or whatever it is, come down to her knees and that's it.

Faura: Anything – any other detail on her appearance, you know, perhaps on her ears or her hands, any marks that you might have noticed?

Fahey: Her fingernails were very close. She wore pink colored nail polish but her nails were real close. Shorter than mine, as a man. And very nervous. You could see that there was something about her that she was on the run or whatever it is.

Faura: Okay. Let's go back there, back to the chase.

Fahey: Now, after she had acknowledged that we were being tailed, she informed me of such and she told me to hurry up and speed up and get away from this guy and she says that even if he does leave us someone else will pick us up. So I proceed to do thusly, and first thing you know all of a sudden it is a blue Volkswagen right on our tail. So then she says to me – er, oh – I says, "What is all this? What's the trouble here? Can't you tell me?"

She says, "Well, I don't want to get you involved." Then she told me real quickly – she says – "They are going to take care of Kennedy tonight." And I say, "Well, what do you mean?" and she says, "I can't tell you, I don't know if I can trust you," she says. "If they knew I was telling you this they would take care of you."

So I am going along up to Malibu. So as we are going along I became a little alarmed, and I says – to myself – maybe this is talk, maybe something else." I figured maybe she was mixed up in an armed robbery or something like this because she had a lot of money on her. Then again I didn't know what to believe.

So as we get up above Malibu heading towards Oxnard, we ran into – there is a big rock to the left of it and you can drive in and look out over in the ocean. So I says, "The best thing to do is to find out if this guy is really tailing me – shoot into the rock – into the parking area there and if he pulls in behind me I will shoot back out."

She says, "Well, you'd better do something, because they are really tailing us."

So as I pull into this parking area by the main rock, he pulls in behind me and pulls around 25 to 50 feet to my right hand side, and he looks right down at me and her and right across to me, and he had blue eyes, he was Caucasian, he had hair like yours – it was dark but much more gray, salt and peppery, like mine. I realized that he was really after us because he looked straight at me in my eyes, and it shook me off because I hadn't done anything wrong for the man to be chasing me so I knew it had to be on her. He never said a word. He got out of the VW, he walked around the other side, and he stretched his arms out like this. He turned around, he looked at us again, he came back around the VW. He got in, he started it up, he backed it up, he came across my tail, stopped. Then he proceeded and he went around this little rock, and he hid behind it with his VW. And I can take you there, and I can show you. I became alarmed. So I proceeded to get out of my car because I wanted to go behind that rock and to see what he was doing. He didn't go down the highway, he just remained right there. So as I started to get out of my car, I glanced at my keys and I caught her glancing at my keys, and so I – I was half way out of my car, and so I got back in my car realizing that she may have, could have possibly taken my car.

So I said, "I better not go." So instead he didn't come out, so I decided to start my car real quick like. I backed up in a circle – in a C-like and pulled around and I headed towards Oxnard, and he was still there. So, in doing so, I was heading right towards Oxnard, he disappeared. I never saw him again. So we are going through Oxnard and in the meantime – on the way to Oxnard she's telling us that they are really tailing us and that – uh, they are out to get Mr. Kennedy tonight at the winning reception, and also that she changed her name again to Betty, this time it was Betty and really I never knew what her name was at the time.

So, I get up into Oxnard and I pick up this Ford again, the same car – the first car – that was following us. She saw it first and she was shook, and she says, "They are really after us." And I says, "Well, what are we gonna do? Would you like to go to the police?"

"No, no, no, just take me back to Los Angeles." Well, I was concerned myself. I says, "Well I want to call on some accounts. There was one account called Cal-Rad-Randler up there. Down Wendy Buick was another one. Then I decided against it, to go out to any company. I felt that maybe while I was in the company they get her or something – I didn't know what would happen. This Ford was on me, so I decided to proceed right on to Ventura which is six miles away. So I get to Ventura and there is still this Ford on me. So I did a couple of figure eights in some side streets and I thought I had lost him and proceeded back through Ventura, and as I get back on the point – I go through Oxnard Boulevard, get over Point Mugu which takes you over to Coast Highway 1. So, on the way back I thought I has lost him, he was gone, then she relaxed a little bit when she realized we weren't being tailed then. Er – she proceeded to tell me that her real name was not Betty or Jean or wasn't the other name she'd given me either. Her real name was Gildeen Upenheimer (Oppenheimer?) and she said it real easy, real softly, she says that she was mixed up in something that she could not tell me about and it concerned what was gonna happen tonight, and I sort of believed her almost then – uh – and this was on our way back from Oxnard heading towards Malibu.

I had a flat tire then, so I pulled over to the right and proceeded to fix my flat tire and a truck driver came over, he stopped, he left his truck, and he came over to help me. And another car was going in the opposite direction, he helped me, they saw the lady sitting in the car. So they fixed my car, and I offered to pay the gentleman and he said no. He said, "One good turn deserves another," and he says, "Next time it may be me." I says, "Thank you, sir," and I went back on the road. So we proceeded down the highway heading toward Malibu, when just a little north of Malibu there is a restaurant called Transers or something of the sort.

Faura: "Trancas?"

Fahey: "Trancas, right. She was hungry. At first she wanted a cocktail, and I said, "I don't drink," I said, "I don't care to drink, I seldom have a drink with my wife" – or something – she knew I was married. So – er – then she said she was hungry so we went in the restaurant, we sat down; I said I wanted to go to the gentlemen's room, so she went to the ladies room. In the gentlemen's room there was a phone – I don't know – perhaps there was one in the ladies room, but we both went to the bathroom. I came out first, she was still in there. Uh – she finally came out and sat down and we ordered fillet of sole. We both had fillet of sole. Now she didn't completely eat her meal. This lady was pretty well shook and she ate half her meal, yet she said she was hungry. Uh – I ate mine pretty well and the waitress there was a brunette. She served us and I am sure she is still there. Er – I asked her, I tried to ask her more about this – what was gonna happen tonight, she informed me, "If you come tonight to the winning reception, you will see for yourself." And I said, "Are you going to be there?" and she said, "Well, certainly, you are going to take me back now. I've got to be back there." So we had spent, I'd say about 45 minutes, maybe, or 50 minutes in the restaurant and we headed back and I took her down to Wilshire Boulevard. I dropped her off in front of the hotel and she invited me to come with her and I refused her and she got mad at me because –

Faura: What time was this now?

Fahey: This was about 7, 7:15, and she was sort of angry with me because I didn't come with her. This lady wanted help and incidentally, on the way back, she told me where she lived. Uh – she wouldn't give me the address, but she said that she had lived – she was staying on Kenmore Street, because on the way back she asked me where Olympic was. She said, "Near Olympic" and she says, "I am on Kenmore near Olympic." And I says, "It's not the Kenmore Hotel, is it?" She says, "No, it is close to Olympic." She did not want to give me the address. She knew the address. Uh – so she invited me to come that night, and she was quite upset with me because I refused to come – I refused to go with her and she got out and she slammed the door and she left. And this is the way the story went.

Faura: Is that the last time you saw her?

Fahey: That is the last time I saw her.

Faura: Did she mention any other place where she had lived, or she might have lived, or anything else about where she was staying in Los Angeles?

Fahey: No, she had come from New York. She actually made me believe in end that she came from New York City. She was coming through New York City.

Faura: She was coming through New York?

Fahey: Yes

Faura: She didn't mention – other than Olympic and Kenmore –

Fahey: I asked her in our first conversation at the coffee shop in the Ambassador if she had stayed in the hotel. No. Did she work around or at the hotel? No. Then she told me later on, on the way back from Oxnard, that she was staying on Kenmore Street.

Whether it would be a room or apartment, I don't know what it is. I knew this, that she had a lot of clothes, she said that she had a lot of clothes and she had to move fast and get out of here and go to Australia because she said that they couldn't touch her there. And I asked her who, and she said to me that time "the Chinese." Whether or not that was something to throw me off, or what – but – uh – that's when I was calling her Gilda, then, because she told me that her name was Gilda Dean. I was calling her Gilda then, and she acknowledged me in that conversation with the name Gilda.

Faura: She said the Chinese could not get her in Australia?

Fahey: Right. Right. Definitely.

Faura: Is that all you can remember now?

Fahey: That's about it at this time.

Faura: Give me the description of the man who got out of the Volkswagen.

Fahey: The man who got out of the Volkswagen, he opened his door, he looked pretty stocky and when he got up he was sort of a short (end of tape, resume with new tape) As he was getting out of the car he seemed to be very well built. He stood up after he got out. He was a sort of short, stocky, well-built chap. He had blue eyes. His hair was dark and gray, salt and pepper fashion. A real heavy-set character. He kept his eyes glued on us.

Faura: How was he dressed?

Fahey: He was dressed in a gray pair of slacks, a dark sport coat on. He had a blue shirt with a dark tie. He had no mustache and he proceeded to walk along the car.

Faura: What was the skin?

Fahey: Very fair Caucasian skin.

Faura: In the neck, did it look like a fat neck, could you tell?

Fahey: Strong thick neck.

Faura: Could the man be described as fat also?

Fahey: No, this man was well built.

Faura: Muscular?

Fahey: Muscular. He was in shape.

Faura: Anything else you remember about him?

Fahey: No. Except that he was pretty well built and he kept his eyes glued on us.

Faura: Okay. Thank you. Tell me, which was the manner in which the FBI questioned you?

Fahey: Well, they let me tell my story and then they – er – Agent McCarthy asked me questions, particularly details about leaving the Wilshire Boulevard, Santa Monica Boulevard, and the Coast Highway, and upon being recalled Friday last, he asked me about my time elements in the hotel, at the coffee bar, in the booth, how long I was in the booth, what time we left the hotel and how long it took us to get to Santa Monica, what was said route, time limits heading towards Malibu, how long it took us to get to the rock up in Oxnard, what time I arrived in Oxnard, what time I arrived in Ventura, turned around to come back to Los Angeles, what time – how long it took us to get to the restaurant, how long we stayed at the restaurant –

Faura: How long did you stay at the restaurant?

Fahey: I'd say we were around 5:15. We must have left around 6 o'clock. Maybe a little after, and we ended up getting back at – uh – the hotel around 7:10.

Faura: What was the name of FBI agent that questioned you?

Fahey: Lloyd Johnson.

Faura: What is the name of the other FBI agent who questioned you?

Fahey: Gene Brian McCarthy.

Faura: Gene Brian McCarthy? Anybody else questioned you?

Fahey: No, sir.

Faura: Did they tell you to go to the police?

Fahey: They said – Mr. McCarthy said at the time that I should report this to the police and that they are gonna – wanted to have me come down and report this, and I said that I didn't want to go down there because I was kind of skeptical, and I was – I'm scared. I was pretty appalled at the situation because of what I had seen on TV and what I heard on the radio, it just rung a bell and was pretty well shook about it, and the information that I had at this time – I am pretty careful who I give it to. I don't even discuss it with my neighbor or anyone.

Faura: Have you told this story to your wife?

Fahey: Yes, I have. Not all of it. Just only half of it. While being at the hotel. I didn't want to embarrass myself with her about being en route to Oxnard and Ventura and back.

Faura: I see. In other words you told her that you had met this young lady at the hotel and that you had a brief conversation with her at the table?

Fahey: My wife is also aware that we were being tailed.

Faura: I see. Have you been tailed subsequently? Now, are you being tailed after? Were you being tailed before you talked to the FBI back in town?

Fahey: Yes.

Faura: In other words, when you returned to this town and prior to going to the FBI you were aware that you were also being tailed?

Fahey: Yes. I have been tailed ever since that day.

Faura: Did you tell the FBI that you were being tailed?

Fahey: No, sir.

Faura: You didn't tell the FBI that you were being tailed?

Fahey: I believe I might have. I don't remember, because I didn't think too much about it at the time. Over the weekend and particularly Monday when this man made it very apparent – it was the same Ford, the same man and he came right on my bumper. I was on the San Bernardino freeway on the way to my company when this happened.

Faura: The same Ford that had tailed you before?

Fahey: The same Ford that had tailed me en route to Oxnard that Tuesday.

Faura: Was there any identification marks on the Ford that would lead you to believe that it was the same Ford?

Fahey: The flat front, the color, the shape of the guy, the feeling.

Faura: It was the same man?

Fahey: Same man.

Faura: Now, the FBI is not aware that you are being followed?

Fahey: Not that I know of – no. I don't know, I mean there are so many things that have transpired – I mean – our conversations – that you just don't forget a look when you see one – I mean – there is no similarity – this is the real thing – you don't forget it when you see it again under the circumstances.

Faura: Right. Did your wife also become aware that you were being followed? Was she in the car at one of these times you were followed?

Fahey: Uh. No, sir. (after a long pause)

Faura: Then why do you say that she is aware. Is it because you told her?

Fahey: I believe there was one day, Saturday, she was with me.

Faura: And you told her that you were being followed and she became aware that you were being followed?

Fahey: Right, right.

Faura: And by this time she knew that you knew this information?

Fahey: This lady, this lady, I am sure that if I were to retrack my steps with you, I'll be glad to take a day off and show you my steps and have the people verify that I was with the blond lady and if we could go with some authority, a policeman or a plainclothesman and try to dig this woman out, we could possibly find where she had stayed if she has taken off already. And – uh – because she had a lot of clothes, so she stated and she was en route to Australia real quick and I am sure that – uh –

Faura: Are you afraid to go back to the Ambassador? Could you and I go back to the Ambassador and retrace your steps?

Fahey: I wouldn't go alone. I would go with someone, yes.

Faura: Would you go with me?

Fahey: I would go with you, yes.

Faura: Okay. Let me ask you another question. Uh – did you come to the press because you thought we could give you some protection?

Fahey: Yes.

Faura: Okay. Now, you have heard of *Life* magazine, of course?

Fahey: I get *Life* every day – I mean every week – excuse me.

Faura: Okay, now. Would you be willing to – uh – I am very friendly with the bureau chief of *Life* magazine, and that is a very powerful and big magazine, as you well know. If I invited him – him representing *Life* magazine – and myself representing the newspaper, the three of us could go and retrace your steps through the Ambassador and over to Ventura and see the rock, and so forth, and see if we could locate those waitresses that served you. Are you willing to do that?

Fahey: I am willing to do that; providing that I get protection. I don't want to be got up and routed to Oxnard because I am scared. I just don't want to be caught up there alone.

Faura: Wait a minute. No. You will be accompanied; there will be the two of us.

Fahey: In fact I have accounts in that area. I have accounts in the Valley and I am afraid to come out into the area alone, even as a salesman for my company because of what has taken place.

Faura: How long have you been with your company?

Fahey: About a little over three months.

Faura: Where do you come from before?

Fahey: Well, San Francisco. I used to – I am an ex-employee of the Bank of America. And – uh –

Faura: How long where you with them?

Fahey: I was with them about a year and a half, prior to that I was with a jewelry company for about six years. They went bankrupt and I –

Faura: In San Francisco?

Fahey: Yes.

Faura: Now, please give me a description of the first two men you saw at the hotel when you were entering from the parking lot.

Fahey: Right. The two men that I had – as I was walking up the stairs going into the hotel, I was following, they were preceding as well, and I thought perhaps that they worked at the hotel. As we came to the swimming pool wall, there was a little passageway there. They had stopped and were talking. As I caught up with them – I couldn't make out what they were saying because it was real fast; it was a language that I just didn't understand. My casual glance was that they worked there as a porter or something of that nature. One was taller than the other.

Faura: What size? What height?

Fahey: The short guy was shorter than you. His hair was kinky. His characterization about himself was that – well – he wouldn't be sitting here with you because he is strictly out of character. The other gentleman was much taller than he and he had – uh – well, as I see now – it was Arabic features. And his hair however was not the same as the little guy, it was straight back. And, uh –

Faura: The hair of the little guy, the little guy was thin also, kind of frail looking?

Fahey: Yes. Right. Fair and frail. I guess that's a good description of him.

Faura: His skin was fair or was it – what was it?

Fahey: Well, I saw the gentleman in the corridor. I thought at first that he might have been Greek, Spanish or something.

Faura: He was darker?

Fahey: He was a little darker, yes.

Faura: And his hair was kinky, you say?

Fahey: Kinky.

Faura: Now, you have seen pictures of the accused assassin?

Fahey: Yes.

Faura: Was it that type of hair?

Fahey: Yes.

Faura: Or straighter?

Fahey: No, the taller guy was straighter. The taller gentleman –

Faura: No. Let's stick with the small guy.

Fahey: Small guy.

Faura: Kinky hair, you say, or he had hair like Sirhan?

Fahey: Well, like, he has his hair done and trimmed, you know? It is kinky hair. I don't know how to describe it.

Faura: Did Sirhan's hair look longer from the pictures you have seen? Did this man have shorter hair than Sirhan?

Fahey: No. He had a pretty good crop of hair.

Faura: Are you now believing that this man was perhaps Sirhan?

Fahey: From what I have seen on TV, and from what I've heard, and from the description that I recognized that day, this was the gentleman.

Faura: And you have seen his pictures in the newspapers and you believe it was him?

Fahey: Right, right.

Faura: Okay, let's go now to the big man. The big man was about what height?

Fahey: Perhaps pretty close to his height.

Faura: How tall are you?

Fahey: I am 5 feet 10 and a half.

Faura: Was his hair black?

Fahey: And it was straight back.

Faura: What was the color of his complexion?

Fahey: Uh – sort of fair – olive color. Light olive.

Faura: Did he also look foreign?

Fahey: Yes.

Faura: Was it more or less the same color as the small man or was he small man darker?

Fahey: I think the taller man was darker.

Faura: The taller man was darker than the smaller.

Fahey: Right.

Faura: Was he thin, the tall man?

Fahey: The tall man was very thin

Faura: Did you give me your height?

Fahey: Five-ten and a half.

Faura: You figure that he was just about your height?

Fahey: He looked pretty close to me.

Faura: When you say pretty close, was he a little shorter, or a little larger?

Fahey: A little shorter.

Faura: Did he seem delicate or did he seem well built, muscular, even though he was thin?

Fahey: Thin, lankish, I don't know how to describe it – leanish.

Faura: Do you recall how they were dressed?

Fahey: Casual clothes. I think one of them had a jacket, he had a sweater underneath, and he had a brown jacket with sort of a different color in here, in the vest part, and in sort of a square stripe – it was a different, lighter color. It was still brown.

Faura: This was the small man or the big man?

Fahey: This was the small man.

Faura: He had a jacket and a shirt underneath?

Fahey: Right, with buttons that came up the opening.

Faura: And the jacket – was it like a pull-over? Like one of those golf jackets?

Fahey: Just a casual regular jacket. I didn't pay much attention.

Faura: When you say jacket, was it a sport jacket?

Fahey: I guess it would have to be a sport jacket.

Faura: It is a jacket like this but a sport jacket.

Fahey: Right.

Faura: And the shirt inside had these two stripes running down just about –

Fahey: The shirt inside the jacket – excuse me – the jacket had two stripes on the outside.

Faura: Oh! The jacket had two stripes. How about the shirt? Do you recall?

Fahey: It was a sweater he had on. It was a sweater.

Faura: Do you recall what color the sweater was?

Fahey: No. I really don't.

Faura: Do you recall the color of the jacket?

Fahey: Brown.

Faura: Solid Brown?

Fahey: A brown affair.

Faura: What about the two stripes running down?

Fahey: They were light brown.

Faura: They were light brown?

Fahey: Yes.

Faura: A two-tone brown jacket. Long sleeves?

Fahey: Long sleeves.

Faura: What about the taller man – how was he dressed?

Fahey: I believe the older man had a white shirt.

Faura: Did he have a jacket on?

Fahey: No. He had a sweater on.

Faura: He had a sweater on? What type of sweater was it?

Fahey: This is what made me feel they worked there because this man, having a white shirt with a sweater on, because I felt that maybe he was going or he was coming and I felt that maybe he worked there, both of them and that's why I didn't pay any attention at the time, I just – a casual glance – I realized there was a couple of guys talking here – I couldn't understand them – I proceeded – I was walking slowly, I wasn't walking fast, because I'd just come of a bunch of stairs and I was –uh –

Faura: Do you recall the color of the jacket, the sweater he was wearing?

Fahey: Uh – it was a dark color – I didn't get the color.

Faura: You don't recall? He had a white shirt – no tie?

Fahey: As I believe he had his back to me. That's the way I looked at him. The gentleman – the smaller gentleman was facing me as I went by.

Faura: I see. Did you take a look at the shoes?

Fahey: No. I was going where the voice was and that's the way I stayed. I mean you just don't notice those things as you walk by because you are unaware of anything that is going to happen.

Faura: Now, let's go back over the dialect that you heard. You say that you would recognize if somebody was talking Spanish?

Fahey: Yes.

Faura: Spanish accent you are aware of?

Fahey: Yes, I worked with Spanish people before – with Bank of America – the wonderful people that worked there and I have heard them. They used to tease me and call me "gringo," but I mean that's –

Faura: And you say that it was definitely not a Spanish accent.

Fahey: Definitely. Wasn't Spanish. It was some other language.

Faura: Anything else that you remember at all?

Fahey: Not –

Faura: What about when the girl took you upstairs and you noticed that she had been there before, you said to her, "You say you aren't staying in the hotel, but you know the hotel?"

Fahey: Yes, because she had taken me up a set of stairs that –

Faura: She said, "I know the way out," she said – How did she explain that, or did she give you an explanation?

Fahey: Well, it made me feel funny going up a set of stairs that we were – don't normally go up I guess. I don't know whether it was a public thoroughfare or not, but it had carpet on it and I was unaware of the stairs being there and I said to her, I said, "Gee, you don't stay at the hotel but you certainly know how to get around." This is what I said to her and she said, "I know a way to go out the back way." Well, she was unaware at the time that my car was parked out in the back also, and when I told her that my car was parked out in the back on the street, and then she acted like she knew the way. We went out the back, no question.

Faura: And she didn't offer any explanation on how she knew the way out or anything? How she was familiar with the hotel?

Fahey: No, sir.

Faura: At the time did she indicate to you that she had been at the hotel prior to that day?

Fahey: No, sir.

Faura: But she did say she was going to be there that night?

Fahey: She said she was going to be there and she invited me to, to be there and I said "no" and she became very perturbed because I wasn't going to be with her.

Faura: In other words, that night you were not there.

Fahey: I was not there.

Faura: Now, her hair – was it long? Sort of a pony tail in the back?

Fahey: Well, not in the back, the pony tail came down the side, where you could bring it up and roll it real quick in a bun.

Faura: Did she at any time roll it up in a bun while she was with you?

Fahey: Yes. Yes, up in Oxnard she had rolled it in a bun.

Faura: She did? Then she let it down again?

Fahey: Then she let it down again. She had a little clip she'd put on it when it was down, and it came right down to the – almost touch her shoulder but not quite.

Faura: Now, she – when you left her at the hotel – what time was that?

Fahey: When I left her at the hotel? I pulled up in front on Wilshire Boulevard. This was approximately 7:10 P.M.

Faura: 7:10 P.M.? She did not ask you to take her home?

Fahey: Sir?

Faura: She did not ask you to take her home?

Fahey: No. She asked me to take her to the Wilshire Boulevard entrance to the Ambassador Hotel.

Faura: She asked you to leave her there?

Fahey: This was up when we left Trancas Restaurant.

Faura: When you left Trancas Restaurant?

Fahey: Right. How do you pronounce that?

Faura: Trancas

Fahey: Trancas

Faura: Do you recall any other conversation on the way down to Trancas?

Fahey: Yes. We had quite a conversation going up and coming down. It both – both up and down pertaining to getting a passport, getting out of the country – uh – she had a lot of clothes to be shipped – she was coming from New York and she did not want to stay in Los Angeles. She wanted to get out real quick because she was involved in something with an organization that was following her, watching her, and she had – she told me – she says for me not to repeat our conversation to no one because if they knew they take care of her. She felt she was being watched and we were tailed and I became a little alarmed about it.

Faura: Did she give you any indication as to where she expected to get that passport?

Fahey: No. Other than take a deceased person's name and their social security number and write for their birth certificate and proceed to get a passport – and how they do this I don't know.

Faura: And she didn't know? She did not give you any indication –

Fahey: I explained this to Agent McCarthy and he said this would have been fraud – and as I see it now – it would be larceny.

Faura: Now did she say she was leaving Los Angeles immediately or after Kennedy was taken care of?

Fahey: Er – she wanted to get out the very next day. It was in her attitude and her approach to let me know that she was hot and she wanted to move and she said that she had to – she didn't know whether she was going to go by ship or go by plane but she was going to Australia because they could not get her there and I said, "Who?" She says, "The Chinese," because I kept saying "who" and all she would offer was, "I don't want to involve you, I don't know if I can trust you" – through the elevation of the day this is what she threw at me every time I would throw a question at her. "Who," "why."

Faura: In thinking back, if you had to find that girl again, where would you start?

Fahey: Over on Kenmore Street, and I would take Kenmore and two, three blocks, and I would start with the Ambassador Hotel, go across the street to the Kenmore Hotel and I would go all the way down to Olympic Boulevard on both sides of the street and hit every landlady.

Faura: Could you describe the girl well enough to have a composite made of her?

Fahey: Yes.

Faura: A reasonable facsimile of this girl?

Fahey: Yes. Now her eyes were blue, but if she was nervous and you look at her very quick you would think they were brown. They were changeable eyes – green, brown and blue eyes. There is a name for that, and I just can't put my finger on it. But you look at her for an instant, the way she was talking, and her eyes would be brown.

Faura: And her nose was prominent enough that –

Fahey: Prominent enough where you could see – uh – that she was from – uh –

Faura: The Middle East?

Fahey: Right. The Middle East.

Faura: Could you describe it as a Nasser nose?

Fahey: Not as big, but similar.

Faura: Now, other than what she said, other than starting the search at Kenmore and Olympic, what other – you know – sometimes we get a feeling that – if you were to look somewhere – where would you look?

Fahey: I would check travel agencies. I'd check hotels along –

Faura: No. We know to go about that, but what I was thinking that during the days she might have mentioned a restaurant, a cocktail lounge, a dress shop –

Fahey: Several times, on the way back from Ventura she said that she wanted to have a cocktail, and I said, "No, no, I don't want a drink." I said, "I am going to take you back where you came – where I found you – and that's it – and I am going to leave you there." And she became very perturbed. "I need your help," and – uh –

Faura: Did she get the impression at the time that you were trying to get rid of her?

Fahey: When I turned her down for a drink – in fact I turned her down for something to eat because I became – I was scared – I was at the time because this Volkswagen shook me up.

Faura: This was before Trancas?

Fahey: Yes, before the Trancas.

Faura: So then you decided to have something to eat?

Fahey: So I decided to – I was pretty shook myself – so I says, "I want to get off the road for a while. I've been driving all day." And I wanted to cool it for a while.

Faura: And then from there on down she kept talking about the passport and so forth?

Fahey: Right. She always would say, "They are going to get him." And I would say "who?" "I don't want to get you involved." Then she would say, "I want you to come with me tonight to the winning reception. "They are going to take care of Mr. Kennedy." That's the way she would talk. I didn't believe it. I figure the lady was either nuts, sick or drunk or something of this nature, she wasn't. Now her hands were very nervous,they were soaking wet. In fact you could see water visible with the naked eye in her hands.

That's how nervous she was when the Volkswagen was behind us, the Ford was behind us. She was really shook and she made me shook. And I have been tossing it around – in fact I tossed it around for a couple of days before I want to the FBI about it, because I didn't know which way to turn. I knew –

Faura: Did the FBI ask you back again?

Fahey: Yes. They called my company, and they left a message under another company's name for me to report to them.

Faura: Have you been there since?

Fahey: Yes.

Faura: No, I mean since the second time.

Fahey: No.

Faura: Have they asked you again?

Fahey: No. They haven't.

(End of interview.)

CHAPTER 11

Fahey's lengthy and dramatic tale, if true, boiled down to conspiracy. Throughout the questioning Faura had attempted to keep his mind on one track: to dry Fahey of all information relevant to the senator's assassination. It was absolutely necessary that his story not be contaminated by engaging him in any kind of argument, conversation or interpretation of what he was revealing. Faura made sure that his few remarks, other than questions posed, were only to clarify Fahey's words, and tried to show little emotion or reaction as possible, a difficult task in the face of the revelations being made.

It was important not to encourage him in any one direction or to sidetrack him by going into detail on anything he was saying at the time. The primary goal in Faura's mind was to let Fahey tell his story the way he could and as completely as possible. Later on he could go into specifics and details.

There were two reasons for Faura's extreme care in letting Fahey tell his story without comment. First, he was afraid to lose him. Fahey had already been to the FBI, and it would just be a matter of time before they would quiet him as a potential witness. Fahey could also have second thoughts and change his mind about talking to Faura, as he was shaken with fear.

The second reason was the natural instinctive desire of reporters not to give police or officials the opportunity to discredit the interrogation with charges that the witness had been "led" and his testimony "contaminated" by prompting of the interrogator.

As it turned out the special unit (SUS) formed by the police to investigate the assassination predictably took that path, not only with Fahey but with numerous other witnesses whose testimony pointed toward a conspiracy.

In Fahey's case, the ploy would not work since, thanks to *Life* magazine financial backing, Faura later took steps to protect Fahey's story from being destroyed by police pressure.

But was the story true?

This, of course, was the important element, regardless of who he was or what his motives were, could his story be documented?

From experience, Faura knew that for a man in Fahey's excited and fearful condition, many details could be left out. Further interrogation of people, even at ease and relaxed, always extracted additional details. Rather than offend him and lose the opportunity for further interrogation by letting him know he intended to "check him out," and verify the truthfulness of his story, Faura opted to show keen interest in the story and recruit him as an inside informant.

"Let's get the bastards that did it," Fahey declared, and promised to meet with Faura again for more questioning and to keep him informed of any moves the FBI made in regard to his story, the line of questioning to which they would subject him and any other information regarding the assassination which he might be able to glean by listening carefully and asking a seemingly innocent question that they might be willing to answer.

Fahey, seeming to enjoy the idea of undercover work, asked for nothing in return. He felt that he could compromise his marriage by picking up the girl and was concerned about his wife finding out. He was assured that it was unlikely the FBI would allow it to slip out, and Faura certainly would not.

Not wishing to mislead him either, Faura suggested that Fahey prepare a good excuse since there was the possibility that if a conspiracy was uncovered that involved the girl, he would be a key witness and the whole story would come out in court.

Fahey accepted this and promised to call Faura as soon as there were further developments on his part. They walked to their cars and Faura followed him to the on-ramp of the freeway knowing that Fahey would feel safer. While driving home, the full impact of Fahey's story hit Faura as he went over it in his mind.

The next day, June 13, a transcript of the interview was made, and Faura went over it again. The implications were too serious to delay giving it to the LAPD.

Remembering that Fahey had refused to go to the police alone but was willing if Faura arranged to go with him, Faura cut off the top part of the transcript (where Fahey gives his name, address and employment) and called the police intelligence unit. Arrangements were made for Faura to meet with one of their agents and turn over a copy of the transcript.

If they were interested after reading it, further arrangements were to be agreed upon for turning Fahey over to them.

At this time, everyone believed the LAPD was seriously exploring all leads that pointed towards a conspiracy. They would soon be wiser.

In Hollywood, the morning of the 13th, Faura did some regular work at his office and planned to continue his investigation into the assassination in the afternoon.

The day before, a woman had called the newspaper, talked to Executive Editor Hubbard, and told of having seen Sirhan in the kitchen disguised as a kitchen worker. He was, she said, with two other men.

Faura called the lady and told her he would interview her later in the week.

On his way out, Robbie, a girl working at the front desk of the *Citizen News* stopped him to tell him about a friend of hers who had a friend who managed a restaurant. According to the attractive ex-showgirl, her lady friend had told her that the restaurant manager was claiming that the "polka-dot girl, Sirhan and another man" had dinner at the restaurant on the night of June 4.

Robbie, a Faura fan since his exposé on Medi-Cal and Medicare fraud cheating in California, was always offering "tips" on stories that she thought should be looked into. She did not know he was already working on the assassination on his own time and was pleased when he told her he would check the story immediately. A few minutes later, with Robbie's auspices, he was sitting in the living room of a 60-years-young delightful and lovely lady.

Retired, the songwriter/businesswoman/entrepreneur by avocation, and astrologer by decree of long hours of loneliness, insisted she wanted no publicity, extracting a promise that he would not use her name.

Nearly an hour of her often witty remarks and sly scrutiny to determine Faura's trustworthiness passed before she consented to contact her friend "the restaurant manager" and arrange a meeting.

Before leaving, she asked Faura to come back for a complete chart to learn what the stars had in store for him and laced it with some nebulous and unidentified dangers in Faura's future.

She had been a refreshingly adorable 60-year-old little girl, but he said good-bye expressing gratitude for the "lead" she was providing and making a mental note to make sure not to spoil his "present" by what was reserved for him in the "future."

CHAPTER 12

The *Hollywood Citizen News* was housed in an old building, paint peeling from the walls, gray and dirty, looking like one of the many former Hollywood beauties who joined the plastic culture of the motion picture industry and helped pave Hollywood and Sunset Boulevard with broken hearts and shattered dreams.

On the corner of the block several coffee shop operators had gone broke while an adjoining hotel survived with the homosexual trade.

Across the street from the door marked 1545 N. Wilcox, another hotel catered to more mainstream sexual practices.

It was in front of this door that the police car was parked, a late model, unmarked car with one occupant in the driver's seat, apparently waiting for someone.

The occupant saw Faura cross the street and immediately sensed he had made his contact. A few minutes later, Faura deliberately withheld a copy of the Fahey transcript until all conditions had been discussed to avoid confusion and error.

It was easy to see the eagerness and almost unrestrained desire to snatch the transcript from his hands.

Faura told him the essence of his appraisal of the story and what was in the transcript. The ground rules were laid.

The police would make no effort to get the man by their own means. They were to read the transcript, and if interested contact Faura. If they called for Faura to produce the witness, Faura would accompany him to Police Headquarters at Parker Center in Los Angeles, and would stay with him until police personnel would come to take him under their protection.

Faura stressed that the witness did not wish to go alone and that he had be turned over at police headquarters.

Faura would wait outside the interrogation room and then leave with him. They agreed this was not much to ask for and a copy of the transcript was turned over to the agent. Seconds later, without further discussion, Faura left the agent's car, which stuck out like a sore thumb in front of the hotel into which a "trick" was entering with her companion.

CHAPTER 13

It did not take long for the LAPD to react to the transcript. They wanted to have the witness for their own interrogation.

Arrangements were made to bring Fahey, still unidentified, to the police, at Parker Center at 11 A.M. June 14. They would meet on the ground floor.

Feeling that everything was going well, Fahey and Faura headed for Parker Center. After identifying himself to the desk sergeant and a quick call by him, two detectives working for the SUS unit came down. They identified themselves as Sgt. Paul O'Steen and Detective Michael J. McGann.

McGann, the younger of the two, explained they were busy upstairs interrogating someone and asked if they could come back a little later, say around 1 o'clock.

Faura could not believe his ears. They were going to let him walk out with Fahey. No effort was made to keep them there or to separate them. Realizing the bonus opportunity, Faura suggested 2 P.M. They agreed.

On the way to the car, Faura suggested to Fahey that this could be an excellent opportunity for him to go through all the stops he had made with the girl. Fahey agreed and Faura knew then that the police had made a tactical mistake in handing him the opportunity that would later prove very valuable. Thanks to that slip, Bonfante and Faura would later firm up Fahey's story where the FBI had failed. Neither the FBI nor the police ever got even close.

Fahey and Faura headed for the Malibu movie colony. The beach would be a welcome change.

During the early days of the investigation, the Ambassador Hotel was alive with investigators. For this reason, Faura and Fahey did not enter the hotel during his reconstruction of his travels on June 4.

Faura was thoroughly familiar with the hotel and its basic layout and it was easy to visualize his movement in the hotel as Fahey described it. In a few minutes they were traveling at high speed towards Malibu. Shortly after they hit the beach at Santa Monica, they pulled off the road into a parking lot Fahey said he had entered. There was no attendant, although there was a toll booth.

Fahey remembered paying an attendant for parking and receiving a Kennedy half dollar as part of the change. There was no way to verify his visit to the parking lot, so they continued towards Malibu and Trancas Restaurant.

At the restaurant Fahey pointed out the table he and the girl had taken that night. He described what they had eaten, said it had been the "special" and told the amount he had paid and described the girl who had served them. He showed Faura the men's room to which he went that night and the women's restroom and the telephone on the wall from which he suspected the girl had made one or more phone calls. A few minutes later they were northbound heading for Ventura. A few miles north of Trancas Restaurant, the land juts out into the blue sea in a camel hump fashion. A huge rock shoots skyward from the land fall and looks down on a much smaller rock. A dirt parking area has been carved out between the two rocks where tourists and sightseers stop for a rest and a panoramic view of the ocean.

It was there that Fahey asked Faura to stop. He then proceeded to show Faura exactly where he had parked, the motions that were made by him and the driver of the Volkswagen, how he drove out of the parking lot and described again his ride to Ventura.

According to his story, he had not stopped in Ventura so there was little point in retracing that route. They turned back towards Los Angeles. On the way Fahey pointed out the spot where he believed he had picked up the Volkswagen "tail."

Returning to the scene of his self-described harrowing experience refreshed Fahey's memory. He remembered the girl had suggested that perhaps she could get passage on CAT or Flying Tiger Airlines. Also that she had met a Mrs. Claire Chennault in New York.

CHAPTER 14

Parker Center is a modern, glass and concrete building, named after the celebrated late Police Chief William Parker. It stands tall across the street from the Federal Building on Los Angeles Street.

The building is the heart and nerve center of Los Angeles police operations, which makes their influence felt throughout the state.

The sixth floor houses the top brass. Scattered throughout the building are small soundproof cubicles designed as interrogation rooms.

It was to one of these rooms that Fahey would be taken by McGann and O'Steen for interrogation when they made their 2 P.M. rendezvous.

The two agents asked permission to duplicate the original tape of Fahey's interview at the San Fernando Police station.

"Give me the tape, and I will take it upstairs and have it duplicated in no time at all," McGann said.

Faura asked, "Do you need to break the cartridge to duplicate?"

"No," McGann responded, "we will fit it into a machine and we can make a duplicate without tampering with it."

"Okay, Faura, said, handing over the tape, "but make sure you return it."

They all went upstairs. The agents took Fahey into an interrogation room and Faura waited outside. Faura can testify to the effective sound proofing of those rooms. Not a whisper filters through even when an ear is pressed against the door.

Much later, the agents and Fahey emerged from the cubicle and McGann left immediately. O'Steen appeared to be irritated. His attitude was one of restrained hostility towards Faura. He said Fahey was not to tell his story to anyone else. He also cautioned Faura that he was not to tell the story either.

Judge Arthur Alarcon had previously issued a sweeping and unprecedented order muzzling all public officials and witnesses from making public statements.

O'Steen stopped short of forbidding Faura to print the story, but advised that the court order prohibiting any dissemination of information on the assassination prior to trial applied to him also.

Faura did not like his attitude or his oblique attack to stop his inquiries. He also sensed that very soon they would attempt to shut him off from all contact with Fahey.

"I don't believe that order applies to the press," he said trying to keep cool.

O'Steen strongly suggested it did. "I'll check it out," Faura said, "If it does it should be challenged."

And challenged it was, by D.A. Evelle Younger in one of his grandstand plays, or so it appeared to some members of the press. He got nowhere.

McGann and O'Steen had not returned the tape to Faura, who asked for it. O'Steen explained that the machine had "broken" and that he could pick it up the next day. He sarcastically said that they could buy Faura a "new" tape. "A good one," he said, "not a cheap Japanese one."

His arrogant and insulting attitude left no doubt he was suggesting that Faura was making too much fuss over a "cheap tape."

Faura was to spend the next two years asking for his tape and going up the chain of command to Police Inspector Peter Hagen. Faura appeared on several TV shows and talked about the confiscated tape.

The first week of March 1970, Inspector Hagen called Faura at home and apologized for "embarrassingly" not being able to locate the tape. "We know it's your tape, and it will be returned to you as soon as it is found," he said. He also suggested that "the D.A.'s office might be holding it as evidence in view of the Sirhan appeal."

Faura knew he was lying, inasmuch as not a shred of evidence had been allowed during Sirhan's trial which might point to a conspiracy. The D.A.'s office would have no use for the tape.

Also, Faura surmised, if the tape had been turned over to the D.A.'s office the police would have asked for a receipt and "a chain of evidence" possession would exit.

Seeing the writing on the wall, Faura wrote to Inspector Hagen thanking him for the call and tried to extract from him a written admission that they had received the tape.

On April 10, 1970 his worst fears were confirmed.

Hagen wrote to Faura: "I have been unable to find any member of this department who can remember receiving the tape from you, nor can I locate anyone who can recall having heard the tape in question."

Twenty years later, under pressure to release the assassination records, the tape was given to the state of California where it can be found under CSA-K50. Under CSA-K32 (A and B tapes) you also hear their interrogation of Fahey in which he tells them clearly that he had gone to the FBI with his story before going to Faura, and that Faura was the one who suggested he talk to the LAPD. Later on they ignored all of this and harassed Fahey to change his story, which he did, only to go back later to his original version after he was out of their claws.

On Sept. 1, 1971 Faura sued the LAPD for the return of the tape – among other things. The young Mexican lawyer who had volunteered to handle the case for him failed to show up in court and the case was dismissed. Had they gotten to him also?

Faura could never find him in his office again for an explanation.

CHAPTER 15

After Fahey's police interrogation, Faura took him to his car. The next day, June 15, he visited the lady who had called the newspaper claiming she had seen Sirhan with two other men in the kitchen of the Ambassador. She had also claimed that Sirhan had been wearing kitchen garb.

Mrs. Carlos Gallegos was a thin, frail looking woman. An émigré from South America, her voice and eyes still reflected the pain of the loss of her husband, whom she obviously had revered. A victim of a notorious absentee landlord, she lived in a substandard flat with a son who aspired to be a singer, and a young daughter then on a month visit to her native land.

That Saturday morning the house looked as if she were getting ready to move. Boxes of clothing were littered all over the small musty apartment.

She apologized for the looks of the apartment in typical Latin fashion, explaining that they had been having troubles with the plumbing for weeks and the landlord had refused to fix it. The night before, while she had been out, the toilet had back-flushed and she had returned to find the house flooded and had been forced to save what she could by removing everything from its usual place.

They sat in a couple of chairs facing each other, the recorder sitting on another chair to the side.

The complete transcript of the taped interview of June 15, 1968, follows. No attempt has been made to correct grammar, syntax or expression.[1]

Mrs. Gallegos: We work here, night work in downtown Los Angeles – Ardee Sportwear Manufacturer.

Faura: How do you spell Ardee?

Mrs. Gallegos: a-r-d-e-e.

Faura: Sport wear manufacturer?

Mrs. Gallegos: Yes. They do sportswear, and I do assistant design and pattern maker. I do patterns for productions patterns.

Faura: Now, will you tell me what you did for Senator Kennedy's campaign?

---

1. For some reason the beginning of the tape did not record when Faura asked for her name and where she worked. The rest follows.

Mrs. Gallegos: Well, I start working from the beginning. I knew Senator Kennedy was the man for us in the United States, for the whole world and I – very much and I did all I could and I was all the time named hostess in these receptions for him and I was – I was always careful and watchful because I knew people was very jealous and envious and so many times they say very unpleasant things.

Faura: In other words you were worried about his safety, conscious that something could happen?

Mrs. Gallegos: Well, unconsciously, I don't know, it seems like I was, because I always was watching without anybody telling me really. I always was watching.

Faura: Okay, now, tell me on the night of June 4th what time did you come into the Ambassador?

Mrs. Gallegos: I – was around 7:30 – sometime around there. I was supposed to be there at 7 o'clock but I was late. I was there about 7:30. I was rushing.

Faura: And you were a hostess that night?

Mrs. Gallegos: Yes. I was hostess every night –at Senator Kennedy's parties.

Faura: You told me that you saw three men.

Mrs. Gallegos: Yes – I was –

Faura: What time did you see these men? And then tell me the story from then on in your own words.

Mrs. Gallegos: I went in there and I started – everyone and I was talking to one of the cousins of Senator Kennedy and then I went to the ballroom where the whole people were and I came back with my daughter and I said, "Let's go and see where he is going to pass by." I don't know I always want to be near. And then I saw three men.

Faura: You went to see where he was going to pass by?

Mrs. Gallegos: Yes, yes, because –

Faura: And you were at the ballroom at this time?

Mrs. Gallegos: Yes. And I knew he pass through the kitchen. I knew that.

Faura: You knew he was going to pass through the kitchen?

Mrs. Gallegos: Yes!

Faura: How did you know that?

Mrs. Gallegos: Because one of the cousins – Mrs. Fitzgerald said that we have to get out – everybody from that hallway, so when he pass through he was not too much people that jump on him – you know –

Faura: Right, now, then you saw these three men where?

Mrs. Gallegos: I saw these three men out of the kitchen in the hallway where the senator was going to pass by.

Faura: Immediately outside the kitchen?

Mrs. Gallegos: Yes. And I was surprised because – I – don't think they were supposed to be there and then I approached them and I says –

Faura: How were they dressed? Before you go into that, how were they dressed?

Mrs. Gallegos: Well, they were dressed like the kitchen helper.

Faura: Was that with the – how was that?

Mrs. Gallegos: With the black pants and the white jacket – you know the regular kitchen helper.

Faura: Uhuh – and this was the first time you saw these men?

Mrs. Gallegos: Yes. I saw the three men standing there.

Faura: Tell me what happened then?

Mrs. Gallegos: And then I approached them and I say, "Are you supposed to be in the hallway? This is the way that the senator is gonna pass by. Why are you three obstructing the way?" And they didn't answer. And I says, "I am talking to you. This is the ways it's supposed to be. You are supposed to be out of the kitchen." And then one of them, the short one – really was – I mean the two one, one in the center, one that is – was to the right side, was the short one. He turned and he says –

Faura: Which one turned to you?

Mrs. Gallegos: The last one.

Faura: The one on the right?

Mrs. Gallegos: Yes. He's short. He looked very Latin. He could be Mexican, he could be Filipino, he could be Hawaiian, because the straight head (hair) combed this way, you know?

Faura: Like flat, plastered hair.

Mrs. Gallegos: Yes, kind of round face and –

Faura: What was his color?

Mrs. Gallegos: Dark. And he looks at me. He all the time were like this –

Faura: Looking sideways?

Mrs. Gallegos: Trying not to give me the face.

Faura: Trying not to let you see their faces?

Mrs. Gallegos: Yes, and I says, "Come on answer me." And he says, "I don't –" He looks at me – like this – see – like this, and he says, "I don't speak English."

Faura: Now, this is the one with the plastered hair?

Mrs. Gallegos: Yes.

Faura: Okay, now the man standing next to him?

Mrs. Gallegos: That was the assassin.

Faura: The man standing next to the man who spoke with you and said, "I don't speak English," you say was the assassin?

Mrs. Gallegos: Yes, yes, yes, yes.

Faura: You are positive that he was the assassin.

Mrs. Gallegos: Oh yes, yes. See when I saw the picture in the TV that they says could not identify him, that nobody knew who he was, Immediately I went to the *Citizen* – to the telephone, and I took the *Citizen News* and I says, "Please let me talk to the editor," and I did not want to talk to anybody else because I thought I was going to take it by – you know so many people call for nothing."

Faura: let me ask this, he-you are positive one was the assassin and the other one, the one that said, "I do not speak English," was the one with the plastered hair, and the third one. Would you describe that man?"

Mrs. Gallegos: The third one was about – about your size – probably this short. Not too dark and was wearing glasses and – no – I would say that he was more light complexion. The other one was not too dark either. The darker one was the one who says. "I do not speak English."

Faura: Now, you told me first, originally, that one of them was taller than kind of lean. Does that –

Mrs. Gallegos: That was the one who has glasses. And he was the taller, about your size.

Faura: Could he have been taller than me?

Mrs. Gallegos: No. Perhaps a little shorter, because see, he was slim – he might have looked taller. No, no, because, see, compared to the others he was not – I mean when I recall the man – if he was real tall man he would be huge to these ones because these ones were very short. He was shorter than me – you know like –

Faura: The other men were as short as you are? I mean – like more or less our size?

Mrs. Gallegos: No. They were shorter. See, you are a tall man to me. Stand up, please. Yes, the other was about your size. See, you are a little husky, but the other was thin –

Faura: Thin and leanish?

Mrs. Gallegos: That is why he looked taller.

Faura: Oh, I see. That is the reason why he looked taller? Okay, now do you remember his hair? The lanky one.

Mrs. Gallegos: It seems like he has curly hair, more or less it was like – I mean not too curly. He could be a little more curly hair than you, but I didn't pay attention to him because he was more in the – he was – I don't know, he was moving, moving. He gave me the sensation that he was going like this – (demonstrating)

Faura: Like he was backing away from you.

Mrs. Gallegos: Yes.

Faura: He didn't say anything – did he?

Mrs. Gallegos: And the assassin doesn't say anything. The only thing I remember is that then I – I talked to the short one – I says, "Oh, you don't speak English but you says so well. But anyway, of you no speak English, I am gonna talk to you in Spanish." And I did talk to him in Spanish

Faura: What did you say to him in Spanish?

Mrs. Gallegos: I says, "*Porque no me contesta ud? Que hace ud?*" (Why don't you answer me? What are you doing?)

Faura: Okay, now –

Mrs. Gallegos: But he didn't answer. But not only that he didn't answer, he (unclear, sounds like he skipped his head, skipped ahead) – like this you know. I only saw the profile. Only once saw him when he says, "I don't speak English," but impressed me. I have his face very well on me.

Faura: You mean the assassin's face?

Mrs. Gallegos: And this one, the short one.

Faura: And the short one also?

Mrs. Gallegos: And the short one also.

Faura: You say the tall one had glasses?

Mrs. Gallegos: Yes. He has glasses.

Faura: And they, all three, had kitchen uniforms? They were all dressed the same way?

Mrs. Gallegos: Yes. All dressed the same way.

Faura: Was there anything else that you noticed that was peculiar about these three men?

Mrs. Gallegos: The one that was in the middle that was always with the – some kind of smile – you know some kind –

Faura: Like a smirk?

Mrs. Gallegos: Yes. Something – uh – I say to him I says, "And now you why don't you answer, don't you speak English either"?

But he didn't answer – he kept like that – and then he turned to me again and smiled – but he smiled in such a funny way. I says, "you know how to smile but you don't know how to answer?" And then the other man said, the tall one said, "Come on, let's get out of here." And they just left.

Faura: When the tall man spoke and told them to "Come on, let's get out of here," did he have and accent or did he speak very good English or what?

Mrs. Gallegos: I didn't notice an accent. No, I didn't.

Faura: What did they do next?

Mrs. Gallegos: They disappeared. They went to the kitchen.

Faura: They went into the –

Mrs. Gallegos: They went into the kitchen.

Faura: Did you see them after they went into the kitchen?

Mrs. Gallegos: No. I went to the door and turned to watch, but in that minute my daughter called me and says, "they are – they are needing you, come on, they are needing you in the other room to organize." So I left there and when I came back I didn't see them.

Faura: Now, what time was it more or less when the three went into the kitchen?

Mrs. Gallegos: It was a few minutes after – it might be 8 o'clock – I imagine about 8, 8:30, because you know they always says that the senator would be 8 o'clock but he always was little delayed sometimes you know and – uh – it might be 8, 8:30 but they were there. That's why when I saw the picture immediately I called the *Citizen-News*. I says – I says, "Mr. Editor, please don't take me wrong, but I know that man and if you want to have the identification of the man you have to look in the kitchen of the Ambassador, because the Ambassador must have some record of his employees and this man works there. And this man says, "Are you sure?" I told this editor what I have (been) telling you and he says, "Are you sure?" I says, "I am seeing the picture on the TV and that is why I called you, that is the man I approached to, I talked to, he didn't want to answer me."

Faura: Have you – did you talk to the police at all or the FBI?

Mrs. Gallegos: I did talk to the FBI. And I called one agent – I don't know what he was, and I told the same thing and I says, "Please look into this much better." And he says, "Oh, we have all the details." And I says, "Please see that justice has been done." And he says, "Yes, what is your name? So, I gave him my name and I says, "Please, I don't do this for publicity. You might believe I am looking for publicity, and I'm looking for attention – and I am not looking for anything but justice."

Faura: Was that your only conversation with the FBI?

Mrs. Gallegos: That's all.

Faura: They did not call you or you did not go to them?

Mrs. Gallegos: No, no.

Faura: And the police did not call you or you go to the police?

Mrs. Gallegos: No, no, no.

Faura: In other words this is the first time you are being interviewed on this?

Mrs. Gallegos: Yes.

Faura: Now, these men went into the kitchen about 8 o'clock, and then you were called to go back in and help hostess the affair?

Mrs. Gallegos: Yes.

Faura: And you never saw these men again?

Mrs. Gallegos: No.

Faura: During the evening?

Mrs. Gallegos: No. I never saw him again until –

Faura: Did you daughter see these three men?

Mrs. Gallegos: Yes. She did.

Faura: Do you think that she could give also a description of these three men?

Mrs. Gallegos: Yes. She has more. She has more impression of the tall one with the glasses. She says that – she doesn't know why, but she was kind of scared about that man.

Faura: She was scared about that man?

Mrs. Gallegos: That's what she says. I says, "Do you pay attention? Look that is the assassin," and she says, "yes, but I didn't pay attention to those two men, I paid attention the other one because, the other one was kind of trying to running away. And I says, "Did you remember the tall one?" She says, "Yes, I do." So she does remember the tall man but I didn't, I got more impression of the two ones, because you see – it seems funny to me that they turned the face all the time. But she – she says that she look at the straight and the tall one, so she does have more impression of the tall one than I do.

Faura: Now, will you describe the glasses the tall man had?

Mrs. Gallegos: It seems to me like it was round, round you know those round ones, but I am not sure, no.

Faura: How about the color? Were they black or brown?

Mrs. Gallegos: It was dark rims. I couldn't say if it was black or brown, but they were dark rims.

Faura: Dark rims?

Mrs. Gallegos: Yes.

Faura: And do you recall if they were metal or plastic?

Mrs. Gallegos: No, no, I couldn't say it was metal or plastic. It probably will be plastic, you know? I couldn't say, really I couldn't say that.

Faura: Is there anything else at all that you recall of that night, perhaps any more on the conversation or what was said between you and these men?

Mrs. Gallegos: No, no. I just couldn't think of anything else –

Faura: The assassin did not talk to you?

Mrs. Gallegos: No. No one else; the only one was the short one that says "I don't speak English."

Faura: The short one with the plastered hair.

Mrs. Gallegos: Yes.

Faura: The short one was shorter than the assassin?

Mrs. Gallegos: Yes, a little bit shorter than the assassin.

Faura: A little bit shorter than the assassin?

Mrs. Gallegos: About an inch shorter. He was real short. I mean he was real – like no fat, but uh – husky.

Faura: Husky?

Mrs. Gallegos Yes. The assassin was skinny.

Faura: Now the – on the man that you remember best, you didn't notice the kind of shoes he was wearing?

Mrs. Gallegos: No.

Faura: Where there any marks on his face?

Mrs. Gallegos: No, it's a peculiar face. It's a face that you don't forget easy, because although it might be a common face, but it still – it's something that – you know – like – the ways he look – and he was, it seems, the same – I don't know. You know when you are – you look at it?

Faura: (unintelligible)

Mrs. Gallegos: Oh, sure. Believe me.

Faura: If you saw this man again you could identify him?

Mrs. Gallegos: Oh yes, Oh yes, Oh yes.

Faura: Could you identify the taller man also?

Mrs. Gallegos: Yes I can. Yes I can.

Faura: Did the taller man have straight – a full head of hair? Or did have any entrances, you know?

Mrs. Gallegos: No. More or less like you. He combed his hair in the way you have. It was no long hair. The short one has a little bit longer, but no long hair either. It was, you know, it was kind of longer than you, but not long like they use –

Faura: Did he have any gray hair or was it all black?

Mrs. Gallegos: No, no, he was young. I would say he was about, he impressed me like he was 20, 21, but had, you know-he had a face likes perhaps it can pass by (for) 18. He was young.

Faura: Very young looking.

Mrs. Gallegos: Yes, very young looking.

Faura: What would you say the age of the little short man was? With the plastered hair?

Mrs. Gallegos: That was – impressed me – like he was 20. Although my daughter is a young girl, she can guess ages better than I do. I don't – I don't know.

Faura: Now – this is the one that looked young was the one with the plastered hair?

Mrs. Gallegos: Yes.

Faura: Now, how about the lankish, leanish one. How old did he look to you?

Mrs. Gallegos: To me – it might be – but don't take me for the truth because I am not a good guess, believe me, that's true. My daughter can guess the age of anybody very well, but I don't. But I would say he was 28. Perhaps – I'm – I made a mistake.

Faura: But he was older than the other two?

Mrs. Gallegos: Oh yes, he was older than the other two.

Faura: Definitely older than the other two.

Mrs. Gallegos: Oh yes, oh yes.

Faura: Could you write to your daughter, special delivery perhaps, and ask her to give you the description and the ages as to what she thinks they are?

Mrs. Gallegos: I will. I will.

Faura: And have her answer special delivery so that you can contact me and let me know.

Mrs. Gallegos: I will. My daughter won't be gone too much, she might be a month, no more than a month, because uh –

Faura: But could we get it before the end of the month?

Mrs. Gallegos: Oh yes, yes.

Faura: Do you think you could write to her today and ask her to give you the description of the three men, everything she can remember, and how old she thinks they were and particularly the lean, tall man? What she can remember, anything about him, you know the hair, the glasses, anything that she can remember about the glasses and so forth? Could you do that for me?

Mrs. Gallegos: Yes, I will, and I will tell her to write in English, because, you know, she must have English because she was – I mean – speaks –

Faura: If she wants to write in Spanish, that's Okay.

Mrs. Gallegos: No. In English is much easier for her. In the Spanish she makes very much mistakes.

Faura: Oh, well – good, if she can do it English then better yet.

Mrs. Gallegos: Yes.

Faura: Very good. Okay, thank you very much.

Mrs. Gallegos: Don't mention it, my pleasure. I wish I can help.

(End of tape.)

A quick appraisal of Mrs. Gallegos statements, if true, established elements of Fahey's story: a tall, leanish, dark complected man at the Ambassador the day of the assassination, this time he was in the company of Sirhan, if her identification of Sirhan was correct; and a second dark complected man in the company of the leanish one and Sirhan.

Of equal importance was the fact that she placed the man she claimed was Sirhan in the kitchen disguised as an employee. If she was correct, this would help reconstruct Sirhan's movements prior to the shooting.

Suspecting that the police would take pains to do just that he did not get involved in that kind of investigation. Other things came to mind while reading the transcript of her interview. Why had not the FBI or the police questioned her? It was now ten days since the senator had been killed. Sirhan at the kitchen with two other men in a confrontation with Gallegos would have been a very important lead to follow.

CHAPTER 16

The FBI and the police had been saying that every lead would be meticulously followed and explored, but the agent to whom Mrs. Gallegos spoke left the impression that he had little interest. Her call had been made just after Sirhan's picture was flashed on television screens across the country, a few hours after the shooting. What did the agent mean by "we have all the details?"

The remark could be interpreted as a monumental presumption or lack of interest because the agent thought Gallegos was a crank.

In either case, it was clear the FBI had been lying about every call and lead being followed. They never spoke to Gallegos.

The LAPD was given a copy of the Gallegos transcript and arrangements were made to interview her. An intermediary was to deliver Gallegos to either Captain Hugh Brown, titular head of the investigation, or Chief of Detectives Robert A. Houghton.

This time, both officials declined to meet with Faura, because they were "tied up" with other matters, Gallegos was to be picked up at her job and interrogated.

The FBI had traditionally refused to cooperate with the LAPD, "taking all they could," in the words of LAPD personnel, "and giving nothing." This attitude pervaded and poisoned their relationship creating great friction and lack of cooperation.

It was now clear to Faura that the FBI was playing the same game with him. Were they upset because he was locating and interviewing witnesses before they did? Faura was convinced that was the case.

He felt justified in his actions inasmuch as the FBI was interviewing witnesses and not passing the information promptly to the LAPD. Officially the LAPD was in charge of the investigation, since the crime had occurred in their jurisdiction. The FBI was to assist and assign a liaison agent. This is what the public was told. In fact, the FBI assigned more than 400 agents to the investigation.

Gathering information as fast as it could, the FBI was withholding it from the LAPD or delaying before it relayed the information to the LAPD.

Gallegos was a case in point. Had Faura not turned the transcript of his interview with her over to the police she probably would have never been questioned.

Rabago, the man Faura had traced, and who had spoken to Sirhan at the Rafferty party, was another example. At the time Faura talked to him he had already talked to the FBI, and they had failed to pass the information on to the LAPD. His testimony was important enough to make him a witness during Sirhan's trial.

Determined to learn and pass on to the public all he could with his modest resources, Faura made up his mind not to let official jealousies interfere with the track of his investigation.

He felt this could lead to difficulties with the LAPD and the FBI, suspicious now because of what he felt was unforgivable petty haggling between the agencies. Fearful of a complete whitewash à la the Dallas-Warren Commission on the John Kennedy assassination, Faura made up his mind to ignore the LAPD and FBI and proceed with his investigation.

Gallegos would be the last witness or information he passed on to either of them.

Both the LAPD and FBI sank to the lowest form of character assassination to stop Faura or shut him off from sources of information. Working alone and silently on the leads he developed, Faura managed to stay ahead and prevent them from shutting up witnesses before he got their stories.

Some witnesses volunteered that they would not be shut up under any circumstances and that they would continue to talk to him after they were interrogated by the police or the FBI. Some also acted as inside informants, relaying to him remarks by their interrogators, thus providing other leads.

Sometimes the humor of the whole situation would make Faura laugh, at least during lighter moments or breaks in the grueling pace.

Had the subject not been so serious, it was fitting for a soap opera. The LAPD and the FBI competing like two Hollywood queens, hints of the CIA feebly dipping its toes in the murky waters, the bulk of the Los Angeles press fat, lazy and unimaginative as usual, waiting patiently for police handouts, and a handful of adventurous newsmen weaving in and out of the cloak and looking over their shoulders for the dagger.

It was a game in which the American public and its institutions would be the greatest losers. And a short time later, the accuracy of this comedic analysis would be sadly played out.

Shortly after interviewing Gallegos on June 15, Fahey, Detective Chuck Stein and Faura met at the San Fernando Police Station.

Not wishing to lie to Stein and trying to protect him from involvement on the case, Faura asked if Stein would do a police composite picture of a "girl involved in a case I am now investigating."

Stein, a young, handsome, up-and-comer detective had recently been married but consented to come that Saturday to do Faura the favor. Faura suspected that Stein, in the back of his mind, might have had some inkling that this had to do with the "polka-dot girl." But Stein did not ask, sensing that Faura did not want to tell.

Patiently, Fahey described features, rejected and approved plastic portions of the puzzle that was to give the face of the girl he had been with. Slowly, meticulously, the transparent pieces of plastic shaped up a facsimile that pleased Fahey.

"That's close enough," Fahey said.

Deep set, shaded eye sockets harbored sorrowful-looking eyes. They were to be the most noticeable feature that would trigger the recollections of other people.

Fahey left, and Faura headed for the house of a friend whose fashion-oriented wife subscribed to several women's hairstyle magazines. On the way, he picked up a couple of magazines on women's hairstyles at the newsstand.

John and Phyllis Racky, knowing that Faura was somehow involved in chasing the "the polka-dot girl" but was unable to talk about it, helped search for the hairstyle he was looking for but asked no questions he could not answer.

Vincent DiPierro, a young kitchen employee of the Ambassador, had told police that he had seen Sirhan in the kitchen prior to the shooting, next to a girl in a "polka-dot dress."

According to DiPierro, he had noticed the girl because "she was attractive." He also said she was "well-built, but not pretty." He had added that Sirhan had said something to the girl and that she had smiled at Sirhan as he helped her down from a low perch she was standing on for a better view.

Sandy Serrano, the Kennedy worker, had said that the girl who had run past her claiming to have shot Kennedy had a "bouffant" hairdo.

In everyone's mind, including the police, DiPierro and Serrano had seen the same girl.

Therein lay the search for the "bouffant" hairdo. It was a futile search. Only the people who had seen the girl could reconstruct that hairdo with the help of an artist.

No connection had been established between Sandy Serrano's testimony and Fahey's. Nothing had been said to even remotely link them. Why, then, combine Fahey's girl composite to Serrano's polka-dot girl hairdo?

Faura tried to avoid mixing the two girls in his mind, because if both stories were true, two possibilities existed. First, two girls might have been involved in the assassination. Second, the girls seen by Serrano, Fahey and DiPierro were the same.

The easiest course for a one-man investigation was to make a composite or portrait of Fahey's girl, since he had spent a whole day with her, and show it to Serrano and DiPierro.

If they had never seen the girl in the composite, then he knew he had to track down more than one girl and a decision would have to be made then as to which lead to follow.

If Serrano and DiPierro recognized the girl in the composite, the conspiracy theory would be considerably strengthened and tracking only one girl down would be simpler. It was urgent to produce the best resemblance of Fahey's girl and get the picture to DiPierro and Serrano.

A reporter's salary is hardly adequate to support a family, let alone the most elementary needs of an investigation such as Faura had embarked upon.

Now he needed to consult with an attorney to discuss some aspects of the investigation and engage him for his next move.

Gary Barnett was an attorney just beginning his own practice. He passed his bar exam in 1968 and was associated with Robert Fitzpatrick, the attorney who represented the Beatles in Los Angeles.

Looking as if he were in his teens, but actually in his mid-20s, Barnett approached law in a manner that was mature and thorough but laced with a vivid, fast imagination and a sense of adventure.

Mainly, he was a good friend with whom Faura enjoyed an occasional drink and hours of tall tales along with Gordon Grant, a *Los Angeles Times* reporter and mutual friend. Most important of all, for this project, Barnett could be had free or at least on the cuff. Faura went to him and talked Barnett into joining the project.

CHAPTER 17

On June 16, Father's Day, Faura picked up Barnett, and together they headed for Chinatown, where they found without difficulty a portrait artist.

The idea was to have the police composite, which is usually kind of raw, polished into a finished portrait, much in the same manner a photograph is converted into a portrait.

The Chinese artist took one look at the composite and eyed Faura knowingly. It was not a usual request. "How much," Faura asked.

"How much is it worth to you," he countered with a sneer. "It's a police composite, isn't it?"

Chinatown in Los Angeles is a country by itself, with its own culture and riddled with tunnels, with all kinds of colorful tales told about it. And it is heavily policed. The artist's attitude and slickness told them he was out to gouge them. Also there was a high probability that as soon as he got through, he would call the police and tell them about the request.

Faura suggested something obscene he could do with his chalk and they left. A discrete artist had to be found, someone who would avoid contact with the police as a natural thing in his daily life – a hippie.

A few minutes later they were on the Harbor Freeway southbound for the Ports O'Call; a tourist complex of businesses on the San Pedro waterfront. Several hippie artists worked there.

Within two hours they had two life-sized, full-color portraits of Fahey's girl.

The artist, Tom Moore, was a gentle and talented young man. With a stroke of his pinky finger he would change features, lighten here, darken there, transforming the police composite into a lifelike portrait.

The "polka-dot girl" fever was high in those days. Faura had identified himself as a newsman to Moore, and had given him a cover story for what he was asking Moore to do. If he believed it, obviously a co-worker did not. When the portrait was finished, Moore's co-worker, an artist who worked at the adjoining stall, came over and took a look at Moore's work.

"How about putting a polka-dot dress on her?" he remarked, laughing. Faura and Barnett knew it was time to go.

As soon as they were in the car Faura asked Barnett to look inside his shirt pocket. Barnett did, drawing out a marijuana cigarette and almost fainting, visualizing his career going up in smoke before it began, should he be caught with the drug in his pocket.

Faura explained that the marijuana had been dropped in his pocket by one of the artists as he boldly reached into Barnett's shirt pocket while asking for a match. It had been a gesture of camaraderie and goodwill and a way of letting us know he trusted us in spite of the fact that he suspected we had lied to him.

The marijuana had been dropped in Barnett's pocket while Moore was in the middle of his portrait and they had been laughing over a funny exchange between Barnett and the artists.

Shortly afterwards, the mailbox of the police station north of San Pedro was one marijuana "stick" richer.

Back in Los Angeles, late in the afternoon, they stopped at the Holland House, a restaurant managed by a man who claimed the "polka-dot girl" had eaten there with Sirhan and another man the night of the shooting. The Holland House was next door to the Ambassador Hotel.

Ermon "Buddy" Parr was closing manager of the Holland House the night of the shooting. He told of seeing a girl in a "polka-dot dress" accompanied by two "ruddy complected" men of "slight build," going through the self-service line of the cafeteria and mingling with the Kennedy workers eating there.

He remembered her "legs" and a "purple polka-dot dress."

Her hair was not "bouffant" but "stringy" and "hanging over her shoulder." She and the two men had been there "around six or seven."

Parr said he remembered them "after Sirhan's face was flashed on the TV" and the rumor ran though the restaurant that Sirhan had been there. There was nothing noticeable about her eyes, hair or any other features, "just a girl."

"I cannot be completely positive," Parr said. "From the picture that they flashed on the TV screen, I remember seeing a man of his description, of his looks and of his build, and of the way he dressed come through our line, and he ate with us that evening."

He was positive Sandra Serrano had eaten there also.

The interview did not last long. He refused to allow Faura to talk to any of his employees for more details and verification of what he was saying.

His story was couched in too many nebulous statements. His refusal to let his employees be interviewed did not help any. His statement that he had "reflected" about it after Sirhan was shown on TV and remembered the trio did not strengthen his story.

Knowing that well-intended people get confused with the flurry of information and rumor that comes out at times of sensational stories, Parr's story did not offer any solid leads. Had he allowed his employees to be interviewed and had they confirmed his story it would have been valuable, but that was not the case. Faura transcribed the tape and filed it. It was the first unproductive lead.

Mondays have a bad reputation, and June 17 followed suit. For the first time, Fahey missed an appointment with Faura, who knew there was no point trying to locate him. He would just wait.

In Faura's mind, Fahey had been picked up by police or the FBI and was being interrogated. Fahey was not working these days because he was afraid to drive on the freeways, according to his own account. The no-show left Faura with a headache and heartache, imagining the worst. Tuesday had to be better, and so it was.

Fahey called and said he had been with the FBI all of the previous day and they made an appointment to meet at Faura's office in San Fernando and a tape was made of the meeting.

A good deal of Fahey's conversation at that meeting had to do with his concern about his wife finding out about the girl having been in his car. Faura had pondered that problem and suggested a cover story. During the course of the interrogation, Faura had stressed that regardless of what he told his wife he had to tell the truth to the FBI and the police and not hide anything. Fahey made clear that he understood that.

The relevant part of his debriefing that day included his observations that the FBI had picked him up at 8:30 A.M. and had also meticulously attempted to retrace his actions on June 4.

According to Fahey, he had left Trancas Restaurant with the impression that the waitress had recognized him. The attendant at the gas station where he and the girl had stopped for gas had not remembered him, nor had they been able to find the parking lot attendant who had given him the Kennedy half-dollar for change.

Life magazine's Bonfante and Faura were later to find out that Fahey's impression of having been recognized by the Trancas waitress had been erroneous and that the FBI had failed to do a thorough job. Shortly afterwards, Faura and Bonfante located the right girl by taking more pains.

SUS would also attempt the same approach to verify Fahey's story. According to Chief Robert A. Houghton, Fahey was taken through the same paces by the police and the net result was a waitress at the Ambassador who said Fahey's face was "vaguely familiar" and another who did not remember him at all.

Both agencies failed to heed Fahey's information that the waitress who had served him at the Ambassador was "temporary help," called in to relieve the pressure of the crowds on those days.

Neither agency did the obvious, which Bonfante and Faura succeeded with later on at Trancas Restaurant.

CHAPTER 18

During his interview of June 18, Fahey said the FBI, besides retracing his steps of June 4, had canvassed the area around Kenmore Street, from Olympic north. Every apartment house, every building where they imagined the girl might have stayed, was checked, with negative results. Then Fahey dropped another bomb.

"However," he said, "we stopped at this Kenmore Hotel; we talked to this man who thinks he has seen her."

According to Fahey, the man he was talking about was the manager of the Kenmore Hotel, at Kenmore and Eighth Street, directly behind the Ambassador Hotel, its entrance facing Eighth.

Fahey described how the FBI had gone over the hotel's "transcripts and records" with the manager. The manager insisted that on several occasions he had seen a girl who matched the description they had given.

The hotel manager, Fahey went on, knew of two girls who fit the description. He knew them both. He was positive the one he had in mind was the girl they were looking for, and added that she had been seen going up the stairs leading from Eighth Street to the Ambassador rear parking lot just one week after the assassination. This report heightened everybody's expectations.

The hotel manager was questioned extensively by the FBI, Fahey said.

"How could he see her go up the back stairs," Faura asked.

"Because his hotel and his desk face the back stairs of the Ambassador; right across the street," Fahey replied.

He added that the FBI had left their calling card with a 24-hour number, instructing the hotel manager to call them if he saw the girl again.

The FBI, Fahey said, had also talked to his boss and arrangements had been made to monitor telephone calls coming in for him.

He added that the FBI wanted to see him around 11 A.M. that day and that he intended to tell them about what had happened on the way to see Faura.

"Okay, tell me what happened this morning," Faura prodded.

Fahey: "Well, I was coming up the Hollywood Freeway to the Ventura Freeway. On the Ventura Freeway I picked up a blue Volkswagen on my tail. I cut over to the San Diego Freeway and he was still with me. He followed me all the way out to the Devonshire off-ramp. He attempted like to go off-ramps but he never did. He just kept coming behind me. He was well behind me. He had sunglasses on. He was this slim man again, but he was driving this Volkswagen.

Fahey said he got off on the San Fernando Mission ramp and that his "tail" had left the freeway by the off-ramp before that, after faking to get off but remaining on his "tail."

Faura: And you think it was the same slim man?

Fahey: Same car, same Volkswagen.

Faura: Except that he was wearing glasses?

Fahey: And also that he was driving the Volkswagen this time. He was driving the Ford that day.

Faura: Were you able to get a glimpse of the license plate?

Fahey: Nothing. He was at a good distance. I couldn't see anything but the figure driving and the blue Volkswagen and he attempted to go off of these off-ramps and he did not go off, he kept coming.

The FBI records show that Fahey told them this story when he spoke with them later that day, June 18.

Reading the FBI report, Faura noticed that Fahey's direction of travel was reversed. Was he lying and could not get his direction straight? A careful reading showed that, aside from the direction of travel, the tale was exactly the same.

You do not travel "from the Ventura Freeway south on the San Diego Freeway" to Fahey's Los Angeles office, as written in the FBI report.

The report, Faura concluded, had obviously been written by agents unfamiliar with the area, most likely written hastily. Still, he was watching for such small nuances and discrepancies and planned to be alert for others.

During his interview of Fahey on June 18, they agreed, due to the increased activity between him and the FBI, that Faura's calls should be somewhat disguised.

Since the FBI agents working with him did not know Faura's voice, Faura was to call himself "Larry" on the telephone and pretend to be an old friend.

They could then pretend to meet for a "couple of beers."

It could not have been done at a better time. The next day, Special Agent Johnson questioned Fahey extensively about his connections, if any, with the press – radio, television, newspapers, etc. At that time Fahey informed them that he had told Faura the story of Gilderdine Oppenheimer.

Johnson questioned Fahey about Faura and, according to Fahey, appeared concerned that Faura might publish what was going on and blow the whole investigation sky high.

Fahey accurately told him that Faura had promised not to publish the story until after the girl was in custody or the investigation concluded. Fahey also expressed to Faura his belief that the FBI would soon contact him. He was wrong. They should have, but never did.

Fahey told Faura that Johnson claimed "a girl" had attempted to contact Fahey twice (presumably at work) but had hung up before identifying herself.

Also the agent suggested that Fahey had been "lucky" in doing or saying something that saved him from becoming "an accomplice," "an accessory," or "a patsy."

It had been a slow day, but the evening was to be quite a different story. It would launch the FBI, the LAPD, Faura, and Bonfante on a hectic and frenetic chase that was to put them all on a collision course.

CHAPTER 19

At 6 P.M. June 19 Faura's home phone rang. The call was for "Larry." "I am on the way to the big 'A' Fahey said cryptically.

"Where is that?" Faura asked, missing the meaning of "the big 'A.'"

"You know," Fahey answered, fearful of telephone taps. "The big 'A' – they got the girl and they called me for a positive identification."

In his excitement he had obviously blown their intent to disguise the conversation. It had been Faura's fault for not catching onto the big "A" being the Ambassador Hotel.

The realization of what he was saying exploded like a shell in Faura's brain. The mystery of the "polka-dot girl" would be solved, he thought.

He asked Fahey to delay his departure a few minutes and bolted out the door, yelling at his wife to call *Life* magazine for Bonfante to get there with a photographer right away. Also to call Don Campbell, a photographer friend. He wanted photos of the girl being picked up to back up his story.

A few minutes later, after an insane ride on the freeway, he pulled into the rear parking lot of the Ambassador Hotel.

There was no sign of Fahey or the FBI. He half-walked half-ran into the hotel and quickly checked the cafeteria and lounges. Everything looked normal and neither of the people he had asked his wife to call had materialized. Jogging down to the parking lot, he jumped some hedges to Eighth Street, trying to avoid being seen by the people at the Kenmore Hotel across the street from the Ambassador's parking lot.

Flashing his press credentials to a startled desk clerk, he raced to the roof of a building next to the Kenmore, from where he could command a view of Ambassador's parking lot, the Kenmore and the general vicinity.

From that position, it would be possible to observe the FBI taking the girl into custody, and hopefully, the beginning of the end.

Bonfante and *Life* magazine photographer Julian Wasser were also racing to the Ambassador, having been contacted by Faura's wife.

FBI agents Johnson and McCarthy sped to the Ambassador to rendezvous with Fahey who was, in turn, rushing to meet them in hopes of making a positive identification of the girl.

As Faura went to the top floor of the building next to the Kenmore Hotel, he was unable to have a clear view outside. He ran to and hurriedly climbed an old rusty fire escape on the outside of the building, almost falling from the top in his careless haste.

Bonfante and Wasser, unseen by Faura, had already arrived at the Ambassador and had planted themselves in the coffee shop near the corridors where they could observe people coming and going.

At the Kenmore Hotel, across the street from the Ambassador rear parking lot, the man who had sounded the alarm waited anxiously for the FBI to arrive, unaware of the other forces converging there in response to his information.

Ty Hammond, manager of the Kenmore Hotel, was the man Fahey claimed had told the FBI that he had seen a girl, who answered the description of the one they were seeking, going up the the Ambassador's rear stairs a week after the assassination.

Hammond had also told the FBI that there were two girls who answered the description, that he knew one of them quite well and that he was convinced that she was the one they were looking for.

Less than a hundred yards away from Hammond, Faura anxiously awaited the arrival of the FBI from his precarious perch.

Scanning the parking lot foot by foot, he could see no activity – not a soul walking or driving. Could the FBI have already come, arrested the girl and gone? Was Fahey with them? Did Fahey identify the girl as the one who was with him June 4? Would he be silenced now? All these questions raced through his mind.

On the street below, the traffic ebbed and flowed. At the Kenmore everything was quiet. Parked near the stairs leading up to the second level on the open parking lot was a car identical to Fahey's – same year, same color –Fahey's? Or coincidence?

Twenty minutes had passed and nothing had happened, so Faura decided to abandon his vigil and go down to the Kenmore's desk, where he was told by Hammond's wife that Hammond was not there. Faura walked to the corner in the direction of the building he had just left.

Two men in a coffee-colored Dodge Polara pulled up in front of the Kenmore. One of them got out and went into the hotel. Sensing something was up, Faura crossed the street quickly and climbed over some bushes so he could not be seen going up the stairs. Walking towards the stairs, now still behind the bushes, he observed the car and its occupant.

Unknown to him then, either the police or the FBI had seen him crossing the street and his attempt at camouflage behind the bushes. Weeks later, Sgt. Dan Cook, LAPD Public Information Officer was to joke to him about "reporters hiding behind bushes."

The occupant of the Polara who had gone into the Kenmore spoke briefly with somebody in the lobby, returned to the car and drove away.

Realizing it was impossible for one man to cover the whole area, Faura decided to try to find Bonfante. Walking through the Embassy and Venetian Rooms, just in case they might be wandering around there, he found them at the coffee shop where they had positioned themselves. Bonfante and Wasser, his camera slung under his coat, had been waiting for a few minutes and had not observed anything unusual, they said.

Going on the assumption that the girl had been taken into custody, the three debated whether the police would have her in a private room or the security office. They concluded that the only logical thing to do was to take the girl out through the back parking lot.

Giving Wasser a description of Fahey and the girl, Faura and Bonfante left him positioned just outside the rear door of the hotel where he could photograph anybody going out, and headed for the car that might be Fahey's. It was registered to someone else.

Walking around the lot, they determined that Fahey's car was not there and headed back to the coffee shop, picking up Wasser on the way.

More debate.

They ordered a drink and left before they were served, having decided that the best move was to return to the Kenmore Hotel. A car bearing consular plates was parked in front of the hotel.

Bonfante and Wasser, old hands at playing tag with the FBI and other intelligence agencies, pegged it as an FBI car. Wasser was assigned to check it out while Bonfante and Faura walked into the Kenmore. Wasser did not waste any time; casually leaning against the front fender he checked the antenna and looked inside the car. Instead of the telescoping factory-installed antenna, this was fully extended, rigid. This type of antenna was in fact welded and had a transformer under the fender that ensures good communication.

Hotel manager Ty Hammond had returned to the hotel. Faura was questioning him when Wasser, his mission accomplished, joined them. Underestimating Hammond, Faura began telling him of his interest in locating a girl about 25 to 27 years old, described the prominent nose and was interrupted by Hammond.

"Blond girl?"

"Yes, blond girl."

Having stopped Faura cold, Hammond savored his next line.

"I know the girl."

"Then you know who I am looking for"

"Yes, I know who you are looking for. Somebody else is looking for her too," Hammond declared coyly.

"Oh, the police have been here," Faura said lamely, sensing he had lost the advantage.

"Yes, they have."

"Well, fine." Faura was searching for the proper approach now.

"What can you tell me about it?"

"Nothing. I have been asked not to talk."

"Oh, well, fine." He was losing more ground. "Then you cannot talk. Can you tell me when was the last time you saw the girl?"

"Yes. About an hour ago."Hammond was playing cat and mouse.

"Oh, you saw her about an hour ago?"

"Yes."

"What else can you tell me about her?"

"I can't tell you anything else, but I know who can."

His claws were out.

"Well, who could that be?"

Deliberately, coyly, Hammond answered, "The FBI."

"All right. Can you give me the name of the FBI agent?"

"No."

"Tell me this: Did the girl go up the stairs and do her usual bit?"

"Oh, yes, she went through her regular routine."

That routine was walking down Eighth Street towards the Ambassador's rear parking lot and then climbing the stairs to the rear entrance of the hotel.

"Did you notify the FBI?"

"Yes, I was the one who called them." Hammond was enjoying his role.

"In that case you must have a 24-hour number for them." Faura was fishing. He had to keep Hammond talking at all costs.

"Yes, I do have a number where I can reach either one of them at any time I need them."

"Have you seen the girl before?"

"Oh, yes. She used to live in an apartment house that I owned about six months ago."

"Six months ago?" That was puzzling. The girl Faura was looking for was supposedly a foreigner.

"Yes, six months ago."

A trim, well-manicured man walked into the lobby from inside the hotel. Easterner-pale, well barbered, pants belonging to a good suit, white business shirt, open at the collar. He appeared to have just walked out of his room to inquire about something in the lobby.

Satisfied that they had confirmed the presence of the FBI at the Kenmore and that Fahey's information was holding true, they left and went to a bar a few doors away from the Kenmore.

What had happened to the girl? Where was Fahey? While trying to piece the events together, they noticed the man who had walked into the lobby of the Kenmore come over to the bar and sit close to Wasser. They had pegged him as FBI before his actions firmed up their suspicions.

Whether he was FBI or not, they were not about to let anyone into their conversation; particularly such an obvious intruder. Wasser, ever alert, got up and played a few records on the juke box. The music was so loud they could barely hear themselves. Shortly afterwards they separated wondering how the FBI could advertise its presence in such a neighborhood with a car with a consular plate.

It was crucial to find out what had actually happened after Fahey met with Special Agents Johnson and McCarthy. Did they get the girl? Another girl? Any girl?

CHAPTER 20

Fahey lived on North Harper, a couple of blocks from the ugly scar Angelinos call Santa Monica Boulevard in West Hollywood.

His name was on the mailbox belonging to Apartment 4 of the well-kept, sparkling new building. The apartment, tastefully decorated with period furniture and carefully placed knick-knacks was a credit to Mrs. Fahey.

She gave Faura a drink and Fahey told of the night's events.

"You won't believe it," he said." They lost the girl by three to five minutes." Faura's heart sank and a feeling of anger, frustration and sadness swelled inside him.

Fahey confirmed that Hammond had called the FBI, who in turn had called him, who in turn called Faura, who in turn called Bonfante. It was almost incredible. Faura wondered now if Fahey had, in fact, delayed his departure to give him time to get to the Ambassador. Hammond later said the FBI has missed the girl by approximately 10 minutes.

Why didn't the FBI have a 24-hour stakeout at the Kenmore? How could they make such a mistake and lose the girl possibly forever?

Suppressing his feelings, Faura listened to Fahey.

Having missed the girl, special agents McCarthy and Johnson had asked Fahey to accompany them to an address a few blocks to the east of Kenmore.

Fahey, in the car with them, had seen Faura standing at the corner just after coming down from the fire escape. Sitting in the back of the car, Fahey had tried to signal him but did not succeed in attracting his attention. They had driven a short distance to an apartment house, where they went up to an apartment on the second floor. According to Fahey, the tenants were a mixed group of Chinese, Arabs, Mexicans and so forth.

McCarthy had some trouble with a "fat" man who answered the door and had to get "firm" before he would cooperate and answer McCarthy's questions. The man finally denied that the name posted on the door belonged to him and referred McCarthy to the building manager.

McCarthy "flipped" a name at the fat man that Fahey could not catch and the man said "yes." McCarthy asked: "Where did she go?" "Fat man" did not know and again referred McCarthy to the building manager.

Fahey thought he had seen "Delancy" or "Dolhancy" on the door plate.

Minutes later, while the lady manager was telling McCarthy that the tenant he was looking for had moved, her son, a man by the name of David, according to Fahey, came to the door saying he knew where the girl lived and where she worked.

Fahey caught that she had worked or now worked at a place called "Sandy's." David gave the address of the girl as 744 Kenmore St., and that she possibly also worked at a bar at Seventh and Catalina, one block from the Ambassador Hotel.

According to Fahey, the man called David had also claimed to have been at the Ambassador on the night of the shooting, that he had seen everything that happened, had reported it to the police but that the police had not paid any attention to his story.

Fahey said the man gave his information freely, fast and voluntarily, but Fahey added that he had not trusted the man.

Back in the car, Johnson and McCarthy drove, with Fahey, to the Kenmore Street address given by David. McCarthy flipped. The address was a parking lot. They drove to Seventh and Catalina. Another dud. No such place.

Boiling mad, the FBI agents decided to check a bar at Eighth and Catalina. Cautiously, McCarthy went in through the front door. Johnson and Fahey waited outside the back door. Another dud.

Giving the impression that they were going to stay on the girl's tracks that night, the agents told Fahey he would not be called again on wild goose chases. He would only be called when they had the girl in custody.

Fahey suggested to Faura that he investigate David since McCarthy had at one point asked him if he was sure of the address and he replied, "Yes, that is the number." Fahey reasoned that the man had intentionally given the FBI wrong information.

How had the FBI made so many elementary and disastrous mistakes? Were they intentional? How did their efforts to get the girl tie in with the police and D.A.'s absolute disregard and interest in Fahey's story?

Faura did not know that LAPD officials were maliciously and deliberately doing much worse.

CHAPTER 21

June 20 found Faura and Bonfante more determined to find the girl than ever. Having lost her once by a hair's breath, knowing better than to trust the FBI and convinced that the police were not really interested, they had also come to believe a cover-up might be attempted.

It was clear that there was little cooperation between the FBI and the LAPD. Lacking any coordination, it was impossible for either of those agencies to determine how much the other knew and how much each was holding back.

The rivalry between the two agencies created a problem, but also, occasionally, an advantage. Police sources, asked if the FBI had already given them certain information, would start complaining and revealing other bits and pieces on the assumption that we had already picked up the information from FBI sources.

Independently, Faura and Bonfante moved though the vacuum picking up information from both sides.

By questioning witnesses already interrogated by the FBI or the police, it was possible for them to determine the leads each was following and whether they had advised each other of their findings.

For example, interrogating a witness they would ask, "Has the FBI questioned you yet?" If the answer was "yes" they would then ask how long ago, and if the police had also interrogated them.

Invariably, one of two things was found. The witness had volunteered their information but had not been interrogated by either agency. This raised doubts in the witnesses' minds about the sincerity of the authorities in following all the leads. Faura and Bonfante often were able to capitalize on this feeling, and persuade the witness to tell them everything they knew.

Second, it was found that some witnesses had been interrogated either by the police or the FBI but not both. The time lapse indicated that the agency that questioned the witness had not notified the other and in some cases they never did.

Under these conditions, and as legitimate members of the press, it was felt that their inquiries were valid, in fact, necessary, if the truth was to be told to the public.

The excitement of the investigation, an undeniable narcotic, and the challenge of doing a good job in spite of police and FBI interference, added to their desire to unmask the fraud that was already germinating in Los Angeles.

At 10:30 A.M. Faura and Fahey met at the *Citizen News* office in Hollywood. Faura had previously called Tom Moore, the artist who had done such a good job creating the likeness from the police composite made at the San Fernando Police Station. Not wanting to go to a public place they invaded the office of Dan Moot, the newspaper's amiable public relations man, and proceeded with their work in his absence.

This was the first time Fahey and Moore met. The idea was to have Fahey tell Moore which features had to be corrected in the life-size, full color portraits he had made from the original composite. With luck they would wind up with portraits that would be almost photographs.

Fahey directed and Moore retouched, once again, tediously, carefully. If it was not quite right, it was redone. Patiently Moore worked as Fahey asked for changes or retouches. Faura watched.

Moore was a master at using his fingers to change shades of color. Finally they were finished.

In front of them, life-size and in full color, were two portraits no one would ever guess had started from a crude police composite. One portrait had the girl with the hair arranged in a bun on top of her head. The other with a pony tail hanging to one side of her head just short of her shoulder. This one had her hair pulled back in a style that could be described as "severe" or "school marmish."

Pains had been taken to obtain the closest possible coloration for the hair and even a little bit of disarray and loose strands, as described by Fahey.

Tom Moore's portrait with the input from Fahey. Faura does not possess the original. It was sent to *Life* magazine, but never published or returned. This recently found image had been given to documentary filmmaker Ted Charach by Faura.

It was a job they could be proud of. Through Fahey and other sources, Faura knew that neither the police nor the FBI had made anywhere near this much progress in identifying the girl. He knew that either by neglect or design, no other composite of the girl had been attempted.

In the Mack Sennett relationship between the FBI and the LAPD, the existence of photos of the composites provided some confusion for another reporter's investigation.

Having learned of the existence of the "photos" of the "polka dot girl" the reporter attempted to have the police confirm their existence. His sources told him that they had heard about them but that they themselves did not have them. It was the FBI who had them, they said.

Trying with his sources in the FBI, he was given the same story, only this time it was the police who had the photos. So here was the same comedy again.

Two large investigating agencies with untold resources at their disposal, investigating one of the crimes of the century, each suspecting that the other had information needed but too foolishly proud to ask for it!

Amazingly, to Faura's knowledge, the riddle was never resolved for them. No one ever went to him, and he guarded the secret by making only four prints of the portraits. The prints were made at *Life* magazine's office in Los Angeles, while Faura waited outside the lab. One copy went to Jordan Bonfante, one to a *Life* staff writer who would attempt to show the photo to Sandy Serrano, and one to Faura. The last copy along with the negatives and originals was sent to *Life* magazine in New York, according to Bonfante.

Moore left immediately after finishing his masterful work, and Fahey and Faura drove to New Hampshire Street, to the apartment building where he had been with Agents Johnson and McCarthy the night before.

They cruised by, and Fahey pointed out the apartment Faura was supposed to check out. Attempting to find a parking space, they made a left turn into a dead-end street and smack into an unmarked police car, identified only by a shield on the side door. It was a reminder that the whole area was still crawling with investigators, and they backed off immediately. Unsuccessful in their attempts to find a parking spot, Fahey and Faura switched places. Fahey drove and dropped Faura off in front of the building. He knocked on the doors of the two apartments Fahey had pointed out. No one was home, and Fahey picked him up again. Shortly afterwards Faura dropped Fahey off and continued to his office.

The apartment search incident, unknown to them, had unlocked the beginning of the end of their association. They soon learned of their blunder. At Faura's office, he found Robbie, the ex-showgirl, chatting with another woman. After some put-on and a couple of dirty jokes, the conversation turned serious.

The other woman, who asked that her name not be used, told them of an Arab she knew who "might know something about Sirhan."

She looked like a serious woman and, in keeping with an old axiom of his, "listen to everyone who offers a story," Faura invited her for coffee and together they went down the street to a café.

His new friend prefaced her story by saying she did not believe it, yet she sounded credible. "I know an Arab boy," she said, "In fact, my ex-husband and I saw him grow up, who told me that he knew Sirhan and his family."

Faura just listened, offering no comment.

"He claims that he knows Sirhan's girlfriend, and that she is the girl in the 'polka-dot dress,'" she added.

Faura shifted in his seat and she must have noticed his eyes open a touch wider. She added a little more information about her informant. Faura declared that the story sounded a little far-out but promised to check it out anyway.

The lady told him the name of the young man she was referring to, his brother's name and the name and address of the brother's business, and she added that since the young man was on his way to Vietnam, Faura better hurry if he wanted to talk to him.

After driving her to her home, Faura headed for a 4:30 appointment with Bonfante at *Life*'s office.

They took photographs of the Fahey-Moore portraits. The *Life* writer assigned by Bonfante to show the portrait to Sandy Serrano, came in, picked up her copy and noted that Sandy was not "cooperating much with the press these days."

According to the writer, Sandy was "doing what was good for the country and that was keeping her mouth shut like the FBI had asked." Faura immediately thought this was the wrong person for her assignment but he said nothing, trusting Bonfante's judgment.

Poor Sandy did not know what the police had in store for her and how badly they were to bruise her reputation. The *Life* writer said she would try to get Sandy the next morning, and that they would have an answer by noon the next day.

Bonfante and Faura tried to impress the woman with the fact that there were only four prints in existence of the portrait they had given her and that under no circumstances was she to show it to anyone other than Sandy Serrano. When she had done that, she was to return the photo to Bonfante.

Faura called Ty Hammond at the Kenmore and made arrangements to meet him. About 40 minutes later Hammond answered some questions.

"Do you really feel that we are chasing the right girl?"

"Yes," Hammond answered without hesitation.

"Does this girl have deep set eyes?"

"Yes."

"How about the nose?"

"Yes. They have a man who will positively identify her."

"Oh, that's nice," Faura responded blandly, assuming he was talking about Fahey and not wishing to let Hammond know that he knew of Fahey. This time it was Faura's game.

At this point, Faura took out the photo of the composites and showed them to him. A few minutes later, Hammond had verified all the features of the girl.

"That's the girl," Hammond said, "that is a very good likeness of the girl, only the eyes are not so hard and her face is a little rounder."

Ironically that had been Fahey's observation – eyes too dark – when he first saw the "photos." Faura realized that in reducing the portraits from life-size to 4-by-5, the eyes had darkened and other features slightly changed.

Hammond's identification was a relief and a bonanza. Faura knew now that Fahey's girl and Hammond's girl were one and the same. Hammond confirmed that the FBI had not shown him any pictures of the girl. Fahey had said the same thing. The FBI was working from a verbal physical description. The LAPD was nowhere in sight.

It was apparent the FBI and the reporters were on an identical track and using the same people for information, which was encouraging.

As Faura continued questioning Hammond, it became clear that he considered the girl a ding-a-ling, possibly a "bone head" and "pretty dumb and stupid." The girl loved to stick around "Latin types" such as "Puerto Ricans, Mexicans, Brazilians and Arabs." In fact, Hammond said, he knew she had Arab friends.

"That stupid girl is either a 'hop-head' or a hooker," Hammond said.

He added that she continued to use the same routine of going through the back door of the Ambassador. He said the FBI knew where she was and was merely lying low waiting for her to make some contact at the Ambassador. He added that they were staking out her house, expecting her to lead them somewhere.

Hammond talked about some police work he had done in Dallas and Fort Worth, Texas. Wanting to recruit him as an inside informant, Faura made his move then, by bringing back his interest in the girl. Explaining to him that all they wanted was to witness the capture of the elusive girl, he was assured that in spite of what the FBI might think, nothing would be published until the girl was caught.

After a couple of drinks and a lot of superfluous talk at the bar near his hotel, Hammond loosened up a little.

"Look, Hammond, we know the girl is within walking distance of here, and we are going to turn loose a few men to go around with photos tomorrow," Faura pushed.

"Well, if you do that almost anybody will recognize her, the first two or three homes you hit. She is pretty well known in the neighborhood," Hammond said.

Again the confusion. How can this be the girl everyone is looking for if she is that well known in the neighborhood and not a stranger?

CHAPTER 22

In any case the point of no return had been passed and this lead had to be followed to some conclusion.

"If you do that," Hammond said, going back to the idea of showing the photos around, "she might go into hiding and you might blow the whole thing."

"Well, you can stop that," Faura's tone tried to imply that if he refused to cooperate and they were forced to show the portraits in the neighborhood Hammond, too, would be morally responsible for the consequences. Hammond bit the bait but did not swallow the hook.

"All I can tell you is that the girl is on New Hampshire."

More was needed.

"Listen, we know the girl is on New Hampshire. The question is which building?" Faura didn't tell him he also knew the number of the building and apartment hoping Hammond would confirm it. But Hammond refused to budge.

"Is she a foreigner?" Faura used the time-honored technique of changing direction in an interrogation.

"No," Hammond responded, "she is from New Jersey. She is Irish."

He went on to say that her middle name was "Spanish" sounding but refused to say what it was or to volunteer her first name, or any name for that matter.

He did promise to work together with them after some talk on Faura's part about "being mutually useful" to each other.

He claimed that, because of his closeness to the FBI in this and other cases, he might be told when they got the girl, and then he could tell the press investigators.

Faura already knew better. The FBI was not telling him anything. They were just talking to him, but having nothing to gain by telling Hammond that, he said nothing.

Hammond obviously did not know that Fahey and the FBI had been at the New Hampshire address and that the girl had moved from there. Faura let it slide planning to use it later.

At home Faura received a call from Luke Perry, who said he was having difficulty getting anyone at Kennedy headquarters to talk, since the FBI had instructed them not to.

The FBI was using its reputation and the good citizenship of everyone to make them accomplices of silence in the fraud it was committing.

The reporter wondered how many people would follow instructions from the FBI if they knew the truth about what the FBI was doing, and that there was nothing the FBI could legally do to stop them from sharing what they knew unless that person was specifically forbidden by a court order.

On Friday, June 21, the "all-points-wanted bulletin" for the "polka-dot girl" was lifted. She was no longer wanted. The police refused to comment on the reasons it was lifted. The D.A.'s office, traditionally less scrupulous, did the dirty work.

About 10 o'clock that morning the D.A.'s office had issued a press release claiming the "polka-dot girl" was no longer wanted because the "police had established that no such person ever existed but was the product of a young Kennedy's worker's hysteria after the assassination."

While Faura and Bonfante had been meticulously tightening the noose around the "polka-dot girl," the LAPD had been working in an opposite direction. The FBI was to join them later.

In fact, the police, increasingly better organized and already having decided in the middle of the investigation that there was no conspiracy, had put into motion their campaign of intimidation and pressure to discredit witnesses whose testimony did not conform to their thinking. They would attempt it on Faura also.

Sandy Serrano was nowhere to be found, and efforts to locate her by *Life* magazine were to no avail.

Efforts to contact her family in Pasadena collapsed. Their telephone had been disconnected. Sandy Serrano had for all practical purposes vanished. She was to be the first victim of the police tactics. In those days the question had to be asked: Which is correct, the police accusation of hysteria or Serrano's recollection?

CHAPTER 23

It took months of research to piece together what the police had done. In order to present fully what the FBI and the police did to Sandy Serrano, it is best to quote their official record and her full declarations.

A Federal Bureau of Investigations report of June 10, 1968, File # Los Angeles 56-156, submitted by special agent Richard C. Burris, gives a complete transcript of Serrano's original declarations, on television, minutes after the shooting.

The report reads: "William Bales, News Editor, NBC news, New York, made available to SA Richard C. Burris, at Los Angeles, a magnetic tape recording made during the interview of Sandra Serrano by news commentator Sander "Sandy" Vanocur, at the Ambassador Hotel, Los Angeles, at approximately 1:30 A.M., June 5, 1968 shortly after the shooting of Senator Robert Francis Kennedy.

"This interview is as follows," the FBI report continues:

Vanocur: Ms. Serrano, ah, just take your time. I'll hold the mike in front of you, and just tell me everything starting from when you first saw the Senator come in the room and what happened.

Serrano: Well, he, he – everybody, was in the main room, you know, listening to him speak, and it was too hot, so I went outside, and I was out on the terrace, and I was out there for about five minutes, 10 minutes, you know. I start to get cold, and then, you know, and everybody was cheering and everything and then I was standing there just thinking, you know, thinking about how many people there were and how wonderful it was. Then this girl came running down the stairs and said, "we've shot him, we've have shot him." "Who did you shoot? And she said "We've shot Senator Kennedy!"

And aft – she had – I can remember what she had on and everything. And after that – a boy came down with her, he was about 23 years old, and he was Mexican-American, because I can remember that because I am Mexican-American, and I says, "What's happening?" And all of a sudden all this people start coming down that back end and I walked in, and I was by the bar area, and nobody seemed to know anything about it, and I thought well, you know maybe I misunderstood or something.

Vanocur: Wait a minute did this young lady say "we?"

Serrano: "We" she said.

Vanocur: Meaning "we" the Mexican American?

Serrano: No. She was not of Mexican-American descent. She was not. She was Caucasian. She had on a white dress with polka dots, she was light-skinned, dark hair, she had black shoes on, and she had a funny nose, it was – it was – I thought it was really funny, all my friends tell me I am so observant. So I walked in and I said.. – who was shot? And nobody – nobody was shot, nobody was shot, and I said "oh, alright!" and I waited awhile and then I walked to the telephone, and I called my parents in Ohio, and I woke my parents up and I told them, Kennedy was shot, and my parents, you know, have been following me within the campaign, so I was in the telephone booth then I saw, just masses of people seem to run by the telephone, and I hung up. I went back into the main room and asked who was shot. And it must have been 10 minutes – 10 minutes before anyone on that ground floor seem to have known anything. And I said "who was shot?" And then I – this Marge Jay was on, on the speaker, on the speaker, and she was saying "somebody has been seriously injured! Ah, everybody please clear the way, go to the television set. So I was standing by the television set listening to everything that happened, and I couldn't believe it, and then – so I went in to make sure, so I asked "Who was shot? Was it him?" They says, "Yes, it was," so I went back to the telephone booth, tried to get my parents but the lines were all tied up – I couldn't get through."

Vanocur: Did you work for sen – did you work for Senator Kennedy?"

Serrano: I am co-chairman of Youth for Kennedy in the Pasadena-Altadena area. I worked very hard for him and everybody in the Pasadena area worked very hard for him. In 1965 I met him, Washington D.C. in an elevator, he stepped on my foot, and I shoved him, and it's an unforgettable experience. At the S.R.O. he gave me the speech that he'd made that night.

Vanocur: You did not get close to where he was carried out or where he was shot?

Serrano: No, I wasn't, no, I wasn't.

Vanocur: Thank you very much.

[Interview ends.]

It must be remembered that this is an exact transcript, according to FBI records of what Sandra Serrano told the TV cameras minutes after the shooting.

While understandably excited in front of a television camera, it is quite clear that Serrano's first knowledge of the shooting comes from the woman in the "polka-dot dress" running by and saying "We shot him, we shot him."

She then observed a "23 years old" Mexican-American man run out with the "girl in the polka-dot dress."

Serrano has the natural reaction of asking "Who did you shoot?" Seconds later she investigates and is told no one was shot and she instantly assumes she had misunderstood, still no excitement, no hysteria.

Her observations that the girl running was wearing a white dress with polka dots, was light skinned, with dark hair, black shoes and a funny nose are made under circumstances that could hardly be called "hysterical."

It would require a cold, calculating and well-prepared individual, without notice, to fabricate and deliver in front of television cameras the story Serrano was telling.

By her own account, it must have been 10 minutes before anyone knew what had happened at the location where she was. She underscores, spontaneously, her reputation as being an observant person.

Ten minutes after the incident with the running woman, Serrano learns positively that there had been a shooting, and then there is no certainty that the wounded person is Senator Kennedy.

Had Vanocur continued his interview, he might have publicly recorded additional details that were later recorded by police at the Ramparts Detective Division during their interrogation of the young Kennedy worker.

The police interrogation took place between 2:35 A.M. and 2:55 A.M. on June 5, 1968 – approximately one hour after the Serrano-Vanocur live television interview.

DR: 68-521-466, the police report of that interrogation, reads as follows:

> Interview by E.H. Henderson, 7695, J.E. Chiquet, 5233, Homicide Division. Tape Ft.158/273
>
> No. 1 Fem. Cauc. 5-6, 122/27, Drk Bru hair, (short) Brn.eyes, turned up nose, good figure, wht dress w/blk dots, blk shoes.
>
> No. 2 M Mex-Amer, 22, 5-5, 160, Blk hair, Drk eyes, Wht shirt, Gold sweater, long sleeves, button type, Drk pnts, greasy hair (straight).
>
> No. 3 M Mex-Amer, 23, 130/135, Bushy Blk hair, seeding (sic) appearance, Lt. Sport shirt (wrinkled) beige pants.
>
> I saw the three above persons walking up the stairs together. No one else was around them. They were not talking but they appeared to be together. About 15/20 minutes later, the female told me "We shot him, we shot him." I asked who they shot and she

said, "Senator Kennedy." I thought she was joking and did not take her serious. I don't know where they went.

Calmer now, Ms. Serrano had added details of infinite importance. She had seen the "girl in the polka-dot dress" 15 or 20 minutes before the shooting in the company of two men, heading in the direction of the kitchen where the shooting took place.

Her description of the men approximately matched those given to Faura by Gallegos of the two men she had seen with the man she believed was Sirhan. All three wore kitchen uniforms according to Gallegos.

The fact that Serrano saw the girl twice would strengthen the credibility of her observations. She had expanded the description of the girl by saying the hair was dark brown and short. She reiterated that she thought the "polka-dot girl" was joking and did not take her seriously, making quite clear that there was not great excitement, pressure or hysteria at that stage of her experience. Her statements to Vanocur and the police were consistent and identical in their essence.

Hours later, between June 6 and 7, FBI SA Richard C. Burris filed a report of his independent interrogation of Ms. Serrano.

The first two paragraphs are the usual detailed recitation of names, addresses and movements Serrano made from the time she left home until the time of the shooting.

Pertinent testimony on the "polka-dot girl" and her companions starts in the middle of the third paragraph.

> Two or three minutes later, which Serrano estimated to be approximately 11:35 P.M., three individuals approached her on the stairway: a woman and two men, and walked past her up the stairs. As the woman got to her, this woman said "excuse us" and Ms. Serrano moved to the side so they could pass. Serrano said she felt these three people were together since they were walking together up the stairs and the woman said "Excuse us."
>
> After approximately 20 to 25 minutes, which Ms. Serrano believed was shortly after midnight, she heard what she thought was six backfires from a car. Four or five real close together.
>
> During this 20 or 25 minutes, no other person went up or down this stairway past her. Approximately 30 seconds after hearing what she thought were backfires; this same woman who had gone up the stairs came running down the stairs toward her, followed by one of the men who had gone up the stairs with her.
>
> Ms. Serrano stated that as this woman ran down the stairs toward her the woman shouted, "We shot him, we shot him."
>
> Serrano said, "Who did you shoot?" to which this woman replied "Senator Kennedy." Ms. Serrano could have said, "He, shot him" or "they shot him." She insisted the word was "we" but volun-

teered that she realized that "we" could have meant we as a group of Kennedy supporters or as we as society in general.

The report goes on to relate the same story Serrano had told Vanocur about asking about the shooting and calling her parents.

By this time she, according to Burris, admitted that she was "crying and near complete hysteria and did not know what to do."

Serrano was asked why she would call her parents long distance in Ohio before she had confirmed the fact that Senator Kennedy had been shot. She said, "if you could have seen the expression in the face and heard the way she said 'we shot him,' you would have believed her too."

Burris goes on to detail Serrano's account of trying to tell several friends, whom she named, what she had witnessed.

She could not get anyone to understand or pay attention due to the prevalent hysteria in the crowd, according to the FBI report.

"Serrano then sat in front of a television set and said aloud, 'I saw these people come down the stairs, what am I going to do?'" Burris reported, and continued: "A person in the area told her she should find a police officer to tell her story to. Serrano walked out of the ballroom area and met her friend, Irene Chavez. She tried to explain her story to Irene but could not get her to completely understand. They walked out of the hotel towards the parking lot but found they could not leave the parking area and started to return to the hotel. As they returned to the hotel, Serrano walked up to a man and said, 'I saw them run down the stairs, what can I do?'"

This man identified himself as Mr. Ambrose, a District Attorney from Beverly Hills and asked her to accompany him, and he would find an officer to tell her story to.

Serrano said they found two uniformed police officers and these officers took her to an area inside the hotel where they were keeping witnesses.

It was there that Vanocur found her and shortly afterwards put her in front of the television cameras to tell the world her story and open monumental problems for the LAPD.

Serrano was then taken to Ramparts Police Station, interviewed and then taken to Police Headquarters and re-interviewed.

She stuck to her story and added details, if the FBI report by Burris is to be believed. Serrano described the woman she saw on the stairway again for Burris, adding that the "hair was ear length, bouffant style" and she wore a white "voile" cloth dress with quarter-inch polka dots.

"The dots were about one-and-one-half to two inches apart. The dress had three-quarter length sleeves, a bib collar with a small black bow and it was A-line style. (Serrano said she took special note of the dress since she had a friend with one just like it.) This woman wore black shoes and no purse. Serrano said this woman did not wear glasses and had "a funny nose," which she described as Bob Hope type. Serrano said she felt she could identify this individual again, the report read.

After describing the two men she had seen with the girl in the "polka-dot dress," Burris noted: "She said after seeing the picture of Sirhan Sirhan in the newspaper, she felt certain this was the same person she saw going up the stairs with the woman."

Asked if she was certain of the events described above, the FBI agent said, "She said she realizes she was near hysteria over the shooting, but was sure of the events she described. Serrano said she had had only one drink and was not taking any type of medication or pills."

The report goes on for another two pages about Serrano's movements. It states that she was taken to NBC studios by FBI, Secret Service agents and LAPD detectives to view all film coverage taken by NBC at the Kennedy primary celebration, in hopes of locating on film anyone who might look like the woman or men she had seen.

The little experiment, virtually worthless unless all films from all television stations and independent photographers is viewed, was unproductive.

This detailed FBI report is of major importance on several counts.

- Serrano tells of coming face to face with the "girl in the polka-dot dress" and having had to move for her.

- The "polka-dot girl" said "excuse us" indicating that the two men were with her.

- She clearly states she thought she had heard "car backfires" – not shots

- She told essentially the same story she had told before regarding the "polka-dot girl"

- She said "if you could have seen the expression in the face and heard the way she said 'we shot Kennedy,' you would have believed her too," indicating the strong impression the woman had left on her.

- She attempted to tell the story of what she had seen to several people, one of them a District Attorney, before telling Vanocur and his audience.

- Serrano was so sure about the girl that she stated that she could identify her again.

- She said "she felt" one of the men was Sirhan.

- She admitted that she was near hysteria over the events of the night before but was sure of the events she described.

This, of course, should be no surprise to anyone since all she saw and heard had taken place before she knew of the shooting and before she had any reason to become hysterical.

Serrano, by having to answer how many drinks she had had that night and deny that she was taking any pills or medications at the time, had been put on the defensive.

Barely two days after the shooting, and armed with Serrano's account, a clear implication that others might have participated in the killing, the LAPD was moving it's juggernaut to break down the girl instead of paying heed to her testimony and pursuing the conspiracy premise.

On June 8, Burris filed a second report in which two brief paragraphs document this:

"Detective C.J. Hughes (7313) Ramparts division accompanied SA Richard C. Burris and Sandra Serrano when Serrano re-enacted the incident described by her in which she claimed to have heard some backfires or shots at the time the Senator was shot.

"Hughes stated that he was aware of the kitchen location of the Embassy Ballroom where Kennedy was shot, and that it was his opinion that it would have been impossible for Serrano to hear .22 shots on her location on a stairway described by her. He said this was especially true because of the crowded conditions of the Embassy Room, and he knew many people much closer than Serrano who were inside the building did not hear the shots."

Elaborate tests were subsequently made to prove that shots fired from a .22 revolver in the kitchen could not be heard at the location where Serrano had been.

Having demonstrated the distance from where Senator Kennedy had been shot to where she claimed she had been standing, Burris asked Serrano if she still thought she could have heard shots.

She stuck to her guns and denied she ever said that she had heard gunshots. This whole charade was flawed, on two counts.

First, according to Burris, Hughes said Kennedy had been shot in the Embassy Room. Kennedy was actually shot in the kitchen. Second, neither the police nor the FBI bothered to test if Serrano could have heard backfires from the street or the parking lot.

The most authoritative source on what took place is Robert Kaiser, with access to most recordings and records of the investigation. Here is how Kaiser describes the Burris-Serrano fiasco.

> "I never heard a gunshot in my life," said Serrano. "I never said I heard gunshots. I said I heard five or six backfires."

She was right. But that did not stop Burris. He wanted to challenge her about some other discrepancies. Why, when she phoned her mother in Ohio shortly after the shooting, didn't she mention that she had seen someone she felt was connected with the crime?

"I have always had difficulty communicating with my mother," she wailed. "I wanted to talk to my father."

Burris wouldn't let go. "On television, with Sander Vanocur, you didn't say anything about seeing a girl and two men going up the fire stairs. You only said you saw a girl and a man coming down. And later you told police you saw two men and a girl going up together and one of them was Sirhan Sirhan. That was the most significant thing you had to tell the police and yet you didn't say anything about this in your first interview, your interview on television."

Serrano was close to tears. "I can't explain why," she cried, "You are trying to trick me. You are lying to me and you are trying to trick me."

"Now, where have we lied to you, Ms. Serrano?" asked Burris.

"Well," she sniffed, "once you said it was a black polka-dot dress, rather than a white dress with black polka dots."

"The investigators were breaking Ms. Serrano into little pieces," Kaiser wrote, and he was quite right.

Serrano was not the first decent citizen to come forward with information, feeling it was her duty, and wind up on the receiving end.

But Serrano had no idea of what was yet to come. She was grilled mercilessly by FBI and SUS agents. Where Burris left off, the LAPD took over. Sgts. Hank Hernandez and Tom Strong wired Sandra Serrano for a polygraph test and proceeded to break her down further.

Under questioning, they got the girl to admit she had picked up her description of the "polka-dot girl" from Vincent DiPierro after they had been placed together in the room where all the witnesses had been gathered.

She also admitted that she might have picked up other descriptions at the Ramparts Police Station and that some details might have come from news reports. One thing was established quite clearly during that polygraph test. Sandra Serrano was by this time a very confused woman.

But not once had she retracted her story of the woman running and screaming, "We shot him, we shot him."

To the LAPD, Serrano's admissions of confusion were enough. The all-points bulletin for the "girl in the polka-dot dress" was canceled.

The great coverup, started secretly barely 48 hours after the killing, had bloomed out publicly.

Making its final report, the LAPD claimed that the conspiracy possibilities of the Sandra Serrano story had been investigated and that "she

claimed to have observed Sirhan, accompanied by another male and a female wearing a 'polka-dot dress,' enter the Ambassador by way of a fire
escape prior to the shooting. After hearing shots fired, she claimed to
have seen the other male and the girl exit by way of the same fire escape;
the female cried, 'We shot him.' The evidence of reliable witnesses had
demonstrated that no such entry and exit occurred. A sound test at the
Ambassador has proven that the shots were not audible to Ms. Serrano.
Following polygraph examination, Ms. Serrano admitted that her prior
statement was pure fabrication."

In their haste to discredit Serrano, the police forgot that her statement
and description of the girl in the "polka-dot dress" and her companions
had been heard by her friends and recorded by television cameras minutes after the shooting and before she met Vincent DiPierro!

Having heard the statements made by Sandra Serrano to others right
after her experience and then to Vanocur it was easy to see the only pure
fabrication was the police report itself.

For the purposes of Faura and Bonfante's investigation, Ms. Serrano
had been effectively removed, by the police, from their reach, and her declarations put under serious doubt. But they knew better. And they still had
Fahey and DiPierro.

CHAPTER 24

June 21 marked the end of the police farce concerning Sandra Serrano. Faura and Bonfante wondered how public officials, on whom the public had placed so much trust, could be such barefaced and accomplished liars.

That Friday was also the day the Arab terrorist group Al Fatah first popped its head into the investigation.

While Faura was waiting for Bonfante at the Time-Life Building, Ron dePaolo, a smart *Life* staff writer, informed Faura that he had learned that a Jordanian official had delivered to the FBI two packets of information regarding Al Fatah.

The FBI's interest in the Arab organization had been sparked by information that Sirhan Sirhan had once attended a church in Los Angeles that occasionally showed Arab movies.

Supposedly, some of the movies were pro-Nasser (President of Egypt), for which an admission would be charged or monies otherwise solicited. A portion of this money went to church charities, the rest found its way to the Middle East – and to Al Fatah.

A church official, the story went, remembered Sirhan attending the church several times.

DePaolo assured Faura that the information had come from a highly reliable source and he, of course, believed it. It was not, however, the kind of information that could help in the immediate search.

Much later during Sirhan's trial, Al Fatah would claim Sirhan as one of its "heroes," and they involved themselves in Sirhan's appeal.

When Bonfante arrived, they discussed the possibility that the police were deliberately lying only to protect the conspiracy investigation and would, perhaps, later on tell the truth and explain the need for having lied to the public.

Somehow they still could not fully believe that the authorities would be so brazen as to try to put such a hoax over on the public, particularly when they knew responsible members of the press had access to much of the information they were suppressing.

Faura and Bonfante were underestimating the police plans and had no idea to what extremes they would go.

Hoping for the best, they decided to contact Hammond and Fahey. They might know if the girl had been picked up and if that was the real reason for the "want" being lifted.

Neither was home, and they thought that Fahey and Hammond might be downtown at police headquarters or the FBI office identifying the girl. After a short wait, Faura drove to the Kenmore where he found Hammond. Hammond would not say a word. The cooperative mood of the previous meeting had vanished and had been replaced by an attitude that was mildly hostile and aloof.

Realizing Hammond had been lost to them, possibly for good, Faura tried to lose no time and went straight to the point.

"Hammond, give me the name of the girl," he said rather firmly, "or at least her address."

Hammond, a former police officer, was well versed in interview procedures. He looked Faura straight in the eyes and said, "I have given my word to the FBI, and I will not go back on it."

Angry and frustrated, Faura left and went to his Hollywood office, from where he called Fahey.

Fahey's attitude on the phone was scared and extremely concerned. He informed Faura in no uncertain terms that he could not talk to him anymore.

He said that the FBI had spotted Faura at several places where they had "stake outs" and that they were very "unhappy."

"In fact," Fahey said, "they are furious with me."

"Why?"

"They spotted us together when we went to the New Hampshire address," Fahey said, confirming the obvious.

With undisguised agitation in his voice, Fahey added: "I have been told firmly and unequivocally that I am not to talk to you or give you any more information whatsoever regarding this case."

Sensing that there was little point in trying to calm him down over the phone and that he was on the verge of losing Fahey also, Faura groped for something to say. He also needed to know if the FBI was next to Fahey while they were talking on the phone.

"I am glad to see that they are so interested in your story and that they are giving it so much importance, so I hope they are giving you protection," he said truthfully but also fishing at the same time.

"I can't even tell you that," Fahey replied curtly, repeating that he could not talk to me anymore.

Obviously, Fahey either had company or was afraid his telephone was "bugged."

Reassuring him he understood and would not make any more attempts to contact him, Faura said he was concerned about violations of Fahey's civil rights and that he would be in touch later on concerning that subject.

Shortly afterwards, Faura told Bonfante of the new developments. Nothing new had been uncovered, and they still did not know if the girl had been found or was still on the loose.

One thing was sure. The FBI was doing a masterful job of intimidating witnesses – shades of Dallas and another Kennedy assassination.

The next day, June 22, found Faura sitting across a table from a police intelligence officer of his acquaintance.

On his way to monitor and photograph a demonstration on Sunset Boulevard, they had agreed to meet and discuss the lead about the Arab boy who claimed he knew Sirhan and Sirhan's girlfriend.

He refused to go with Faura to the boy's mother's business without permission from his superiors, so Faura dropped the subject.

He then called Gary Barnett, his young attorney friend who had agreed to help, to come down and help with some work on the assassination that Faura did not want to do alone.

While waiting for Barnett, he called the brother of the Arab youth. He was uncooperative and refused to talk on the phone, so Faura agreed to see him personally.

Calling the lady who had given him the information originally, Faura tried to learn more of what he was getting into.

She instantly straightened something out. Faura had, she said, misunderstood. The girl was supposed to work for the youth's brother at his telephone answering service; she was not Sirhan's girlfriend but the girlfriend of one of Sirhan's brothers.

That straightened out, she added there was nothing to worry about, since they were supposed to be very decent people.

Barnett arrived and he and Faura went to the Kenmore Hotel to give it another try with Hammond. He was not there.

Barnett agreed to show the "photos" of the girl Faura had produced around the neighborhood and they began.

Although they believed bars would be a good place to check out, they decided not to hit them until the last minute.

Cleaners, stores, coffee shops, they went to all doors with no luck.

Next door to the Kenmore, the operator of a Chinese restaurant recognized the girl immediately. He remembered her because, he said, she had come in three times "in a row." No, he did not know her name or where she lived.

Several other places were negative. Then they started in the opposite direction, toward New Hampshire.

Another shopkeeper, a lady, said the photo appeared to be the wife of a man who lived at 811 S. Kenmore. She added that the couple was getting a divorce because the girl had been going "to pot" in the past few months.

Faura and Barnett tried a little further down the street for confirmation. Instead, they got a positive identification.

"Yes, of course, I know her, but I can't tell you her name; she works at Langer's, at Seventh and Alvarado." The lady sounded positive.

"You can find her there. The only thing, her hair now is redhead [sic], she voluntarily added.

Her reaction had been so strong; they drove straight down to Langer's. Before sitting down they had spotted the girl.

Deep set, shadowed hazel eyes, prominent nose, same shape of face but – wrong girl. The girl they were looking at was heavier than 125-27, older than 25-27 and perhaps taller.

The resemblance to the photo was uncanny. It was easy to understand why their informant had been so positive. The "uncanny look-alikes" brought to mind that the same thing had occurred in the John Kennedy investigation, with several Lee Oswald "lookalikes."

They had a bite to eat and left.

CHAPTER 25

The real payoff to the Langer's visit was, at that moment, one block away and walking towards them as they walked towards their car.

On Alvarado Street, going towards Eighth, they passed a thin, kindly looking Mexican-American. Something in Faura's mind clicked. Not being the shy type Faura stopped the Mexican-American. "You look terribly familiar. Where have I seen you?"

"You were at the Ambassador the other night," he said, "I work there." In fact Faura had been practically living at the Ambassador in those days. As was his practice, whenever he went anywhere where the service people spoke Spanish, he had exchanged some pleasantries in his native language with the busboy that was now standing in front of him.

Within minutes Jose Carvajal was telling them one of the most important things ever to happen in his life.

He had been in the Ambassador kitchen within seconds after the shooting had begun and he was happy to impress Faura and Barnett with what he had witnessed. Neither Barnett nor Faura made an effort to tell him he was talking to an attorney and a newsman who were investigating some aspects of the assassination.

Carvajal related how he had run into the kitchen in time to see the "polka dot dress" run straight into a dead-end hallway.

According to the busboy, the girl realized she was running in the wrong direction, stopped, turned around, ran in the opposite direction and, finding an exit, ran through it and kept going.

Had anyone else in the kitchen seen the girl?

"Fifteen to twenty people must have seen her run," he replied.

The "girl in the polka-dot dress" had been seen by one of the kitchen helpers talking to Sirhan at length on a little terrace in front of the rear door of the Ambassador, Carvajal said.

Jose Luis Miranda, Carvajal continued, a dishwasher who was standing in front of Sirhan near a dishwashing machine, had been picked up by the FBI and had not returned to work.

The mysterious Miranda never returned to work, nor was he listed as a witness by any of the authorities. No one knew whatever happened to him. The fact that he was allegedly an illegal immigrant might have had something to do with his disappearance. No one knew for sure.

Carvajal had more to tell, and they let him talk. His narration became more interesting.

He had seen another man run away from the shooting. According to him, others also saw the man run. One of the porters and a kitchen employee ran after him as he went to a telephone booth. He was overheard to say "the job is done" or "it's done" or something to that effect, according to Carvajal. The man was immediately turned over to the police, the busboy said.

"What was the description of the man?" Faura asked.

He replied without hesitation: Hair black, taller than Sirhan, thin, leanish, light Indian kind of skin.

It was identical to the description given by Fahey and Gallegos. Could it be that Sirhan's companions had caught that night?

Carvajal concluded his narration with something Faura had come to live with.

"The FBI asked the employees not to talk about it." And they didn't. With the exception of Carvajal, tripped by the historical event he had witnessed, innocently talking without knowing who he was talking to, poor Mexican-Americans avoided inquisitors like the plague.

Many of the Mexicans were terrified. Some hardly spoke English. Others, fully aware of the local police because of abuse and discrimination against Mexicans, did not want any contact with anyone with a badge, and the rest lived in constant fear of "Emilia" or "Emily," their tag for the Immigration Department.

It is a common practice of California farmers and businessmen to hire illegal aliens, known as "mojados" or "wetbacks," and to pay them substandard wages. There were "mojados" in the kitchen that night. Understandably, no one ever heard from them, except the FBI and the police.

If the police or the FBI had arrested anyone else that night, they were not saying anything. The secrecy under which they work is a threat to the public interest, but the public does not appear to mind. So Faura was left to his own devices to prove his case in spite of the police forces.

He resolved to firm up Carvajal's story as best he could, using the Spanish language and his Mexican Foreign Correspondent credentials.

He and Barnett left Alvarado Street and drove to pick up Faura's car and then proceed to Barnett's apartment. Once there, Faura gave Barnett the "photos" of the girl and asked him to go down the street to see Vincent DiPierro, who lived barely a block away, on the same street.

Faura waited at the corner while Barnett went to the house. Barnett returned a very short time later saying there was nobody home. Faura left the photos with Barnett and asked him to try again the next day.

CHAPTER 26

S unday June 23 was of great import to the independent investigation. DiPierro was the young man who had seen Sirhan smile at a "girl in a polka-dot dress" as he helped her down from a dish cart at the Ambassador's kitchen just seconds before Sirhan shot Kennedy.

It was his testimony and description of the "polka-dot girl" that had firmed up Serrano's "polka-dot girl" story. Together they were the basis for the international "all points bulletin" from the LAPD.

DiPierro had been so close to the Senator when he was shot that he was splattered with blood. He was one of the witnesses of events before and of the shooting itself.

Son of the maître d' at the Ambassador and a college student at the University of California, DiPierro worked in the Ambassador kitchen to pick up some extra money. A clean-cut, decent young man, still living with his family while he went to college, he was a most credible witness when, under oath, he told the Los Angeles grand jury investigating the murder of Senator Kennedy: "The only reason I noticed him (Sirhan), there was a very good looking girl next to him. That was the reason I looked over there."

DiPierro had been asked by the grand jury, "What did you notice about this person (Sirhan)."

The testimony takes place under oath and is documented on page 91 of the transcript of the secret hearings held by the grand jury.

On page 89 of that transcript, DiPierro had been asked if he had noticed a "certain individual in the area."

DiPierro responded: "Yes, two people, I noticed. Whether or not the second person was involved, I don't know."

The grand jury was not interested in such details at the time. They did come to them later on.

Page 104 of the transcript:

Q. Now, going back to just before this shooting, you observed a nice looking girl?

A. Yes, sir, I did.

Q. Could you identify her again if you saw her?

A. To some degree, yes, sir, I could. I could never forget what she looked like because she had a very good-looking figure – and the dress was kind of – lousy.

Q. Flousy?

A. Lousy.

Q. Now, after the shooting, you remained at the scene, did you happen to see her again?

A. No. After the shooting I did not see her. I only saw her before.

Q. You did not ask her name or anything?

A. No, sir, I didn't.

Q. Did any of the fellows or guys you work with by any chance?

A. No, no one had, other than myself, had seen her, I don't believe.

Q. You have inquired around, I take it, since?

A. I have only talked to one fellow who was across from me, that had seen me, that was with me the whole time. I asked him, and he said that he had seen her but that he didn't know where she went or what her name was.

Q. Could you describe what she was wearing?

A. Yes. It looked as though it was a white dress, and it had either black or dark polka dots on it. It kind of had – looked like a bib in the front, kind of went around. It's like that (indicating).

A GRAND JUROR: A lacy dickey, probably.

THE WITNESS: It was like over the material itself; it was the same as the clothing. And then she was –she — the person who is accused of the shooting him was – like I say, they were both on the – standing together.

Q. Back of the tray stand?

A. Yes, and what happened he looked as though he either talked to her or flirted with her because she smiled. This is just before she got down.

Q. So, at least, their association, in proximity of the tray they were smiling, perhaps –

A. Together. They were both smiling. As he got down he was smiling. In fact the minute the first two shots were fired, he still had a very sick looking smile on his face. That's one thing – I can never forget that.

Briefly, the grand jury and DiPierro went into other testimony no longer involving the girl. On page 107 of the transcript they come back to her.

Q. Would you describe the facial characteristics first of all, of this girl?

A. Yes. She had dark hair that was cut, I would say, just above the shoulders (indicating). And it kind of looked like it was messed up at the time. I mean. She could have changed that — she could have come with curls. I don't know, it was just messed up at the time, her face – facial expression, she had what looked like a short nose. She wasn't too facially – she was not that pretty. And like I say, figure — she had a very good figure.

A couple of minutes later, DiPierro was excused.

It is important to underscore some things other than the character and credibility of Vincent DiPierro.

• The secret Grand Jury proceedings in which he and others testified were conducted on June 7, barely two days after the shooting of Senator Kennedy.

• DiPierro did not know and still does not, to this day, know John Fahey.

• John Fahey could not know what DiPierro was telling a secret grand jury.

• DiPierro's observations were made from very close range, about five feet.

• None of DiPierro's testimony was known to the press or to the public.

• DiPierro was talking to the grand jury just about the same time Fahey was making his first contact with the FBI.

• They were both responsible, working, sober, upstanding members of the community with no interest in personal publicity.

We must also bear in mind that DiPierro and Fahey were providing descriptions of a woman they saw June 4 (or, in Di Pierro's case, a few minutes after midnight June 4, since the shooting took place approximately 20 minutes into June 5).

The similarities in the descriptions of the features they remember are identical:

• Good body shape, not so good face

• Hair just above the shoulder

• Hair kind of messed up (DiPierro said "could have been in curls"; Fahey said it was curled on top in a bun, and then dropped "just above the shoulder.")

CHAPTER TWENTY-SIX

• DiPierro said "dark hair"; Fahey said "dark blond"

Most important, both men were volunteering information, as they considered their duty, without pressure or offer of reward. Neither knew at the time that the Los Angeles Police Department was to pressure them both and force one of them to ridicule himself in court for the benefit of its planned fraud on the American public. The other was ridiculed publicly by the police.

Faura had secured Barnett to show the "photos" to Vincent DiPierro for two reasons: first, to pin down his girl, Sandra Serrano's "polka dot girl" and Fahey's girl, as being one and the same, eliminating the search for any others; and second, to protect DiPierro and Fahey's testimony and descriptions from possible police attempts to discredit them.

Predictably the police did just that and succeeded until challenged by the publication of Robert Kaiser's *RFK Must Die*.

Barnett was a natural for the assignment. Very young and just out of UCLA, DiPierro would easily identify with him. He was also living a few hundred feet away from DiPierro and his family on Beverly Glen Boulevard in West Los Angeles, which Faura hoped would inspire confidence in DiPierro.

Faura had chosen to send someone to confront DiPierro, preferably an attorney, so it would not be said that Faura had influenced DiPierro, as the police were later to charge in Faura's relationship with Fahey.

To this day, Faura has never met DiPierro, but is very grateful for his contribution that day.

CHAPTER 27

What transpired between DiPierro and Barnett is of primary importance to the search for the "polka-dot girl." For this reason Faura's interview of Barnett after his visit with Di Pierro was recorded in full, on Sunday, June 23, 1968.

Faura: Okay, Gary, will you give me your full name and the spelling?

Barnett: Gary B-A-R-N-E-T-T.

Faura: All right. And who are you associated with?

Barnett: I am associated presently with Robert Fitzpatrick, an attorney.

Faura: You are an attorney?

Barnett: Yes, I am.

Faura: What is the address of your business office?

Barnett: 9000 Sunset Blvd., suite 1100.

Faura: I asked you to visit Vincent DiPierro, a witness of the Kennedy assassination who was at the time in the kitchen, and I gave you two photographs to show Vincent DiPierro to see if he would recognize this girl as the girl he saw standing next to Sirhan Sirhan, the accused assassin. Now, will you tell me in detail from the moment that you knocked on the door, what happened?

Barnett: Well, I knocked on the door, the father answered the door. They were both getting ready to go somewhere. The father invited me in and brought his son, Vincent DiPierro. Today is Sunday, so, I went there approximately at 10 o'clock.

Faura: That was today that you did this?

Barnett: That's right.

Faura: This morning? (Faura was trying to determine the time lapse between the time Barnett saw DiPierro and the interview to assure himself that the details would still be fresh in Barnett's mind.)

Barnett: This morning. The boy came out and didn't recognize me, of course, and probably the question in his mind was who I was. But I introduced myself as Gary Barnett and that I lived approximately a block up from where he was, which is true, and I told him that I had just recently been through UCLA and was now an attorney, and it was quite a coincidence that I had been hired – or directed – by a man to show him this photos to ask whether or not, he recognized this girl, and as we were sitting in the couch – a temporary couch they made – and as I said that I turned over the piece of paper in a notebook and showed him the photograph.

First, the photo of the girl with the bun on top of her head. He showed no sign in one way or another of recognition, or intense interest. He did not change the expression on his face. And he said something like "well –" and I said "perhaps, this – you recognize this photograph?" And I put the girl with the bun on her head – the photograph – behind the other one, which is the girl with the pony tail on her left side.

Faura: The second one you showed him is the one with the pony tail?

Barnett: That's right. He said, "Yes, this has to do with the shooting, doesn't it?" I said, well, yes, possibly." I said, "Do you recognize this girl?" He said, "Well, the face is a bit broader but the hair isn't the same, the hair, actually the way I saw her, was shorter, so were the eyebrows – weren't quite the same, and she had a pudgier nose." And when I asked him whether it was turned down or not – I pushed my nose down and asked him if it was turned down, he said, "No, no it was shorter and up a little bit."

Then he said: "But that's the girl."

Then I asked him –

Faura: Let me stop you there, Gary, after he made the corrections he made the statement, "but that's the girl"?

Barnett: Yes, if the statement differed it could be "mmm – that's the girl."

Faura: In other words the girl looked terribly familiar, he had associated the girl to the shooting already, because of the prior question he had asked you, and after looking and making a couple of corrections – that the girl possibly had a rounder face and that the eyebrows needed a little bit of correction, and that the nose was "pudgier," to use his word he did make the statement, "that's the girl."[1]

Barnett: He did positively make that statement and I can say this, that he naturally assumed, when he saw the photograph, and he naturally concluded that that was the girl without any kind of hesitation whatever. His only hesitation was in so far as concentration and recognition.

Faura: What did he say after that?

---

1. This was, of course, repetitious but had to be done to make sure that there was no mistake in what Barnett understood DiPierro had said.

Barnett: After that he said that "that's the girl" and then I asked him, "What kind of dress was she wearing?" And as a matter of course, as though he assumed that I knew, he said, "Well, you know a polka-dot dress." Whereupon I asked him, because of the discrepancy between this girl wearing a mini skirt polka-dot dress, as some people had observed, an a lengthier polka-dot dress, I inquired as to what kind of dress she had. I said, I think I said, "Was it a mini skirt or what kind of dress was it?" But I did mention the word "mini skirt" before he replied "Oh, no, no it came down to just above her knees and it was a clinging kind of dress." Those weren't his exact words but it was either "clinging" or "contour" or "formed" dress – in other words giving the connotation that it clung to her body – a tight dress and well fitting. Then he said, "but of course, I can't tell you anything about what happened, because I've been instructed not to." And he showed me the court order that essentially said that no witness or potential witness shall talk about the case for public dissemination.

Faura: Did he say anything else?

Barnett: No. That's all he said, except that he reiterated again – a total of two or three times – that he really could not talk about it, but the rest of the conversation was trivial as to – "Well, I hope I see you again sometime," "nice meeting you," "thank you very much" – that sort of thing.

Faura: That was the end of your interview with him?

Barnett: That was the sum total of the interview, and I left and came back to my apartment.

Faura's interview with Barnett ended a few seconds later with the usual trivia.

CHAPTER 28

Exercising extreme care and without any hint of what was about to happen, they had surprised a primary witness, one of the two who had seen the "polka-dot girl" at close range, with photos of Fahey's girl.

Fahey, DiPierro, both: "That's the girl."

With some minor corrections, understandably, since they were working with "constructed portraits," DiPierro had identified the same woman Fahey claimed had foreknowledge of the assassination.

DiPierro had also said, under oath to the grand jury, that the girl appeared to have been with Sirhan in the kitchen just before Sirhan shot Kennedy and that she and Sirhan had smiled at each other.

DiPierro's admissions to Barnett had narrowed down the search.

According to DiPierro, the "polka-dot girl" and Carvajal had been with Sirhan up to the shooting of the senator. Earlier in the day for reasons unknown, she had attempted to recruit Fahey into helping her leave the country and had warned him of the impending assassination.

With Sirhan in custody, but unwilling to give even a scrap of information, and no other prime suspects of a conspiracy in hand that police would admit to, it was clear that the "polka-dot girl" was the key to unlocking the truth about the assassination.

By this time it was getting difficult treading a middle line and keeping with the "one killer" theory of the police.

The shot in the arm by DiPierro prompted Faura to call Hammond again. He tried another approach: Does the name Dolhancy ring a bell with you? he asked. "Yes," Hammond replied, "that was one of my customers here, one of my tenants."

"That's the boyfriend or husband of the girl, isn't it?"

"No," Hammond replied, "He has his own wife, and they are getting a divorce shortly."

Obviously it was the wrong name.

"Do you manage the house at 811 South. Kenmore?"

"Yes, that is where she was staying at the time I knew her."

That was all Faura got that day from Hammond. He still refused to give the name of the girl. Of some consolation was the fact that she had been pinpointed as being at 811 South Kenmore.

On Monday June 24, a little after 10 A.M., Faura called the police intelligence contact he had been speaking to and asked for arrangements for the interrogation of Gallegos by the LAPD.

He had to go through the motions since he had told police about Gallegos before realizing the coverup they were planning.

The contact asked Faura to make arrangements with Gallegos and then he would try to match them with Captain Hugh Brown, a high official in Special Unit Senator – SUS, the so-called elite unit investigating the assassination.

Not being able to contact Gallegos that day, Faura failed to make arrangements for her to tell her story to the police – the story she had tried to tell the FBI shortly after the killing, but was of no interest to the FBI.

In her search for "justice," Gallegos was willing to go through the police grilling. But it was not to be that day.

Faura went to the *Life* magazine office, first with De Paolo, the *Life* staffer, and then, with Bonfante, they listened to the Barnett taped interview. They all drew the same conclusion. DiPierro had identified Fahey's girl as the "girl in the polka-dot dress." There was no doubt.

Knowing that all they could do was to work forward from the last known address of the girl, they agreed it was most urgent to find her – if possible before the police did.

First, they had to ascertain that she had not been picked up already. That was top priority.

They also wanted to investigate if Jose Luis Miranda, the dishwasher, was under arrest or in any kind of custody.

Bonfante called Dave Marcus, the attorney, to find out if it was legal to hold Miranda or any other witness or conspirators without some sort of record.

Marcus said it was. Besides, the police could book them and then "lose" the record to guard against noisy reporters. Marcus also promised to check with Immigration about Miranda. In the long run Marcus could not develop anything and Miranda was never located.

Bonfante agreed to meet with Faura near the Kenmore for another excursion showing the photos in the neighborhood. Having some time to kill, Faura went to the Gallegos home, but she was not there. He noticed that there were two bullet holes in her front window. He looked through the window and everything inside appeared normal.

Bonfante was notorious for being late to appointments, and he was holding fast to his reputation. So, for the next hour, Faura showed the "photos" around the neighborhood with no positive results.

When Bonfante finally arrived, they went to 811 S. Kenmore. The Kenmore Towers, just around the corner from the Kenmore Hotel, was joined to it and part of the same complex, something they had not noticed before. Because of this and realizing that Hammond being the manager there could cause trouble if they failed to consult with him, they went to his office to ask permission to knock on doors at the Towers. They were told he was asleep and would be back at 6 P.M.

It was then 20 minutes to 6 P.M. and not wanting to leave the neighborhood, they went to 731 S. New Hampshire, the address where Fahey had taken Faura. They walked to the apartment Fahey had pointed out as the one he had gone to with FBI special agents McCarthy and Johnson. The door plate bore the name: DOLHANCY.

No one was home.

They went back to the Kenmore Hotel, where they now found Hammond.

Somewhat less reluctant to talk, the strain apparently gone, Hammond stated he did not know if the girl had been taken into custody or not but that he felt the FBI would tell him if they had.

Knowing that the FBI needed only Fahey for an identification, they disagreed with that assumption, but did not tell him so.

"Can you suggest any place where she hangs around?" Faura asked, not really expecting any help. Hammond surprised him.

"Why don't you try Sandy's Cafeteria at Sixth and Western. She used to work there."

Sandy's was one of the names agents McCarthy and Johnson had attempted to track down, only they were told it was a bar, which might account for their failure to find it. The location was also on Western, a few miles west of Eighth and Catalina where the agents had gone.

Time was of the essence, and Faura and Bonfante headed immediately for Sandy's Cafeteria. The place was moderately crowded at this hour, and they waited in turn for a hostess. Instead of asking for a table they asked for information.

"Does this girl still work here?" they asked the lady, showing her the "photo."

"Yes. Maureen. She used to work here, but about a month ago she went to the Sheraton West."

The Sheraton West is a few blocks from the Ambassador Hotel, so they drove there. They asked for Maureen Dolhancy. She was off until June 26, two days hence.

Capitalizing once more on the language bond with the kitchen help Faura asked: "Is this Maureen Dolhancy?"showing the picture.

"Yes. She will be back on Wednesday."

After some maneuvering, they obtained a phone number of the girl, but no address. They sat down, had a drink and tried, soon afterwards, to call the number given. It was disconnected. Plans were made to have the number traced and obtain the address where it had been installed.

An hour later at his office, Faura called Barnett. He had previously told Fahey that if he felt abused, harassed or pressured by the FBI or the police he should call Barnett, with whom Faura had made arrangements to represent Fahey.

Barnett told Faura that Fahey had not called him.

CHAPTER 29

Fahey never took advantage of the offer, but he should have, as events later proved.

Faura planned to go to Gallegos house again that night but didn't make it.

The morning of Tuesday June 25, he spent going over reverse directory telephone books, courtesy of the phone company, looking for Dolhancy's address. No luck. The telephone lead on Dolhancy died then and there.

From his San Fernando news bureau he called the contact at police intelligence. It was now twenty-one days since the shooting and they had not talked to an important witness. How about the arrangements for Gallegos?

He was told that the SUS unit had been working 24-hour shifts for a few weeks and were worn out.

Captain Brown could not make it.

Faura suggested that perhaps he should provide them with a transcript of his interview with Mrs. Gallegos, let them read it and, if they decided it was something they did not have and would like to have, arrangements could be made to for her to talk to the police.

That was acceptable. Faura mentioned the two bullet holes in the front window.

"Oh, my god," the man at the other end gasped.

Faura offered to investigate and try to locate Gallegos that day and turn over the transcript the next day, Wednesday the 26th.

Calmly reviewing the events of those days Faura realized that he should have been invited or summoned "downtown" for a thorough voluntary interrogation. It was obvious that he had been trying to help and that he had come across important information. It never happened. Soon they would start trying to discredit him and stop his investigation.

Surely the possibility that someone had taken a couple of shots at the home of what could turn out to be an important witness warranted more than "Oh, god," a gasp and a promise from a reporter to locate the intended victim.

But that is how things stood as Faura went home early, after some once more failing to locate Gallegos.

He wondered about the next day, Wednesday the 26th: Would the girl be at the Sheraton Hotel? Was she the girl they were looking for? Was she really the "girl in the polka-dot dress?"

Faura arrived at the Sheraton at 9:30 A.M. Walking into the restaurant he came face to face with Maureen Dolhancy. Unaware of what was about to happen, she gracefully smiled at her new customer as he sat down.

She was a knockout, a dead-ringer for the girl that had been described and a model for the "photo."

Faura called Bonfante and told him the girl was at work. Bonfante said he would be there in thirty minutes, the approximate driving time from his office to the Sheraton.

It was to be two hours of sweating and anxious waiting before Bonfante showed up with Julian Wasser, the Time-Life photographer.

Prior to their arrival, the girl had served Faura a glass of juice and he tried to engage her in conversation. It didn't work and he had to go back to reading the *New York Times* and sweating out his wait.

Once his party had joined him they discussed the best way to take pictures of her.

Bonfante left to make a phone call while Faura and Wasser discussed the strategy for the unauthorized photo session.

Wasser rejected Faura's suggestions as too subtle. An aggressive and thoroughly professional young man, he explained that he could not take any chances in losing either good pictures or the girl. The best approach was a bold, if brazen, sure-fire one.

"Call her to the table," he said firmly. Faura did and they were launched into an adventure which landed all three of them at the Ramparts Police Station.

CHAPTER 30

B ack at the table, Bonfante ordered breakfast when the girl came to the table. She was standing right in front and very close to the table writing the order when Wasser suddenly pulled the camera from under his coat and started snapping pictures, while crouching, and leaning over the table at point-blank range.

Faura had never seen such rapid snapping of pictures as the display Wasser put on. Click, click, click, click – maybe a dozen pictures in the blink of an eye.

Dolhancy was shocked. Giving him an angry look, she stomped away to another table. The air had been super-charged around the table. Everything happened so fast. A minute or so later, Dolhancy was back.

"I don't appreciate you taking my pictures. Do you mind telling me why you are taking my pictures?" she demanded angrily.

"Because I love the way you look," he replied cynically and, jamming the camera in front of her face, again started shooting fast.

Obviously very angry now, she rushed to the kitchen and coming out with a serving tray, started serving the table that was back-to-back to the trio of newsmen.

Wasser would not let go. Kneeling on his seat and shooting over the barrier separating the two tables, he tried joke with her.

"The way you are serving that, you must be British."

Dolhancy, avoiding the camera, repeated, "I don't appreciate you taking my pictures."

The customers she was serving didn't know what to make of it. She finished serving the startled customers and told the hostess what was going on.

The hostess became alarmed. There was a commotion beginning to grow with the other employees, and all eyes were on the newsmen as they sat at their small cubicle.

Dolhancy came back and demanded to know who they were and asked for identification. Wasser said he was a tourist and had no identification. She left in a huff again. Faura predicted to his companions that it was sure the hotel security and the police would come now.

"They are going to demand the film," he said.

Wasser took the roll of film out of the camera, gave it to Bonfante and inserted a fresh roll. Quickly they decided the situation was getting out of hand, and they should identify themselves and try to placate the girl.

Once more, she headed for their table looking livid. Bonfante, a smooth talker, tried to cool her down.

"You shouldn't be upset," he said. "Apparently this is a case of mistaken identity."

She was beyond placating. She insisted they identify themselves.

Faura let her glance at his LAPD press credentials.

"Oh, you are LAPD," she said. "Next time you are downtown give my regards to Pereira." The cynicism in her voice made it clear she was not buying it and was still seething mad.

"No. It is not LAPD," Faura hastened to correct. "It is press."

She nailed him with her angry and beautiful eyes.

"You are not planning on publishing or printing those pictures?"

"No. Obviously we had the wrong girl," he said, meekly, unconvincingly. She gave him an unexpected bonus.

"Last night the FBI stopped me, and they wanted to know about Gilda D. Oppenheimer," she said.

"Who?" Bonfante said.

"Gilda D. Oppenheimer."

"No, never heard of her," Faura lied, knowing full well this was one of the names the "polka-dot girl" has given Fahey.

"What's this about? Dolhancy insisted. "It has something to do with the assassination."

There it was. She had slung it at the fan. We were getting deeper.

"Well, she is actually not involved," Faura tried to throw water on the fire. "We are trying to locate the girl because she knows one of the witnesses."

"Well, you shouldn't have taken my picture; you shouldn't have taken my picture. You were here last night looking for me," she accused. The girl was full of surprises.

"Not last night; we were not here." Faura knew it was a half-truth but wanted to make no more admissions that he had to.

"Well, one of you guys said that you were an old boyfriend of mine."

"No, we didn't say that." In fact that had been the ploy used with the kitchen help.

"Well, you gentlemen were looking for me the other night."

The statement was now fully accurate.

"Monday we were here. You were not here, and we asked about you."

She was not calming down any. Bonfante made a mistake by giving her a credit card to pay the bill. Had he paid in cash they could have gotten up and walked out without further fuss.

While signing for the expenses Bonfante spoke with her.

"Look, we would like to ask you about last night with the FBI. Perhaps we could have a drink or a cup of coffee later, after you are through?"

"Well, it is almost 1 o'clock. I am through now. How about here?" Her attitude and tone made it almost a challenge.

"Well fine, here or outside?"

"Anywhere you want. How about my boss's office?" She was in command.

"Fine. Who is he?"

"Mr. Roberts."

"Well, that's Okay," Bonfante said resignedly. They had been maneuvered into something they did not want.

The girl took the credit card and receipt from Bonfante again and walked away. It was obvious she was up to something and she was stalling. Amongst themselves they agreed that the best course was to take back Bonfante's credit card and get out.

They tried that but the girl had taken the card to "Mr. Roberts," who was in fact the person in charge of security.

They walked to his office. On the way, Faura suggested that Wasser get out and wait in the car, having been the one who shot the pictures. He did.

Bonfante and Faura walked to the security office, and Dolhancy was not there yet. They started back and saw her coming down the stairs. She was very agitated. She was so upset, she wasn't even listening to what Bonfante and Faura were saying, trying to calm her down.

Mr. Roberts appeared.

In his office, he demanded identification. Not wanting to rock the boat further, they handed him their credentials. He looked pretty upset also as he made notes from the credentials. They tried to apologize to Roberts and the girl but they were so upset they would not listen.

Roberts told the girl that she should sue. Obviously he was not aware of the aggressiveness of the press in the United States, a fact underscored somewhat by his slight British accent. He should have known that they had every right to ask questions. Whatever he knew or did not know, he knew enough to call the police before even talking to the newsmen.

As the four of them verbally charged and dodged in Roberts' office, they were joined by Ramparts detectives. Four in all, ranks of sergeant and up.

Very politely they asked for their credentials. The newsmen showed them and once more tried to apologize. There was a chance Roberts and the girl would calm down and accept their apologies with the police there. No such luck. The police were not taking the bait either and asked them to come to the Ramparts police station.

On the way out, Bonfante and Faura created another commotion in front of one of the shops in the hotel. The girl wanted to know where "the other man" was – "The one who took the pictures."

Wasser had been coming back in when he saw the group arguing. He quickly sat down on a bench and opening a newspaper hid himself.

"Who? What man?"

"You know, the one who took the pictures."

"Oh, you mean him?" Bonfante made his second mistake of the day by calling attention to Wasser.

Wasser joined them.

"You want the film?"

"Yes, where is it?"

"Okay, Julian, give her the film," Bonfante said, just as Wasser opened his camera.

Taking the 35mm roll out of the camera, Wasser deftly yanked at one end and the film was exposed.

"There, now it's spoiled," Julian said. "No one can have your pictures now." Of course, he did not tell her that he had exposed a fresh roll of film. By yanking it out, there was no way for anyone to know of the deception. The whole charade had been planned before.

"Here, you can have it," Julian generously offered the dangling exposed film to the girl.

Bonfante and Faura now joined by Wasser were courteously nudged to the police car waiting outside. The film with the precious pictures of the girl was still snug in Bonfante's pocket.

CHAPTER 31

The man in charge of the team that had picked them up was Lt. Hagen. On the way to the station they trade stories on other cases and everything was very amicable.

At the station, they surrendered their credentials and gave names of people who could identify them at their places of employment. The check they were going through was unprecedented. While telephone calls were being made to verify their authenticity, they asked why all the elaborate security over press credentials.

They were told that late the night before (Tuesday), the FBI had been asking questions at the Sheraton. Later, kitchen employees leaving work had been accosted by two men flashing some sort of credentials and claiming to be police.

The two men questioned the employees and disappeared; so many people asking questions about the girl had aroused suspicions and the police had been alerted.

One of the detectives that had taken them to the station remarked: "Perhaps you are looking for the "polka-dot girl?"

"She doesn't exist," Faura remarked cynically, reminding him the police had said so.

Hagen called Faura to the telephone.

Abe Greenberg, managing editor of the *Hollywood Citizen News* at the time was on the phone.

"What's wrong?"

"Nothing. I have been picked up for asking too many questions."

"Don't you have any credentials with you?"

"Yes, but this area appears to be too sensitive, and they are not enough, a further check is being made."

Returning to the desk where Bonfante and Wasser were, Faura saw a detective he recognized. He was the same man, the police Intelligence agent had taken him to Ramparts after his first contact with them.

Faura went over and said hello. They conversed in low tones.

"I recognized you but did not know if you wanted to be recognized. That's the reason I ignored you," he said.

Faura realized the detective had been thinking that he was an undercover agent for the Intelligence Division, whose agents are not known to the other departments.

The detective had given Faura the courtesy of ignoring him and protecting his cover, he thought.

Not being one to lose an opportunity handed him on a silver platter, Faura played along and told him it was all right. Faura implied his cover was intact and told the detective that he had casually asked for him.

When Faura asked for him, Hagen had asked if he knew the man.

"No," Faura said, "but he has seen me before and knows who I am. He can identify me."

"I am glad they took me off this thing," the detective said in a conspiratorially low voice.

Keeping up the pretense, Faura said, "I am glad too. This is not the kind of a bugger where anybody is going to come out a winner."

The detective nodded silently.

"There is going to be a lot of political play and anyone in it is going to be in a difficult position," Faura added.

"Not only that," the detective said, "this is no longer a common murder, no this is not a common murder."

Faura perceived that the detective was suggesting a conspiracy but realized it might have been his frame of mind because of the other information he was aware of.

The man he was talking to was a highly placed detective in the Ramparts Division, where the early stages of the investigation had occurred and the first flow of information, together with Sirhan Sirhan and all the other witnesses had come to rest before the investigation was moved "downtown" to police headquarters.

The first impression of the brief and apparently insignificant conversation is that nothing of any significance was said – until the following is considered:

- The man was under the impression that he was talking to a fellow undercover officer with more access to information than he himself had, because of having seen Faura in conversation with Hagen.

- He had conducted and had access to many of the interrogations done the night of the murder at the Ramparts police station.

- The detectives at the Ramparts station had developed the information on which the "wanted bulletin" had been issued for the "polka-dot girl."

- The man must have been aware that the police were claiming there was no conspiracy and the "polka-dot girl" was not wanted.

- He was glad to be off the case because "it was not ordinary murder." He had said it twice.

As it often happens in this kind of situation, Faura could not continue to sit there and hope for more information from him.

To do so would arouse the curiosity of the others at the station and any investigation would easily reveal the fragile game the press was playing with the police. For this reason, he cut the conversation short.

Hagen had not been satisfied with Faura's credentials or their verification by Abe Greenberg and was checking further. He was doing the same with the others.

Meanwhile, the roll of film shot by Wasser was burning a hole in Bonfante's pocket. There was no telling what the police would do next.

Bonfante passed the film to Faura, who put it in his pocket and hoped he would not have to bluff his way out of surrendering it by calling on the man he had been talking to before, something he was prepared to do to save the film. The whole situation was delicate and unpredictable. You could feel the tension in the air.

Hagen approached them and said, "Okay, fellows, it's all right." They all relaxed.

"I just talked to Manny about you," he said to Faura, "and he knows you."

Faura had written a story on the retirement of Manny Pena, a well-know detective (known to some in the D.A.'s office as the "house killer" for waiting for armed robbers to come out of the establishment they had robbed and shooting them down before asking them to surrender). Pena left the police and went to work for the State Department's Agency for International Development, a CIA front.

Pena had quietly returned to the LAPD a few weeks before the assassination and was literally in charge of the Senator's death investigation.

Faura's complimentary piece on Pena on his retirement to go work for the "State Department" had saved the day for him.

Pena was in charge of the "day watch" of the investigation. He determined which leads to follow and which would be discarded. Why an AID/CIA agent was in that position was never explained. His "clearance" of Faura was a complete surprise to Faura, who did not know that Pena was back from training foreign police forces, mainly in Latin America, for the AID/CIA.

Turning his attention to Bonfante, Hagen told him that he had been OK'd by someone in Pasadena, whose name escaped Faura.

Surprised, Bonfante remarked, "Hey, I am impressed. How did he find that out?"

Hagen told him Pena had suggested that perhaps that party knew Bonfante.

Bonfante insisted, "I am really impressed, how did Manny know?"

Hagen did not really have an answer. "Obviously, he knew. They know a bit about these things. You guys move in pretty high circles," Hagen said, and walked away to his desk asking a detective to take them back to their car. The incident had been very tense but courteous. But they had successfully removed them from the Sheraton, where the trail for the "polka dot girl" had ended.

On the way out of the station the crew for Jack Webb's TV show, *Dragnet,* was in the parking lot. It didn't escape Faura that the whole episode they had just gone through belonged more in a TV soap opera than not.

CHAPTER 32

They were driven back to the Sheraton and their cars. The film was still in Faura's pocket, but the hottest trail to the "polka-dot girl" had collapsed.

Faura went through, in his mind, the late nights and weeks of hard work they had done. Had something important escaped them?

Driving to Barnett's apartment for a drink and a report on his efforts to contact Fahey, Faura sifted through the highlights of the quest for the "polka-dot girl" in the prior few days.

- Hammond's tip: the FBI was chasing the girl they found.
- They had tracked her from Kenmore to New Hampshire, to Sandy's, to the Sheraton.
- There was no question this girl was the girl sought by the FBI since the name Dolhancy appeared at the 731 S. New Hampshire address. The name was confirmed at the Sheraton, and the FBI had questioned her about Gilda D. Oppenheimer.

There was no doubt they had found the girl – the same girl the FBI had found. Was she the same girl Fahey had picked up and DiPierro had identified as the "girl in the polka-dot dress?"

If she was, their search was over, but there was no gold at the end of the rainbow. The fact that the girl was still loose meant she had been cleared by the FBI, her whereabouts on the night of the assassination checked out by the agents who were chasing her. That much the FBI could be trusted to do, right? Faura thought.

Two things of importance had been established:

- The FBI was still looking for the girl in the "polka-dot dress" one week after the LAPD had denied her existence. Sandra Serrano had been vindicated in Faura's mind, if not publicly.
- The FBI had asked for "Gilda D. Oppenheimer," which meant they were checking Fahey's story.

This also meant the FBI and Faura's team were positively concentrating on the same leads, and he was neck and neck with the FBI in following them. That was some consolation.

Hammond's description of a "hop head," "a bit of a nut" and "a ding-a-ling" certainly did not fit Dolhancy, who appeared to be a serious and responsible girl.

What did it all mean?

From Barnett's apartment Faura called Fahey three times without success; the same with Hammond. His spirits were low.

It came to mind that the only thing left to do to close the "polka-dot file" was for Fahey and Hammond to identify Dolhancy as the girl they had been looking for.

Now that they knew where to find her, that would be no problem. They went to work on that.

After seeing Dolhancy, Fahey said she was not "his girl." Hammond said the FBI had located a "lookalike."

Had Faura known what the future held, he would have celebrated rather than mourned the end of the Dolhancy trail.

Bonfante was meeting with Dave Marcus, the attorney, and Mrs. Sirhan to gather some background for a story in *Life* magazine on June 27th. It was a low-key day, but new leads were developed.

Don Campbell, Faura's photographer friend, said he knew a girl by the name of Pam Russo who was at the Rafferty party the night of the assassination and who had some information Faura might find interesting. Campbell agreed to arrange a meeting.

Meanwhile Faura drove to the house of the man who had the telephone answering service, the brother of the youth who had claimed to know Sirhan's brother and his girlfriend, and found him sick in bed.

He denied that his brother knew any of the Sirhan family or their girlfriends or the boy who was on his way to Vietnam. It was he, himself, who knew Adel Sirhan and his girlfriend. He said that because of the description given over the radio and television he had thought that it could be Adel's girlfriend.

He proceeded to give Faura some background on Adel and the girl, all uncomplimentary. Faura let him talk. He said he had a picture of the girl in his office, which Faura could see any time.

Faura then produced the two "photos" of the girl he was interested in. The man examined them closely. "She doesn't look anything like this girl, except in the eyes."

It had been a waste of time. Back at Faura's office, he called Fahey.

"I have been fired," Fahey said dejectedly.

"I am sorry to hear that. I know the head of the San Fernando Employment Office. I'll talk to him about you."

"I'll appreciate that."

"I hope they are not bugging you anymore," Faura said, referring to the FBI's pressure to stop talking to Faura.

"No," he replied. He seemed more calm and relaxed in spite of his low spirits. Not wanting to push Fahey in the state he was in, Faura said no more and hung up.

He called Dave Marcus and told him he had made arrangements for a job for Saidallah (Said) Sirhan, the brother of the assassin who had been at dinner that night at Marcus' house.

"Well, wait a minute. Said is here, you can talk to him," Marcus said.

After the usual pleasantries they got into the subject.

"Yes, I appreciate very much everything that you are doing."

"Saidallah, the thing is you are going to have to have transportation because this place is in the San Fernando Valley."

"I can't take a job outside of Pasadena."

"Why, are you forbidden?"

"It's not that. Because of security, I don't feel I should leave the area."

He also expressed concern about accepting a job and being held responsible for any incidents or damages which might occur. Faura told him that a confidential interview had already been arranged with the employer.

"Frankly, I really appreciate very much." He declined to go to the interview because it was out of Pasadena.

Faura told him it was up to him. He was only redeeming his promise to find him a job. Saidallah reiterated several times that he was really appreciative and expressed his surprise that Faura had kept his promise. He gave Faura his new telephone number at home and spoke courteously as if they were old friends.

Faura's next call was to Pamela Russo, the girl who had been at the Rafferty party and who had been referred to him by Don Campbell.

Yes, she said, she had been questioned by the FBI. Come to think of it, she had questioned the FBI back, she said. She was that kind of girl – sharp, aggressive and very much aware.

According to Russo, the FBI agent had told her that Sirhan had said that he had given a $20 bill to one of the hostesses at the Rafferty party.

According to the FBI agent's version, as told to Russo, Sirhan had remarked that he had entered the Rafferty party and everyone had looked at him and he didn't like that. He said no more, realizing he was talking too much. She also said that a co-worker in the Rafferty campaign had tackled a man running away from the shooting and that he had seen a girl in a polka-dot dress.

Faura stopped her and told her he would see her later to tape her story. She agreed. Three days had passed since Faura had promised to locate Gallegos. In the excitement and urgency of finding the "polka-dot girl," he had gone only once to her house and failed to find her. He questioned some people at an apartment house next door and learned that she had been seen working on her laundry. Everything appeared to be normal with her, they said.

On June 28, he finally connected with her by telephone and confirmed that everything was all right, she had been very busy looking for another place to move because of difficulties with her landlord.

"What about the bullet holes in the window?" Faura asked.

"Yes, isn't that terrible? She didn't sound terribly upset. "We were in the back of the house when they crashed through."

"Who shot at you?"

"We don't know."

"Did you report it to the police?"

"Oh, that was some time ago, a few weeks at least." That was the end of that. Obviously the shooting had no connection to her involvement with the investigation. Faura asked her if she still wanted to talk to the police and tell her story. She consented.

CHAPTER 33

By lunch time a Police Intelligence officer sat across the table from Faura at the Paprika Restaurant on Cahuenga Boulevard in Hollywood. With them was a newsman-police/undercover-CIA informant. It had not been planned that way. He had seen them there and joined them.

They chatted for a few minutes and the "tripe agent" left. Faura and his companion concluded their business. The policeman got the transcript of the Gallegos interview, and Faura the assurance that she would be contacted at her job and taken "downtown" for questioning. He later learned from Gallegos that they had interviewed her once with little interest in her story.

The LAPD had their man. They were not interested in his companions.

The next day brought some more information on the "polka-dot girl," with the interrogation of Pamela Russo.

Russo, besides being a lively, attractive and smart girl, was also in a very responsible position in the Rafferty organization. Rafferty was running for the U.S. Senate seat of Thomas Kuchel. Russo was the administrative assistant to the state press director for Rafferty.

After the usual preliminaries and what time she arrived at the Rafferty party, who else was there and a general description of the setup at the Venetian Room, where the party was being held, they went straight into the rest of her story.

Faura asked her to tell him about the young man who had tackled or had seen the police tackle a man running away from the shooting.

> **Russo:** Yes, I recall that we were talking about the assassination and I'd say that this was approximately 45 minutes – maybe an hour – after this had happened, and he said, "I tackled one of them" or somebody that was running out of the hotel. And I said, "Well, why did you tackle him?" and he said, "I thought maybe he stole something, and I wasn't sure exactly who the man was or what he was." He said that he had tackled this fellow and knocked him down and then the police came running in and the police either dragged him out, or chased this fellow further, and this is all he said. He said he was young, he said it was a young fellow.
>
> **Faura:** Did he give any description of the man?

Russo: No, he didn't. He did not give a description, to me, of the man.

Faura: Now, if they tackled the man and the police later chased him out, does that mean that the man got away or did the police actually take custody of the man. Did he say?

Russo: He said to me that the police grabbed the man. He said they ran after him and grabbed him. Now, he said that he couldn't tell if there were four or five policemen running out there, and they had grabbed him but haven't heard or read anything about another man being caught, or anybody else being apprehended that night.

Faura had. From Carvajal, the kitchen helper, what she was saying was confirming Carvajal's story. Faura said nothing. It was obvious that Faura would have to locate her co-worker to get the story first hand. But she did not know her co-worker's identity.

She did know he drove a van used to deliver campaign literature and run errands. He was young, very blond and a volunteer worker. He operated from Rafferty headquarters at 3584 Wilshire Boulevard. But she was sure she could get the name of the young man. Faura dropped that line of questioning and moved to another area.

Faura: Now, let's go to the FBI who came to interview you. What was his name?

Russo: Robert Morneau.

Faura: Tell me what happened when he came to see you.

Russo: According to Morneau, Sirhan had said that he entered the Rafferty party and everyone turned around to look at him – which I think is impossible unless he was there extremely early, because there were so many people in that room that night that nobody would have noticed another body walking into the room."[1] He said (Mourneau) that Sirhan had said that he tried to get a drink from one of the hostesses, something about they wanted a ticket for a drink and they said no, and he had said something like, "Well, here's $20. Is that enough? Keep it," and walked away. This is what Sirhan had said – that he had given $20 to one of the hostesses.

Faura: He told you that Sirhan said that?

Russo: Yes, he did.

Faura: Is there a possibility that you may be confusing what the FBI man said with newspaper and *Life* magazine's account of what Sirhan said?

---

1. The remark was to prove significant when her co-worker was located.

Russo: No, because to tell you the truth, I really haven't read all the accounts. I look mostly at pictures. Unfortunately I haven't really kept –

Faura: You have not read the *Life* magazine account?

Russo: No I read (sic) the pictures. There was a caption right next to the Rafferty picture up on the left hand side that said something about "Sirhan was earlier thrown out of the Rafferty party."

It was important to Faura to establish that she had not been confused and that the information had come from the FBI.

Faura: So you are positive that your information came from the FBI?

Russo: Yes, because as a matter of fact, I was quite surprised.

She went on to relate some more about Special Agent Morneau's questioning. Morneau had told her that Sirhan had been with an Indian friend earlier in the evening whom Sirhan had invited to play pool.

The friend had declined, Morneau had said, and went to buy a newspaper to look for a job in the classified ads.

Keeping the want ads section, the friend gave Sirhan the rest of the newspaper. Five hours later Sirhan shot Kennedy, Russo says the FBI agent had concluded.

This incident, unknown at the time, has since been reported and confirmed by Chief of Detectives Robert Houghton.

Faura: This is all from Morneau?

Russo: From Morneau. That's right. U-huh.

Russo is one of those persons who can't sit still, went on into a lot of other details not relevant to the subject. Faura steered her back to his area of interest.

Faura: All right, now, let's to back now to the leanish, lanky looking man who came over to you and asked for a press pass. (She had mentioned him before in one of her impulsive rambles.)

Russo: Yes, a man came up to the table and he asked for – he said, "Could I have one of those tickets?" – he said – he did not call it a "press pass." He said, "Could I have one of those tickets for a drink?" and I said, "Well, do you represent any of the working media?" And he said, "Yes," And he told me something that I can't remember, and I said, "I can't give you any without identification." He didn't and got kind of aggravated and he hung around for a few minutes and he just sort of hung around the table and then he went on. This man was olive complected, slight almost skinny. I'd call him for a man – about 5'8." I imagined he weighed about 135 – maybe 140-135 pounds.

Faura: Now, I am 5'8," of course, a little stockier. But was he about my height?

Russo: He may have been a little shorter than you.

Faura: Shorter?

Russo: U-huh.

Fahey's and Gallegos description of one of the men they saw were already ticket-taping through Faura's mind. This was identical to those descriptions, and Gallegos had seen him with Sirhan.

Faura: Definitely, olive complexion?

Russo: Yes, yes, in his early 30s.

Faura: Could he have been 27?

Russo: Sure, easy, u-huh.

Faura: How about his hair?

Russo: His hair was long – not excessively long as the standards today. But he looked like he needed a haircut, and he wore it kind of a haphazard pompadour-type style. It looked a little messy – looked like he might have had – you know – cream oil on his hair or something, but, uh –

Faura: Could it have been straight back hair?

Russo: Yes, it wasn't curly. It wasn't curly, it was straight. It looked like some Latin types who have very straight hair – the Italian types – the Mexican-Americans who have real straight hair. Well this was –real straight.

Faura: Kind of plastered?

Russo: Yes, kind of plastered and parts of were in a pompadour and the other was sort of hanging a little bit. He had on a white shirt, what I would call it is one of the surplus store type shirts, for you know $1.99, with, you know, the very starched (collar) and no tie. It was open at the neck, and the sleeves were rolled up one time. He had on dark pants.

Faura: It was a short sleeve?

Russo: Short sleeve, that's right.

CHAPTER THIRTY-THREE

Faura: White?

Russo: White.

Faura: Now, when you say dark pants, where they dark blue, black?

Russo: It was very hard to tell. I couldn't really tell you whether they were blue or black, because the lighting was so bad.

Faura: But the pants were very dark. Did you see any of the kitchen's help that night or the help of the hotel? How did the pants compare to those of the kitchen help?

Russo: They were lighter. The kitchen help, as I recall, were black. And the pants he had on – I am trying to remember – they were kind of baggy. By the way, he spoke with a slight accent.

Shortly thereafter Russo would run dry of the details she remembered about the man. She related again how he hung around the table and then drifted into the Rafferty room without the "press credential" he had asked for. She never saw him again.

Like Fahey, Russo also said the man's accent was not Spanish, Italian or German. She just did not know what it was.

Further questioning developed that Russo had seen Sirhan as he was brought out by the flying wedge of policemen and people.

"He is just a kid," she remembered saying.

She added lengthy details about the scenario at the time. Faura let her live the experience again and then brought her back to the FBI man who had questioned her.

Faura: Let's go back to the FBI man. Anything else comes to mind that he said?

Russo: Well, he told me about the woman.

It turns out Morneau had told her about a woman who had come forth claiming she was at the Ambassador wearing a polka-dot scarf.

According to Morneau, this girl, a belly dancer, had been polygraphed and was found to be lying for publicity reasons.

Russo claimed that Morneau had told her this piece of information one day before it was released to the press.

The FBI questioning of Russo had taken place over a period of two days. Each time she had asked questions, and they had been answered. While some of the information had already been made public, Faura wanted to make sure she had run into a talkative agent. Faura had visions of breaking the FBI security again. A female Fahey, of sorts.

She unknowingly encouraged his thoughts by her next remarks.

"In a way it felt it was kind of strange that he would tell a lot of these things or discuss them with me when it seems to me that – I'd always heard that the FBI is petty tight-lipped, and I thought – I wondered if he wasn't just saying some things just to sort of – to pacify me, just to sort of, you know, cordially answer my questions, and I wondered if they were true."

The information was true all right – that was what was giving Faura the idea of recruiting her to use Morneau for information. But that would be later. Right now he wanted to hear about the girl she had seen that night at the Rafferty party. The girl had been wearing a polka-dot dress.

Faura: Now tell me about the girl, describe the "girl in the polka-dot dress" that you saw over there.

Russo: The girl I saw in the "polka-dot dress," the reason I remember her is because I have a dress very similar. There are a lot of dresses – there is an Arpegio, they have them now, there is a copy they sell I believe at Zody's that has purple dots on it and white buttons – square buttons – the dots look round from far away but they are definitely square upon a closer look. It has long sleeves, its A-line, it is short. It has a large collar on it, large white cuffs. The girl was maybe about 5'5" -5'6" – she wasn't real tall. I think she was a little taller than I am but I – it is hard to tell with women – their hair. She had a kind of bouffant hairdo. It was jet black. It had almost like – you've seen wigs of this sort that are very, very bouffant, they all look the same – they are kind of tucked under, they come a little bit toward the face. The girl had a long thin nose. It was – it was almost when you looked at it – it looked a little bit crooked. It was thin between the eyes. It came down – it broadened at the nose, and then it narrowed again toward the base of the nose, but the nostrils were a little bit wider.

This is what I remember. I remember that nose. I saw the girl enter the Rafferty room. She had a drink in her hands. She didn't talk to anybody that I can remember, and I saw her again out in the lobby outside the room later on, but I don't know how much time had lapsed. I had gotten up to just – I think I was going upstairs – as I recall I was going to the Rafferty room.

Faura: She was with nobody when she –

Russo: Nobody.

Faura: And she was with nobody when she was outside the room?

Russo: No.

Faura: Did it appear that she was looking for somebody?

Russo: Yes, she could have been looking for somebody – but she was just standing around and looking –

At this point Faura showed her the "photos." Russo remarked about the nose.

Russo: Yes, the nose was something like that – and the face is familiar to me – I don't know from where – the hair – it couldn't have been on that girl. It was black.

Faura: And it was a different style?

Russo: It was a different style. It looked short. Now – I can see this too, that the girl could have been wearing a wig, because you can cover up any hair color with it, and if you have long hair, wear it on top of your head and wear a wig.

Faura: How short was the dress?

Russo: Uh, a little above the knees – it is not what you would call really a "mini."

Faura: Above the knees?

Russo: Above the knees, yes.

Faura: (pointing to the "photo") That nose was definitely the nose you saw?

Russo: That nose – yes, I would say.

Faura: But you don't recall that the eyes might look the same.

Russo: No. I don't. And yet the face, with that hair on top of her head is familiar to me.

Faura: Where you at the Ambassador the day before also?

Russo: Yes, I was.

Faura: But, you don't recall that you might have seen that girl the day before?

Russo: No, I don't recall. There were a lot of people around. Uh, a lot of Kennedy people, Kennedy followers … (she goes into details unrelated to the question).

Faura: Now, your only association with those features is from the night of the Rafferty party?

Russo: That's the only time I can recall.

Faura: And you saw the girl twice?

Russo: U-huh. I saw her twice. I saw her once inside –

Faura: And you recall her because of the dress and the nose?

Russo: And the nose. That's all I recall. Mostly because, uh, now I would – as I said before – that the things that strike me are maybe the things that were a little out of the ordinary – (like) the man that was a little strange and wanted the ticket for a drink.

Faura: And the fact that the girl had the kind of dress like yours?

Russo: Like you know – similar to mine. Mine is brown, but there's – there are different colors and –

Faura: What color were the polka dots? How dark?

Russo: Purple, purple. Not purple like this (pointing to a shade of purple on the table). They could be – if you were far away – in the lighting – they could have been black, if you were far away they would look like black dots, but when you got close, uh, they are small dots if this is –

Faura: Very small dots?

Russo: They are small, yes.

Faura: About what, size of a penny? Size of a quarter?

Russo: No. They are not that big, they are smaller than that.

Faura: A nickel?

Russo: Like a dime.

Faura: The size of a dime.

Russo: The size of a dime – maybe even smaller than that, yes. Now my dress has smaller white polka dots. You know, now that I think of it, I believe Zody's sells a dress like this, that is similar to this, with dots on it. It's a copy. But they were real small – you know, they weren't big purple polka dots.

Faura: They were about the size of a dime?

Russo: No. I'd say they were even smaller than that.

Faura: Smaller than a dime?

Russo: I don't know if this could possibly be the girl, except that that nose is familiar.

Faura: But the polka-dot girl that you saw in the room and outside in the polka-dot dress – it was an A-dress, the way that you describe it, and the polka dots were purple but were smaller.

Russo: They were smaller, yes, they weren't the size of a dime, they were –

CHAPTER 34

Painfully, repetitiously, Faura had forced the issue of the size of the polka dots as an important feature. Big splotches or pin heads? The question was important since no one had publicized the size of the dots.

Russo had given a description of the girl she saw at the Rafferty party that was almost identical to that of the "polka-dot girl." Was it the same girl? Pains had to be taken to break down the description and find discrepancies, if there were any. If none, she had just raised the possibility that the "polka-dot girl" and Sirhan had met or made contact at the Rafferty party.

Russo and Gallego's descriptions of men with the girl were identical in all respects.

The details of the dress described by Russo could have only been supplied by an eye witness, since Serrano's detailed description of the dress had not been made public.

Russo's description also matched those of Fahey and DiPierro's of the girl or girls they had seen and whom DiPierro had identified as the notorious "girl in the polka-dot dress."

While her description of the hair matched Serrano's it was different to that described by Fahey. Russo had instinctively suggested an answer – a wig.

Regardless of hair style, DiPierro, another witness who had seen the "polka-dot girl" close up, had identified the face.

His girl was Fahey's girl, who on June 4 had told Fahey, "They are going to take care of Kennedy tonight."

The girl Sandra Serrano had told of answered the same description.

The "polka-dot girl's" companions' descriptions also matched those of the men seen by Fahey and Gallegos, including the man they believed to be Sirhan. It does not require a particularly talented mind to conclude that they might have participated in the planning and the actual execution of the murder.

Russo's declarations were closing some of the gaps. The polka-dot girl had now been placed early in the evening at the Rafferty party, the same place where Sirhan was later proven to be at just about the same time. Was the Rafferty party their rendezvous place?

Less than a week after the Russo interview, Faura located her young co-worker, with her help, and he provided the answer to that question.

Asking questions about Special Agent Morneau, Faura intending to plant her to get information from Morneau, once Faura learned that Morneau was attending CalState.

Two years later FBI infiltration of colleges would become a controversial issue in the country. It was nothing new as SA Morneau can attest.

Faura's plan to use Russo to get information from Morneau did not work, and Morneau never knew it had been tried.

Three weeks had gone by since the fateful day of the murder. It was Sunday, and Faura and Fahey were still working together, but the relationship was strained and tenuous because of FBI pressure.

They tried again. This time Fahey told Faura that the FBI agents had defamed Faura's character and called him all kinds of names to influence Fahey's opinion of him. He didn't even understand some of their diatribe.

"They said you were 'irreprobable.' What does that mean?"

They both laughed. But it was really no laughing matter. Faura knew they would go far beyond calling him names, and felt sure they would succeed eventually in eliminating Fahey as a source of information. In retaliation Faura called the FBI office to needle one of them.

"This is Fernando Faura."

"I know of you," he said curtly.

"I want to talk to you about the Kennedy killing," Faura said.

"I am very busy. I can't see you."

"You are afraid I am going to ask some questions, but perhaps, I am just offering some answers," Faura was cocky, knowing the agent was at a disadvantage.

"We are busy." The agent was hard and inflexible in tone.

"I'll come down anyway. In any case, I want to record you telling me you are not interested in leads volunteered by the public." It was meant as a challenge, and he knew he had the agent in a corner.

"Okay, I'll call you Thursday and let you know when to come in." He never called; as Faura suspected all along, knowing their fiction about following all the leads. Faura had no intention of going anyway, they would have to come to him if they wanted the information he had.

To that date, Faura had statements they never had, conclusively proving that all leads were not being followed.

The Feds attempt to discredit him had failed on their first attempt with Fahey. They were not to give up. The LAPD, far cruder, in method and approach, would try its hand later on.

Tracking down the young Rafferty driver and co-worker of Russo was the order of the day for July 3. After several misses in West Los Angeles, they succeeded.

The name of the young man was Greg Clayton. He lived in Palisades Park, an exclusive section near the beach outside of Santa Monica. They obtained a phone number but no address.

Reasoning that a phone call from a stranger asking questions about the Kennedy assassination would be highly suspicious they decided to try to learn the address of the young man and just drop in on him.

The phone rang at Clayton's house and was answered by the mother. The caller asked if she had requested telephone service or repairs. She said no.

"Well someone there did. What's your address?"

Without hesitation she gave the unknown caller her address. Immediately after, armed with Greg Clayton's address, Faura and Russo headed towards the beach community, stopping on the way to pick up a newspaper that headlined an attempt on the life of Saidallah Sirhan, brother of the assassin, as he drove on the Pasadena Freeway.

When she replaced the receiver, Mrs. Clayton had become suspicious and called the sheriff's substation in Malibu. By the time Faura and Russo arrived at their street, the neighborhood was being heavily patrolled by sheriff's cars. They spotted the first one just off Pacific Coast Highway.

"I won't stop at the house," Mrs. Russo said, "I will drive past the house and check the neighborhood."

Another sheriff's car cruised close to Clayton's house.

Using a public phone she called the house and asked for Greg.

"Hi, Greg," maybe you don't remember me, but I need to talk to you. I am Pam Russo from the Rafferty campaign."

He remembered her.

"I am in the neighborhood and thought of you for something coming up for a Nixon Project. Can you come and meet me?"

Yes, he could.

Minutes later they sat at a cocktail lounge at the Malibu Pier, having been joined by Gregory Ross Clayton.

A personable, clean-cut and alert young man very much involved in the politics of the country, Clayton enthusiastically exchanged some pleasantries with Russo and proceeded to tell them about a little excitement at his home.

They had received an anonymous call asking for their address. His mother, he said, was very wary because her husband, a high bank official, was the only person with the combination to the bank vault.

There had been an attempted kidnapping once, and the whole family was now worried about another try. After the call had been received, he related, his mother had checked with the phone companies in the area and found out no such call had been made by them. They had then called the sheriff and the house was being staked out.

Faura could not help but feel guilty about the trouble he had caused them. Faura had not learned how the address had been obtained until it was handed to him, and by then, it was too late. This was the kind of thing Faura had meticulously avoided so as not to give the police an excuse to detain him.

Clayton's story finished, Russo told him that he might be needed for some campaign work for Richard Nixon and asked if he would be available. He agreed.

They then discussed the events in which he participated the night of the shooting of Senator Kennedy.

According to Clayton, he had seen Sirhan early in the evening with three other men and a girl in a "polka-dot dress." He knew it was Sirhan because he had seen Sirhan being taken out of the Ambassador by police after the shooting. After hearing the whole story, Faura asked if it would be alright to put it on tape later on. He agreed and his story was taped a week later.

CHAPTER 35

Faura: What time did you get to the door – when you were guarding the (Rafferty party) door – what time did you start more or less?"

Clayton: Between 9 and 9:30.

Faura: What time was it that the man who appeared to be Sirhan and the (girl in the polka dot dress) and the rest of them go to that door, approximately?

Clayton: Well, I didn't see. I saw them leaving the Venetian Room, [Where the Rafferty function was held.] when I was finished bringing in my last load of Rafferty signs – that would be around 9 o'clock.

Faura: You saw them leaving the room?

Sirhan, three other men and the polka-dot dress girl were reported leaving the Rafferty party, less than a hundred feet from the Embassy Room and the Kennedy party.

The time was close enough to the reported altercation between Sirhan and a girl at the Rafferty party over a drink. Sirhan's presence at the Rafferty party had been confirmed because of that altercation. Now, according to Clayton, he was there with other men and a girl.

Clayton went on to tell about how he had stopped two of the men he saw with the man he believed to be Sirhan from entering the Rafferty party.

Clayton: They didn't look like they belonged,.

Faura: You saw them again at 11 o'clock?

Clayton: Yes, that's when – right after I had some trouble with the youth identifying himself with the Continental News Service, and after I had refused admission to him, I watched, and he went over to half way between the Venetian Room and the fountain and I was watching him, and at that time I noticed the "polka-dot girl" and what appeared to be Sirhan in a white shirt – you know, the hair – I saw the back of him and two other youths stand on the far side of him facing me, one youth whom I later thought was standing with them.

Faura: I noticed that when you talk about a guy who you observed standing near the fountain – you say you saw someone "who appeared to be Sirhan." Earlier you said – you said you saw the man coming out of the room. Are you not sure?

Clayton: They looked very similar. I haven't seen a real good picture of Sirhan yet. The ones I have seen look very much like him. The clothing was the same, so I presumed it was him.

The word "presume" is not one to instill confidence in any investigator. They would have to come back to it.

Faura: How many in the group you saw with Sirhan?

Clayton: There were three "boys," the person I think was Sirhan and the "girl in the polka dot dress."

Faura: Why do you call them "boys"?

Clayton: They were what you would call a college age, or under 25."

Asked about the "polka-dot girl," Clayton gave a description of her matching almost every detail given by others who had provided descriptions for the girl.

He also described the other three men in the group. One of them was "not skinny but slender," about 5'8," "foreign looking." The others were smaller and closer to Sirhan's build.

Faura then asked Clayton about the man he had tackled while he ran out of the Embassy Room and the direction where the Senator was shot.

Clayton: So I ran into there, and the (guard) walked a few feet in front of the door, and I saw two men, one with an object in his hand, it appeared to "flash," and another one was knocking – the one I caught, was knocking a newspaper photographer all over the table there and some chairs.

Faura: Now, when you say he was "knocking," he was not fighting, he was just running?

Clayton: He just shoved him all over the table.

Faura: While he was running?

Clayton: Yes. Trying to get him out of the way, at that time I took about two steps back toward the door and yelled to the security guy – and at the time I yelled, the other guy switched and ran back to the hallway.

Faura: The guy had something in his hand?

Clayton: Yes. That flashed.

Faura: Ran through the hallway?

Clayton explained the man changed direction and "ran back [out] another entrance." The other one kept coming toward him, and he was tripped by him (Clayton) and tackled by a guard.

In the ensuing struggle the guard asked the man questions. According to Clayton, the man with a "look of madness in his eyes as if he had rabies" kept saying, "Let me go. Gotta get out of here. Let me go."

The man was handcuffed by the guard and Clayton, and then taken to the security office. Clayton picked up some papers the man had been carrying when apprehended. They were bumper stickers reading: "KENNEDY ASSASSINATION A DEATH HOAX?"

The description of the man? Clayton kindly complied:

"He was about 5'6" and very tiny looking, looks foreign, had some sort of brown color real short, curly hair. He was wearing a coat but I don't think he was wearing a tie, and the thing I noticed the most about the coat, is that he had four flags across the one lapel of his coat. I didn't recognize any of the flags."

Slowly, thoroughly, they broke down the description of each of the other men for future reference.

Clayton was asked if during the capture of the running man, he had seen any of the other men he had observed with the group earlier that evening.

"The one that ran back through, I didn't get a look at him, the one with the object in his hand," Clayton said and pitched in a little more irrelevant detail before saying, "at the time I noticed two youths were running down the hallway that parallels the Venetian Room (Rafferty party) out to the outdoor patio, and one of the two I recognized as being the tall one in the group."

"The tall guy with Sirhan and the 'polka-dot girl' group?" Faura asked.

"Right," Clayton said.

Clayton went on to describe how he had been almost run over by a "flying wedge" of police and people as Sirhan had been taken out of the Ambassador.

He had tried to get an LAPD sergeant to go with him to the office where they had taken the "running man," but was unsuccessful.

"What about the girl?" Faura asked.

She had vanished. Clayton claims to have circled the lot several times as the hotel was being sealed off and never saw her.

"The last time you saw her was with the group around 11 o'clock?" Faura pushed.

"Well, when Sirhan, one boy and her started walking towards the Embassy Room."

How come Clayton remembered so much about the group, Faura wondered.

"Well, they were like discussing something, and the reason I was watching them, I thought they might try to cause some trouble in the Rafferty headquarters, and the one kept pointing toward the direction of the Embassy Room, I had assumed that maybe he was going to come down the hallway and go into the back entrance of the Venetian room."

Apparently Clayton was speculating that Sen. Kennedy would transit through the Venetian Room.

Faura asked if he had he contacted the police with all this information. Yes, to no avail, the young man stated. He had originally called the West Los Angeles police station, the one closest to his home, and they referred him to the Ramparts Division, where the investigation was being conducted in those days. He had called, they had taken his name and phone number and promised to call back.

CHAPTER 36

C layton's story dovetailed perfectly with Russo's. They had both observed a girl in a "polka-dot dress" from the door of the Venetian Room where the Rafferty party was taking place.

Clayton claimed she was with men who answered the descriptions of those described by Fahey and Gallegos.

Clayton had claimed one of the men was Sirhan, and that Sirhan, the girl and another man from the group had been walking toward the Embassy Room and Kennedy's party the last time he had seen them.

Two ran out the back door immediately after the shooting. One of them was recognized by Clayton as being with Sirhan and the "girl in the polka-dot dress." As chance would have it, Clayton did not chase the two men running out because he had his hands full with another one.

The one he helped capture was Michael Wayne, a man who looks like Sirhan and had been in the kitchen at the time of the shooting. Police investigated and cleared him of any association with Sirhan.

The one Clayton recognized as being with the man he believed was Sirhan and the "polka-dot girl" escaped out the door and into the parking lot, never to be found again.

Ironically, this was the twin version of Serrano's "polka-dot girl" story.

Faura and Russo interviewed Clayton, October 11, nearly four months after the "polka-dot girl" had been declared a "figment of the imagination" of Sandy Serrano.

Clayton gave essentially the same story to Robert Miller of the LAPD as he had given to Faura, but the interview was not recorded and only document I-4611 exists of the interview. Based on the account in this document, Clayton left out some important information that he had given Faura.

Clayton said, according to I-4611, that he saw Sirhan with a girl and three men at the Rafferty party but the document does not mention that the girl was in a "polka-dot dress." There is no recording, so there is no way of knowing if he did mention it or that fact was redacted out of the interview.

During Faura's interview of Clayton, Michael Wayne, the man he tripped and help capture, was heard to say "let me go, got to get out of here. I am not answering any questions, I am not going to say anything in public."

The last two statements, at least, would lead any reasonable investigator to presume he had something to say. They are not the words of an innocent spectator trying to get away from the scene of a crime.

There is no way of knowing if Clayton told this to the police.

I-4611 also says that Clayton failed to identify a photo of Sirhan. When shown a "mug shot" of Sirhan, Clayton did not recognize him but confused him with Munir Sirhan when shown a "mug" of Munir.

It should be remembered that Clayton saw Sirhan being taken out of the kitchen and recognized him as one of the men with the girl, according to his interview with Faura. This in a short span of time and when the actual events were happening. Three months later the police expected Clayton to distinguish between Sirhan and his brother.

Clayton had seen the group close by and even talked to one of them. Their looks were fresh in his mind when Sirhan was taken out and he recognized him as one of them.

If we are to believe him, Clayton had heard the first shot, and ran to the kitchen door with a guard in time to block it for two men that were trying to exit that way. One of them with something in his hand that "flashed." None of this appears in his interrogation by Miller. Did he fail to tell Miller, or did Miller fail to report it?

Wayne had displayed a lot of enterprise in managing to get into the kitchen and was also a Sirhan "lookalike." He became of interest to the LAPD.

Lisa Pease, a tireless assassination investigator, quotes an LAPD supplementary report on Michael Wayne in which the investigator says the business card of Keith Duane Gilbert, was in the possession of Wayne at the time of his apprehension after the Kennedy shooting.

"Gilbert is reported to be an extremist and militant who has been involved in a dynamite theft, previously." Wayne denied knowing Gilbert and did not remember having his card. According to Pease, Gilbert's file, when checked, had a Wayne business card in it. Wayne was polygraphed by LAPD Sgt. Hank Hernandez, who found him to be "truthful." Wayne has Gilbert's card but denies knowing him. Gilbert has Wayne's card but Hernandez finds them to be "truthful" about not knowing each other. They decided that the Michael Wayne card in Gilbert's possession belonged to another Michael Wayne. Incredible coincidence.

CHAPTER 37

On July 4, Fahey and his wife had dinner and a few drinks with Faura's family and their neighbors.

Thanks to a friend in the San Fernando Police Department, police protection was arranged for Fahey, Faura and the rest of them to go watch a fireworks display to redeem Faura's promise to his children.

The next day, July 5, found Los Angeles Police Chief Thomas Reddin disagreeing with the Pasadena Police Department about the alleged attempt on Saidallah Sirhan's life on the Pasadena Freeway.

Bonfante said that Reddin did not believe the story told by Said Sirhan. He was told of statements by Capt. Wright of the Pasadena police, indicating that an investigation was continuing on the assumption that Said was telling the truth.

Bonfante called Pasadena, since Wright was a good friend.

Wright said that he was taking Said's statements to be fact, and that the trajectory of the bullet holes in Said's car indicated the shots could have been fired from a Volkswagen bus, as Said claimed.

Another instance of Reddin claiming there was nothing to a story before it was really investigated.

On Sunday night July 7, Fahey telephoned Faura. It was important, he said, but "we cannot talk on the phone." Could they meet at the San Fernando Police station the next day?

On Monday, Fahey was at the appointed place at high noon. He had remembered something important, he said.

"McCarthy and the other FBI agent had blocked my mind by saying that CAT airlines and Flying Tigers were not passenger airlines, that they carry freight only, and to stop thinking about them because there was nothing there," showing annoyance towards the FBI agents.

He was referring to the fact that the girl he had been with had suggested that perhaps she could obtain passage on CAT (Civil Air Transport) to get out of Los Angeles. Faura knew CAT carried freight only, so he wondered how she could fly out on it, unless she knew someone to authorize it.

He also knew Flying Tigers Airline had morphed into CAT, which had morphed into AIR AMERICA, a CIA proprietary reported to be the carrier for the drug trafficking of the South Vietnamese generals helping the United States during the Vietnam War. He did not want to alarm Fahey, so he did not mention it.

Fahey said he was feeling angry with himself for not remembering more. In recollecting and going over every detail of his adventure, he had remembered that the woman had shown him a picture of a girl claiming she was also named "Oppenheimer."

In mentioning that she could get passage on CAT or Flying Tigers Airlines she had referred to a man also named "Oppenheimer." Fahey could not remember the man's first name.

The man named Oppenheimer, Fahey continued to recall, was an official of the Federal Aviation Agency in Guam.

"He either operates out of Guam or Taipei," Fahey said, "or travels between the two of them quite frequently."

Fahey said that the woman, upon showing him the picture of the girl, left the impression that she had to contact the girl sooner or later. Fahey underscored that he was positive of his statements and recollection.

"I am positive you will find this man there. It you just determine that, then we can go from there."

Faura got the feeling that Fahey had something else in mind that he was not telling him. The girl whose photo the woman had shown him was in some kind of school "back east" – he had said before. He suggested that they find the man in Guam and then go for the girl "back east."

He seemed positive and confident about what he was suggesting. Faura doubted if CAT Airlines was still flying. He advanced his thoughts that they had merged with Flying Tigers, a cargo airline.

This, of course, was in error, as Fahey demonstrated in short order. He suggested that a client to whom he sold chemicals would know. The client was on Foothill Boulevard, a couple of miles from where Fahey and Faura were, and Fahey suggested they go check with his client.

A few minutes later they drove into the parking lot of China Air Lines and walked into the office of Mr. Woo, the purchasing agent.

Fahey introduced Faura as a newsman working on a story and, after showing his LAPD credentials at Woo's request, Faura asked if he knew of CAT airlines.

"Yes," said Woo. "I know of Civil Air Transport."

He did not know if CAT was flying freight or passengers and proceeded to give the name of CAT's president. They learned that CAT flies to Taiwan, Hong Kong, and that part of the world.

Weeks later the LAPD would use the incident for fabricating the most incredible and vulnerable lie to discredit Fahey and Faura.

This fabrication was introduced into the investigation record where it stands as testimony of the police cover-up and their fragile lies. According to the police record, a team of investigators checking out Fahey's story found out that Fahey and Faura had visited Mr. Woo in the middle of May, thereby providing a link before the assassination and implying that they had concocted Fahey's story together!

Faura's notes, which would stand in any court of law, clearly show that they visited Woo on July 8.

The secret polygraph test the police gave Fahey to break him down further, a copy of which Faura obtained, clearly shows that Fahey met Faura on the day he walked into the *Hollywood Citizen News* editorial office seven days after the assassination.

Fahey had also gone with his story to the FBI before ever knowing Faura. The FBI had the truth on tape and Fahey's declarations to them. The question must then be asked: how many more fabrications?

CHAPTER 38

It is also interesting to note that the LAPD never contacted Faura personally to confirm or deny any of what they introduced into the record regarding Fahey, or Faura's investigation of this story.

The handling of that portion of the investigation and the fabricated records introduced are enough evidence that the investigation was an unadulterated fraud.

After leaving Woo, Fahey expressed and displayed eagerness to meet "Oppenheimer" the man, face to face. He volunteered to go to Guam with Bonfante and Faura to track the man down. He insinuated that he had more information but that he would give it only after we found "Oppenheimer."

"Look, we'll get to this point, and we will take over from there," he declared. "I think we are very close to striking blood."

Back at his bureau at the San Fernando Police Station, Faura placed a call to one of his sources in a federal agency and asked for assistance in locating "Oppenheimer" with the little information they had available.

His source said he would try with the FAA and Immigration. He understood Faura's request that the FBI be kept out of it. His source too had had experience with the FBI.

Driving home that day, Fahey's story disturbed Faura. While he believed that in trying to remember Fahey had broken through a mental block placed there by the harping police and FBI agents, Faura did not like the idea of Fahey holding back information. The time had come to investigate him and determine the truthfulness of his statements.

Faura started a check on Fahey's background and arrangements for a polygraph test.

There were other loose ends to tie up. After trying for a few days, Faura finally caught up with Jose Carvajal, the Ambassador kitchen helper who had told him and Barnett a man had been apprehended as he spoke on the phone.

The man, according to Carvajal, had said, "we shot him," or "we got him," or the "job is done," or words to that effect – and also that the "polka-dot girl" had run in one direction, trapped herself, turned back and ran out the door. Many witnesses had seen this, he said.

Now he retold his story.

This time he gave the name of the man that had apprehended the man in the telephone booth. He gave the name of Jesse Gonzales as the man whom Sirhan had asked if the senator was coming through that part of the kitchen. Carvajal said that the FBI had given Gonzales protection for a few days but that he was back to work now.

According to Carvajal, Gonzalez had observed the "polka-dot girl" conversing with Sirhan for a long time outside on a small terrace behind the kitchen where the senator was shot. Gonzales had told him, Carvajal claimed, that he and several others had heard the "polka-dot girl" cry, "We shot him. We shot him."

The FBI had shown him several composites, Carvajal went on, and appeared to be attempting to connect the "polka-dot girl" to the girl seen talking to Sirhan and to the shooting.

The information was very interesting but all secondhand. It was necessary to talk to Gonzales. Because of the fact that Carvajal and Gonzales worked in the kitchen, the information would be as good as gold.

The fact that Gonzales had been asked by Sirhan if the senator was coming through the kitchen had been confirmed and was encouraging, but all in all Gonzales had to be interrogated before Carvajal's story could be accepted. This proved to be wishful thinking.

Carvajal promised to see Faura the next day and take him to Gonzales, but did not show up. The next day Faura located Carvajal. He was to never again get another word from Carvajal.

"The police say I can't talk," he said, and he never did.

The investigation was slowing down considerably. The LAPD said 45 specialists were assigned to SUS in addition to more than 400 FBI agents working on the assassination investigation.

While Faura and friends had been able to move fast, unhampered by policy and procedures, and make remarkable progress while the police were beginning to gear up to the investigation, by this time it was getting very difficult and police and FBI were closing doors that would never open for them again.

They kept trying. On July 30, Luke Perry telephoned. He had met a man named Teddy Charach who claimed to have pictures taken in the kitchen the night of the shooting. Faura arranged to meet with Charach the next day.

CHAPTER 39

Theodore Charach gave the impression to Faura that he was a nervous and cagey young man who appeared to be propelled by a fanatical desire and drive to strike it rich. They met at the Sportsman Lodge in San Fernando Valley. For two hours Charach beat around the bush, measuring, feeling Faura out.

Finally he produced several still pictures blown up from a motion picture. One of the pictures showed a man who looked very much like Sirhan, very close to Senator Kennedy as he gave a speech.

In another, a woman in a polka-dot dress was discerned in the crowd. Charach was full of information that he shared somewhat guardedly. He said the stills were parts of a motion picture documentary being prepared by a young UCLA student by the name of Alvin Tokunow.

Charach had met a man called Richard Lubic, who was interested in buying the film and the stills for District Attorney Jim Garrison of New Orleans, who at that time was investigating the John F. Kennedy assassination. Would Faura be interested in meeting Lubic?

Perhaps Lubic would cooperate with Faura, making the film and blow-ups available after Garrison got what he wanted.

That would be fine, Faura agreed. There was little question in Faura's mind that Charach was out for a fast buck. Regardless of his motives, Faura realized that Charach was correct in assuming that he had something of value, and that it was worth going along with anything he suggested within reason.

Would Faura introduce him to *Life* magazine in case his negotiations with Lubic collapsed? Yes, Faura agreed, as long as he understood that it was Charach's deal and that Faura wanted no part of it.

Would Faura work with him on a record he was planning? Maybe. Faura did not like Charach's aggressiveness or his commercialism. The meeting over, they agreed to meet again two days later.

Two things happened the next day in relation to Faura's chase of the "polka-dot girl" that, although they contributed nothing to it, Faura would never forget.

By pre-arrangement, Faura was at the Marcus law firm when Mary Sirhan came in. The sad-looking, suffering, small woman and Faura chatted briefly while Marcus busied himself calling Russell Parsons, Sirhan's defense attorney.

Mrs. Sirhan had come in relation to her divorce from Sirhan's father. The burden of the assassination seemed to rest on her shoulders invisibly, only to be reflected in her eyes and her soft speech. One could not help but feel admiration for her stamina and stoicism.

They spoke, avoiding all mention of Sirhan or the killing. A little later, Marcus invited them to his home in Pasadena.

Cagily, Marcus asked Faura to drive Mrs. Sirhan in his car, and he would take another client who was in the office.

Someone mentioned the police and the protection they had over the Sirhan family home, and Marcus changed the traveling arrangements. She would go with him, the other client with Faura.

At Marcus' palatial home they got out of the cars, and Marcus was instantly surrounded by his grandchildren. A lovely handsome boy, around 5 or 6, years old, came to Marcus and hugged him. Marcus turned around to introduce him to his guests.

"Meet Fernando and Mrs. Sirhan," he said. The boy looked at them with a smile. He had a beautiful face.

"What's your name?" Mrs. Sirhan inquired, bending down a little to take him by the hand.

"Bobby," he replied.

In Faura's mind the next few seconds froze into eternity. He stopped breathing. Time stopped. Mrs. Sirhan smiled kindly, Marcus tending to another hugging child, had lost the exchange and had started to turn towards them.

Faura was inexplicably shocked by the boy's answer, as if it had been the wrong thing to say. Her son had just killed "Bobby Kennedy," as he was known to his followers.

"Bobby," Mrs. Sirhan echoed and after two or three seconds, "That is a very nice name."

Straightening up and moving towards the house, Mrs. Sirhan returned the whole scene back to reality. It had been to Faura as if a camera had stopped the motion at the word, "Bobby," and returned it after she released it with her comment.

A few minutes later, Marcus' driver took her back home. It was to be the last time Faura saw her. He thought of what a fine woman she was, he thought of his mother, and he thought that his investigation could only add to Mrs. Sirhan's hurt.

The other incident that he would never forget was provided by Marcus himself.

Throughout that evening there had been no opportunity to discuss the Sirhan case. Marcus, sipping a drink in his den, broached the subject during a few minutes alone with Faura.

"Mrs. Sirhan tells me that to her knowledge the rights to a book about her son have not been sold in New York or anywhere else," Marcus said.

The idea had never occurred to Faura.

"How much would that story be worth?" Marcus asked.

"Anywhere between $100,000 and 250,000," Faura guessed, not really knowing.

"Fine," he chimed in, "I will get it for you, and I will represent you."

Marcus laughed at his own suggestion, but he was serious. If anyone could do it, he could. Faura left that night with the feeling that Marcus was going to attempt to make a deal for a book that Faura would write.

Faura made up his mind that night that he would not get trapped into writing a book about the assassin when he was investigating a conspiracy. The offer was never made, and he never had to articulate his decision.

Sometime later, Robert Kaiser, the *Life* magazine stringer he had met with Bonfante at Marcus' office, was, through his own initiative and talent, to secure the rights to such a book. The result was *RFK Must Die*, a mine of invaluable information and research into the assassination.

Leaving Marcus' home that night, Faura stopped by a public phone booth and called his city editor. It was 11 P.M. but he had a story too important to pass up.

"Russell Parsons will plead not guilty for Sirhan," he told his editor. There had been a great deal of speculation about the plea, what will it be: insanity, diminished capacity or what?

Here was a scoop picked up from the horse's mouth. This is what Parsons had told Marcus, and Faura had overheard the conversation.

Since the *Hollywood Citizen News* hit the stands before any other newspaper, it would be a clear lead over the other newspapers: a national scoop.

The editor went back to bed, and the story was missed. That timidity could have been one of the reasons the newspaper folded two years later, after being the second oldest newspaper in Hollywood.

"Teddy" Charach, as his friends called him and Faura met at 2 P.M. Aug. 2, when Faura took him to *Life* magazine's office to meet Bonfante. Bonfante looked at the pictures, paid little attention to the girl and showed restrained interest in the man who looked like Sirhan.

He could not, he told Charach, make a decision then and there. He would be talking to his editors in Miami, where he was to meet them for the Republican convention, and upon his return he would make a decision about the movie and the stills.

He asked Faura, in the meantime, to take a look at the movie and give him his opinion of it.

CHAPTER 40

S hortly afterwards Charach took Faura to Richard Lubic's office on the famed Sunset Strip.

Lubic went over his involvement with the Jim Garrison people, said they suspected the girl Faura sought was the same girl a New York newsman and a Garrison agent had been tracking.

According to Lubic's account, the pair had been shadowing two suspected anti-Castro Cuban revolutionaries. One day they were followed to one of New York's international airports, where they picked up a young woman answering the description of the "polka-dot girl."

The two Cubans drove her to a midtown hotel. They later left the hotel with some luggage they did not have when they entered. They then drove the girl to the Newark, N.J., airport, where they were to put her and the luggage on an American Airlines plane bound for Los Angeles, where the trackers lost the girl.

All this had happened three days prior to the Robert Kennedy assassination, coinciding with the statement of Fahey's girl, that she had been in the country three days.

Therein was their interest in Faura's investigation would he help? Faura was not sure of the ground he was treading on. He told Lubic he would cooperate and exchange information with Garrison if they would show good faith.

Lubic claimed that they had a picture of the girl and suggested that Faura take a look at it. Faura agreed. Lubic also suggested that Faura meet and talk to a Garrison agent living in Palisades Park.

Faura also agreed to that. Lubic asked that Faura talk to Garrison personally the next time Garrison was in town, and Faura agreed provided that it was done very discretely.

Garrison had unleashed the wrath of the establishment and was under the most vicious and discrediting attacks ever to be heaped on a public official. While Faura believed and had confirmed some of the information Garrison had, he had no intention of allowing himself to get into the same predicament as Garrison. He knew full well some in high office who would be interested in scuttling any investigation into the Kennedy assassinations.

Leaving Lubic's office, Charach was dismayed. They had talked about "their interest" – that having to do with the assassination – but not "his interest" – that of making money.

He honestly, if crudely, remarked that he had made a mistake in introducing Faura to Lubic. As it turned out that was the first and last time Faura saw Lubic and Lubic produced nothing.

In spite of his disappointment, Charach agreed to meet Faura the next day and take him to meet Alvin Tokunow, for a private screening of the film.

In contrast to Charach, Luke Perry continued to help, receiving no financial help and expecting none. That night he called with yet another lead. An acquaintance by the name of Chuck Dirks, a teacher, had been questioned by the FBI and might have useful information.

Faura invited Luke to go with him to the screening of the film the next day. Luke was delighted. Dirks lived near Faura's home in the San Fernando Valley, and Perry and he went there about 1 o'clock the next morning. He told his story and they arranged to tape it later on. At 11 A.M. they met Charach at the corner of Westwood and Wilshire Boulevard.

Before noon they were all huddled around a "movieola" running the movie Tokunow had made the night of the assassination. The little room in the School of Cinematography at UCLA was hot and cramped as they viewed it once for overall effect. Then, running it again, it was stopped at the point where the man resembling Sirhan appeared. The same with the girl. Back to the Sirhan frames. Now in slow motion, from a few feet before the man's first appearance to a few feet beyond. Again and again and again, frame by frame.

There was no question that the man could not possibly be Sirhan. In watching the film in slow motion, one could see that the man they were looking at had a suit coat and a tie on.

The same procedure was used on the frames of the girl. She was not the "girl in the polka-dot dress."

Somewhat disappointed, they left UCLA. Charach admitted that he had known all along what the results would be. Faura was angry but stopped short of insulting him.

Faura told Bonfante that neither Sirhan nor the "polka-dot girl" were in the film and related the incident with Charach, then forgot about it. That was not, however, to be the end of the film caper. A few days later, someone broke into the UCLA film department and the original print was stolen. Prime suspects, in Charach's mind, were the Garrison people, and Faura and Bonfante.

The whole idea was preposterous, but Faura also wondered who might have such an interest in the film as to risk stealing it. It was interesting speculation, but he decided to forget about it. But the little, useless film, would not leave them alone.

About three weeks later, *Newsweek* magazine got hold of the "film story" and ran an item in its "Periscope" section. This attracted the attention of *Life* magazine's editorial offices in New York. *Life* called Bonfante. Buy the film and the stills, just in case. Bonfante bypassed Charach and bought a copy of the film directly from Tokunow, without telling Faura. The LAPD, trailing them as had become their habit, obtained a poor copy of the film.

Life published the pictures, almost half a page, of the man who looked like Sirhan, very close to Kennedy while the senator gave his last speech. Faura wondered what was the point since it was not Sirhan. Unknown to Faura, Charach sued *Life* magazine.

Months later, Bonante called Faura.

"We have a problem," he said smacking his lips characteristically.

"We do?"

"During the trial today, every third word coming out of Charach's mouth was Fernando Faura," he said. "The bastard spilled his mouth to the press."

"Hold it right there Jordan," Faura stopped him. "What trial? What are you talking about?"

"I told you. Charach sued *Life* over the pictures we published."

Faura had assumed the transaction had been consummated with Charach. It hadn't, and Charach had sued.

Caught by surprise, Faura listened to Bonfante tell about their day in court.

Life had won the suit, but Charach had been cornered by the press at the Beverly Hills court and, for a half hour, expounded on a conspiracy, claiming that Faura knew there was one, that he had pictures of the "polka-dot girl," etc, etc.

Months of undercover work shot to hell by a disgruntled man. Faura called every news bureau in Los Angeles, asking if Charach was to be put on the air with his wild stories and demanding equal time if they did. Not one station ran the story that night. After seeing the film of Charach's interview no one would.

CHAPTER 41

Two years later Charach was to develop his own information on a second gun theory and sue the Los Angeles Police Department to block the promotion of DeWayne Wolfer to head the police laboratory. Charach charged that Wolfer erred in his ballistics procedures with the Sirhan gun and bullets extracted from some of the other victims and the senator himself.

Charach claimed that there were two guns firing at the Senator, and that a total of 11 shots had been fired, instead of eight as is the official version.

Amazingly Charach named a second gunman: Thane Eugene Cesar. Cesar, a maintenance worker, at Lockheed Aircraft, was also a part time security guard. On the night that Robert Kennedy was killed, he was part of the security set up by the hotel to control the crowds.

Cesar was in the kitchen when the shooting began. He claims to have dived for the safety of the floor behind Kennedy while drawing his gun. He also claims he did not fire a single shot.

Under questioning, Cesar admitted that at one time he owned a .22 caliber gun of the same make as that used by Sirhan, but added that he had sold it a few months prior to June 5.

The night of the shooting he claims to have unholstered a .38 caliber weapon but never fired it. Charach publicly charged him with being the actual killer. It is now a matter of public record.

Cesar has yet to sue Charach, because "Charach has no money to get, and it would be a waste of time and money."

The strange developments did not end there.

Charach also claimed in his suit that the bullets Wolfer had claimed came from Sirhan's gun had in fact come from a different gun. Using court records he proved it beyond any doubt. Charach produced the serial numbers of the two guns in the controversy.

Police claimed they had Sirhan's gun but the other one had been destroyed. Now District Attorney Joseph Bush, successor to Evelle Younger, waded into the fray and charged that the evidence under the custody of the County Clerk had been tampered with and damaged.

This was interpreted by most independent investigators as a smoke screen designed to draw the heat from Charach's charges.

A grand jury was convened.

Several dozen witnesses were subpoenaed, Faura among them. The farce lasted several weeks while D.A. Busch privately admitted to close associates that he wished he had kept his mouth shut, and postponed the airing of the findings on several occasions while he jockeyed for a tenable position.

The conclusion of the grand jury was announced and the results were predictable. The blame was put on the county clerk for not properly safeguarding the evidence and allowing it to be tampered with.

What that had to do with Charach's charges no one cared to explain.

It did give the police an easy way out, and they took it. Wolfer had mislabeled the bullets that he had sworn in court came from Sirhan's gun, the district attorney said.

The one thing many were hoping would take place did not. The district attorney resolved that the testing of Sirhan's gun a second time was not necessary. Charach's charges could have been put to rest or proven by testing the gun. It was not done.

The police position is further eroded by the fact that they had consistently said there were no other guns in the kitchen and that there were no other persons with known right-wing connections or philosophies. The presence of Cesar in the kitchen with an unholstered gun blows both of them sky high.

Charach had dropped the suit a week after he filed it. The last Faura heard of Charach, he was still trying to sell his record.

Five days after the UCLA screening, Faura taped an interview with Chuck Dirks at his home in Mission Hills.

Dirks looks more like a student than a teacher, his youthful appearance somewhat tempered by a serious no-nonsense face. He was very cooperative and promised to do whatever was necessary to help. He proved as good as his word.

Dirks had been questioned by Robert Miller of the LAPD rather than by an FBI agent, as Luke Perry had said.

Miller, in giving Dirks the old "We are checking every possible lead" public relations story, had also let slip something that, coming from an LAPD officer, underscores the lies being told the public by the department.

During his conversation and interrogation of Dirks, Miller had said the LAPD wanted to be through with the investigation by September, one month later.

By that time the Reddin Report on the assassination would be prepared. He claimed the LAPD did not want it to have the "flaws" the Warren Report had.

Then Miller had made a mistake. He asked Dirks about a "girl in a polka-dot dress" standing by a camera set-up. He also asked if Dirks had seen anyone answering the description of the "polka-dot girl."

These questions in reference to the "girl in the polka-dot dress" were posed by LAPD's Miller on Aug. 2. It becomes quite obvious then that on Aug. 2, the LAPD was still looking for a girl they had claimed did not exist back on June 21!

Miller had shown Dirks some photos of Sirhan for possible identification and, not getting any results, questioned Dirks about two "Latin looking" men he had seen entering the kitchen. Dirks had complied and started his own questioning.

Miller told him of a man who had been at Kennedy headquarters to register, as volunteers, a "group of Arabs" who were coming from the Middle East. Checking that lead and the Kennedy people, Miller told Dirks, that neither the man nor the "group of Arabs" could be located. The man, Miller had gone on, had "influence and contacts," "traveled quite a bit," was from the "far east" and "worked for the Rand Corporation" in Santa Monica.

Miller, realizing that he was talking too much, had cut himself short and reversed himself: "We found him," he said.

Dirks interpreted this to mean that the man had finally been tracked down by the police. No further reference was made to the subject during the remainder of Miller's half-hour visit with Dirks.

Knowing that Dirks was intelligent and perceptive, Faura suggested that he be put under hypnosis by an expert to help him recollect the events of the night of June 4. He agreed and this was done two weeks later.

Having deliberately left Fahey alone all this time to allow the FBI and the police to cool off, Faura and Bonfante decided it was time to start working on his story again. There was little doubt that the "girl in the polka-dot dress" was a real, live, breathing body.

DiPierro had identified her, and Fahey had said she had prior knowledge of the assassination; now they had to firm up or discount Fahey's account.

A check on Fahey's background had come through showing that he had had some trouble when he was a young man but indicating that he had been an upstanding citizen for the last 20 years, through all of his adult life.

On Aug. 18, Faura and Bonfante set out to prove or disprove that Fahey had been at Trancas Restaurant in the company of a woman at the time he had claimed.

On the day that Faura was to turn Fahey over to the LAPD, there had been a delay of three hours. He and Fahey had used the time to go over the route Fahey followed, and Fahey had shown Faura the restaurant table where he claimed to have been sitting with his companion.

Sometime later, both the FBI and the police had taken Fahey through the same paces. The FBI being more thorough in this instance had taken him to Trancas Restaurant to identify the waitress who had served them.

Fahey had pointed to a waitress as the one that most looked like her. The FBI, excluding Fahey from the questioning of the waitress, determined that Fahey had not been at Trancas. The waitress did not remember him, so they concluded he was lying.

The FBI approach was obviously elementary and simplistic in its conclusion. Faura had another approach – to find the tickets for June 4, select those for the shift between 4 and 8 P.M., and determine from the tickets who had been serving the table at which Fahey had eaten – table No. 14.

With this done they could question the waitress who served Fahey and his companion and see what she remembered. They were confident that the looks of Fahey's companion would be remembered. With this plan in mind, Faura and Bonfante headed for Malibu and Trancas Restaurant.

At the restaurant, they asked the manager to let them see the sales tickets for June 4. He politely refused and said only the owner could do that. They suggested he call the owner, and he did. Bonfante talked to the owner and asked for permission to go see him at his home, which was nearby. The owner agreed.

At the owner's home, a palatial residence in the Malibu hills, the owner offered them a drink, which they accepted. He was Italian, and he looked it, between 40 and 50 years old, sophisticated but obviously very street wise. Hovering near him was an attractive woman about his age whom he introduced as his wife.

She served the drinks and the host asked Bonfante if he spoke Italian, and Bonfante answered in Italian. They started a conversation in Italian, which Faura did not understand, so he tried to make a word here and there while enjoying the beautiful panoramic view of the Malibu hills, the Coast Highway lights, and the black ocean. "My god," he thought, "this is a scene out of the 'Godfather,' and here we are in the boss's mansion asking for permission to take a peek at these files to solve a murder." The conversation was brief, animated and punctuated with laughter.

Bonfante had charmed the "boss," and he called the restaurant and gave his permission to let us look "at whatever they need to see." A little more than two hours after they had started on their mission they had a box full of restaurant "tickets" in front of them at the restaurant's office.

Quickly finding the month of June, they narrowed it down to the fourth, then to the proper table. Fahey had told them what they had eaten, that it was on "special" and how much it cost him. No beverages. Bonfante with one batch and Faura with another, they looked through the tickets.

Bingo! Only one ticket had the amount Fahey had paid. Check No. 536938. It showed that two people at table 14 ordered "2 fillet of sole-mash special," price $3.90, plus tax .20 for a total of $4.10.

A waitress came in. She had been sent for by the restaurant manager – having been the waitress questioned by the FBI.

She said Fahey had identified her as the one who had served him. She told the FBI that she could not remember him, and they had left in a huff. Later in the day, she claimed, she had remembered that she did not even work June 4, therefore could not have been the girl they wanted.

Fahey had fingered the wrong girl. Had the FBI known that this girl was not working on June 4, they could have realized Fahey's mistake and perhaps tried harder.

Taking a more difficult but more accurate approach, Faura and Bonfante instantly eliminated that error.

"Is this your handwriting?"

"No. I didn't work that day?"

"Whose writing is it?"

"Jan Page."

"Did she work that day?"

"Yes, she did. It was also on her shift that they had the 'fillet of sole' on special." The manager confirmed this information but refused to give them Jan Page's phone number and address. Instead he called her himself to ask if she would come and meet them. During this time Bonfante took photos of the ticket.

Minutes later they met Jan Page at a beach cocktail lounge near her home on Pacific Coast Highway. The atmosphere was quiet and relaxed. The sun was setting and the Pacific Ocean, living up to its name with a small surf, added to the peaceful feeling of the lounge where they sat at a corner table. Jan Page was instantly relaxed and talking.

CHAPTER 42

"I remember the day of June 4th because it was before Kennedy was killed, and I was terribly upset that evening. I did not know why at the time, but about 6 or 7 in the evening I became unexplainably upset," she said.

"I was working in the coffee shop that day and I vaguely remember the couple because they sat at table 14, against the window, and very few people sit there. The girl sat against the window and the man sat on the inside.

"I don't remember if they had a drink, I only remember they had something simple and didn't stay very long. I remarked to myself that they were very nice-looking people, and I wanted to take a better look at them.

"The girl was very nice looking and so was the man, and I wanted to look at them some more – I don't stare at people, but I like to look them over if they look interesting, you know, to look what jewelry she had and so on.

"They didn't stay long," Page repeated, "and they were quiet the whole time. They certainly didn't laugh and whoop it up. In fact they looked strained, as though there was a wall between them.

"I didn't see much of him because his back was to me. But she gave me the impression that she might have been very nervous."

Page then added, without prodding or having been requested, a description of the girl that was identical to that given by Fahey.

"The girl was slim, chic – slim, not skinny, and could have been anywhere around thirty years old. She was well dressed in some neutral shade. She wore a pony tail, on the right side. Her eyes – they could have been gray – were very strange."

The reporters showed Page their "photo."

"They were not as deep set as the exaggerated way they are in this picture – a little fuller face, a mouth slightly fuller, and eyes not so exaggerated," she repeated.

"Her complexion was sallow, as though not entirely healthy, very fair and sallow," Page concluded.

She had, to Faura's satisfaction, given a very close description.

Page had also provided the reason why Fahey had pointed out the wrong waitress. He had not had the opportunity to see the girl who was serving him, except when she was taking the order.

"I didn't see much of him because his back was to me," Page had said. For the same reason Fahey could not have seen much of her.

Page's recollection left no doubt Fahey had been at Trancas with the girl as he had said. The cooperative Page agreed to undergo hypnosis also to attempt a total recall. Bonfante called her two days later to tell her of the arrangements made for the hypnotic session. Page had changed her tune.

"Since I never took that second look I wanted to take, I am afraid now that I wouldn't be able to contribute anything very much about that girl," she said.

It later developed that, in attempting to check Faura and Bonfante out as legitimate newsmen she had called a friend at the sheriff's office. He, in turn, called the LAPD.

A few hours after our meeting with her, LAPD Sgt. O'Steen – the same man who had illegally confiscated the tape – was battering her down. After a brief visit to her home, O'Steen had gone "downtown" and called her on the phone. "What is the color of my eyes?" he demanded.

Page did not remember.

"If you cannot remember what you just saw how can you remember what you saw June 4th?"

The embarrassed waitress got the message and refused to cooperate further with the reporters.

We had lost Page, but we still had Dirks for the hypnotic session.

Dr. Raymond LaScola had come highly recommended by Lt. Charles Sherwood, who was with the San Fernando Police Department and a friend of Faura's. Sherwood claimed LaScola was used by the police because of his reputation in having helped a victim's memory with hypnosis, thereby solving the crime.

Dr. LaScola agreed to help us, and on Aug. 24, we took Dirks to him. We also brought Fahey along to become familiar with the process so that he, too, could be hypnotized in the attempt to extract more details. We did not know that the defense and the police where to use the same techniques with Sirhan later.

Dirks was put into a deep hypnotic state. He recalled the shots and the screams and relived his experience narrating it to us and the silent tape recorder next to him. Then LaScola guided him to another area.

Dirks recreated his attempts at helping a fire marshal direct people to another room to prevent their entry into the Embassy Room. He remembers two men: "I guess they were about student or graduate student age. One was taller than the other. He had brown – they were looking kind of drab. Neither had their hair combed. They couldn't care less, I should say, obviously about their appearance."

"Move back, I said," Dirks continued, "but they did not want to move back with the rest of the people and go downstairs. Instead they moved across in front of us from the right.

"One was taller than the other. I guess that one was about 5'9." One was shorter. They instead went to the left and in through some doors."

Dirks said he did not know where the doors led to and added other details.

"Later on I did find out that the doors led to the kitchen. I had wondered at the time just where they went."

Dirks lost sight of the men and went back to his wife and friend.

LaScola asked him to describe the men further.

"The tallest man had a brown jacket. It looked like an older jacket. Thin faces, both thin faces. And both dark hair. They are both dark, somewhat dark complected – they aren't Negro, but they were dark complected."

LaScola placed Dirks into deeper hypnosis and asked him if one of the men he had seen was Sirhan. Dirks was incoherent. There were too many people, too much light when Sirhan was being taken out by the police. He might have been one of the men he saw earlier, but he was not sure.

LaScola moved Dirks to yet another area.

"I was startled to see this girl standing on the platform," Dirks said. Faura realized Dirks was talking about the girl LAPD officer Miller had questioned him about.

"The reason I was startled is because she didn't look like she belonged," Dirks continued in his trance. "She just sort of stuck out."

A description of the girl was obtained shortly afterwards.

"Cheap white cotton dress, with polka dots, wiry stringy, hair, etc."

Dirks was shown the "photo" the newsmen had. He said the "photo" looked like the woman he had seen. Yes, that could be her.

Dirks was taken out of hypnosis. The description of the girl he had seen near the TV cameras was close to the other descriptions we had.

We chatted briefly, and Faura asked Fahey what he thought of submitting to hypnosis now that he had seen there was nothing to it.

Faura knew he was skeptical and wanted to reassure him. That had been the only reason Faura invited him.

"I guess it is all right, but not now," Fahey demurred.

"There is no pain, just relax and watch, close your eyes, now! You are under, John, see, there is nothing to it," LaScola said, touching and closing Fahey's eyelids.

Faura could not believe it himself. Fahey was under hypnosis instantly. Earlier that day he had a tooth pulled and some oral surgery. He had been complaining of a toothache or neuralgia most of the afternoon.

Now LaScola was making a post-hypnotic suggestion.

"John when you wake up there will be no toothache. It will be gone. Your mouth will heal much sooner than you expect. You will be surprised."

He repeated it several times. He then asked Fahey to wake up. Leaving LaScola's office, we went to a restaurant across the street for a cup of coffee.

Fahey declared that he didn't feel he had been under hypnosis, but said nothing for fear of embarrassing the doctor.

What he failed to realize was that people under hypnosis rarely feel they are and that they are fully aware of what is happening. Events two days later would prove that he had been very much under hypnosis.

CHAPTER 43

The following Monday, Aug. 27, Bonfante and Faura visited Fahey at his new job in Los Angeles. He was now in charge of a small store that sold electric shavers. Fahey lost no time in broaching the subject.

"Something strange has happened," he said in wonderment.

"My mouth has healed almost completely. It is almost like a miracle."

"It was no miracle," the newsmen corrected him, "it was hypnosis."

"I still don't believe I was under," Fahey countered.

"Never mind that. Did you remember anything new about the girl?"

"I can't explain it," he said, "but I did." He still resisted the fact that he had been hypnotized.

"I remember the girl told me she was going up north somewhere. It was to some place near San Francisco, to a conference or convention. She belonged to some organization called the Rosylings or Rosichristy – or something like that."

"The Rosicrucians," Faura exploded. "Their headquarters is in San Jose!"

"That's it, that's it," Fahey cried. "The Rosicrucians."

The Rosicrucian Temple and headquarters is in San Jose, a 45-minute drive from San Francisco.

Jordan Bonfante looked at Faura with a surprised and knowing look. Sirhan was a Rosicrucian.

His first request in jail was for his Rosicrucian membership to be paid up to date and for Rosicrucian literature. He was known to practice Rosicrucian exercises for self-hypnosis.

Here then was what appeared to be a good and solid lead. Perhaps a much closer link between Sirhan and the girl could be developed.

Bonfante and Faura left Fahey and on the way to their car, purchased a Rosicrucian magazine. The inside cover confirmed their information. The Rosicrucian headquarters was in San Jose. The magazine had a calendar of events, past and future. There had been several seminars in June. In fact, they had one almost every week.

Encouraged by the new development, they decided to expedite the polygraph examination of Fahey. That was to be the real test. Was his story true or not?

Three days later the answer was provided for them by Chris Gugas, one of the foremost polygraph experts in the country.

Gugas' credentials were impeccable. Formerly a CIA agent in Europe and Asia, he had established the polygraph program for the U.S. Marine Corps and trained many of its examiners, as well as those of many other government agencies.

A columnist for a police newspaper, he held a teaching credential in Criminal Investigation and Police Science from the California State Board of Education. He was also the founder and first president of the National Board of Polygraph Examiners and was, at the time, the President of the American Polygraph Association.

A man of Gugas' background and reputation was necessary to protect the integrity of the polygraph examination, inasmuch as they felt that it, too, would be challenged. He was obviously the right man for the job.

Polygraph examinations are not allowed in court as evidence since trained professionals (CIA agents, undercover operators of all agencies, and other cloak-and-dagger operators prone to be tested) are trained to defeat the polygraph. However, it is still widely used by police agencies and others with the general public because they don't know how to fool the machine, and is usually very useful in detecting deception.

On Aug. 30, while a personally autographed photo of FBI Director J. Edgar Hoover stared down at them, Gugas took Fahey though his polygraph examination.

Bonfante and Faura had picked up Fahey at his job and, fearful he might change his mind about the polygraph, had agreed not to let him out of their sight, not even to go to the bathroom.

Faura and Bonfante were both edgy, knowing the importance of the examination and, realizing it should have been done before, wanted to take no chances. Fahey was calm and cooperative. He signed a statement agreeing to take the test without promise of reward, threat or immunity.

Gugas Professional Security Consultants office at 9301 Wilshire Blvd., provided and excellent view of Santa Monica Bay, for those with the time and inclination to look out the window while waiting for the elevator. This is where Bonfante and Faura waited while Gugas put Fahey through the polygraph test.

They paced the corridors anxiously, occasionally stopping at a window to look at the city and bay below. Early evening was settling softly over the city and neon lights were turning on to adorn what was promising to be a beautiful night.

They debated going downstairs for a drink and decided against it in case "something happened," and Gugas needed them. "What are we going to do if Fahey refuses to be tested and comes bolting out the door?" Bonfante asked.

"We'll grab the bastard and throw him out the window," Faura responded, walking to the window again. The tension grew with every tick of the clock.

Pacing from opposite directions, Faura and Bonfante found themselves shoulder to shoulder at the same window. Staring into space, Bonfante muttered: "It would serve the bastard right."

They looked at each other. For a few seconds they tried to recognize each
other and sift their own minds. Then they exploded into spontaneous, uncon-
trollable laughter. Bonfante, a man with a keen wit and a highly developed sense
of humor that occasionally splashed the pages of *Life* magazine, released the
tension with his remark. They laughed and laughed until their stomachs hurt.

In retrospect, they realized that the tension was released after Fahey had
been in Gugas' office long enough for them to know that he was not going to
balk. While the night outside grew darker, Gugas, inside, was shedding light
on Fahey's truthfulness. Bonfante and Faura felt they had reached the zenith of
their investigation.

Inside the efficient office, an efficient man was determining whether
or not all of their efforts had been in vain. The late nights, the tedious
hours of waiting in dinky nightclubs and cocktail lounges, the hundreds
of phone calls, the thousands of miles driven, the hopes and disappoint-
ments, the arguments and the fights, the furtive looks over their shoulders, the Dick Tracy-next-to-the-James-Bond syndrome, the embarrass-
ments and the dirty name-calling – they all came with them to watch the
most important performance of John Fahey, storyteller. A hit or a miss?
Only the polygraph knew.

The LAPD and the FBI had systematically closed every door they
had opened. With threats and intimidation, they had successfully used
their advantage to slowly choke one of the air passages of the truth legally
pursued by the press. Fahey's polygraph examination was their last ditch
defense. If he passed the test and was telling the truth, the police force
trying to suppress the story would suffer a telling blow.

While the news team articulated their impartiality in their search,
Faura, deep inside, after all his efforts, wanted Fahey to pass the test. There
was nothing to do but wait. And wait they did for the next four hours.

Gugas and Fahey emerged. Faura and Bonfante nearly choked trying
to be "cool" and refrain from asking questions in front of Fahey.

Bonfante conversed with Fahey as he gently, unnoticed, pushed Faura
towards Gugas. They all conversed about nothing in particular.

While Gugas was placing his equipment in his car, Faura got one lick
in. "How does it look?" he barely whispered.

"It will take me a day or so to carefully analyze the results," Gugas,
replied. "Be patient." His cool and detached manner was no consolation.

"I know that, but you must have gotten some kind of impression,"
Faura insisted.

"Yes, it looks good," Gugas responded, enjoying Faura's layman anxiousness.

A few days later Gugas had the results of his test.

CHAPTER 44

Fahey had passed. He was telling the truth.

Gugas would make a written report. Having been given a transcript of Fahey's story prior to the examination, Gugas had discussed the story with Fahey before commencing the test.

His report read: "The examiner discussed the transcribed statements made at the San Fernando Police Department with the subject. All the critical and key questions were read and thoroughly discussed with Mr. Fahey prior to the examination. The following critical questions were asked the subject:

1. "Is the information you have given the FBI and to me regarding the Ambassador Hotel incident true in all respects?"
The subject answered YES. No deception indicated.

2. "Did a woman tell you, 'They are going to take care of Mr. Kennedy tonight'? Or words to that effect?"
The subject answered YES. No deception indicated.

3. (This question was of a personal nature as a control).

4. "Have you made up this story for personal gain?"
The subject answered NO. No deception indicated.

5. "Have you lied to Fernando Faura or Jordan Bonfante about out this case?"
The subject answered NO. No deception indicated.

6. "Did you have dinner at Trancas Restaurant with a woman on June 4th of this year as you stated?"
The subject answered YES. No deception indicated.

7. "Have you told the whole truth about the Ambassador Hotel affair and the trip to Oxnard with a woman on June 4th, 1968?"
Subject answered YES. No deception indicated.

8. "Have you lied to me?"
The subject answered NO. No deception indicated.

On page two of his report, Gugas explains that three examinations were given on the first series of questions listed on his first page.

Gugas then explains a test made to see if Fahey would be responsive to a "lie question" and concluded that he was. He then went to another set of questions.

The report said: The following questions were asked the subject on two examinations.

1. "Did you tell the LAPD and the FBI the truth about the Ambassador Hotel and the Oxnard incident?"
   The subject answered YES. No deception indicated.

2. "Were you actually followed on June 4th, 1968 as you have said?"
   The subject answered YES. Reaction indicated here.

3. "On June 4th, the woman said she did not want you to get involved?"
   The subject answered YES. No deception indicated.

4. "Did you believe that your life was in danger on June 4th 1968?"
   The subject answered YES. Reaction indicated here.

5. "Have you answered all these questions truthfully?"
   The subject answered YES. No deception indicated.

After this series of questions Fahey complained of being tired and hungry, and Gugas stopped his testing.

He explains in his report: "The subject was asked why he had reacted to questions #2 and #4. He stated that he was disturbed thinking about what happened. He would offer no other explanation, other than to say that he was tired, hungry and that his arm bothered him.

"Since these two questions indicated a specific reaction, the examiner asked the subject if he would be willing to come back later for additional testing in order to clear up those two reactions. He stated that he would be more than willing, because he wanted nothing to show against his statements. Because of the limited number of examinations on Series Two, the examiner will not make a definite determination on these two questions or the two charts because of the subject's condition."

Fahey might not have failed the two questions after all, Gugas was saying. It could be that the two questions about being followed and being in danger might have created enough anxiety to cause a reaction.

Fahey himself had said from the beginning that the woman might have been a "nut" but he later became convinced that she was not. This could explain why he was not afraid on June 4 but became so after the assassination and the realization that the woman knew that it was going to take place.

In any case, there was ample room for doubt in favor of Fahey in those two questions. All the other critical questions had been answered by him. He had passed with "flying colors" or "like a champ," and those were the expressions Faura used when he called Fahey to tell him the results of the examination. Faura figured it would brace and cheer him up.

Keeping in mind the experience and credentials of the examiner, the following portions of the report are of primary importance:

"All attempts by the examiner to 'trip up' the subject were fruitless because his story was virtually the same story as in the transcript."

"In evaluating the subject's story and in trying to knock holes in it, the examiner was unable to shake the subjects at this interview."

The last paragraph in Gugas' report, dated Sept. 20, 1968, states: "It is the examiner's opinion Fahey is sincere in his statements and that there is a need for continued investigation by your office and the police to obtain additional physical evidence to back up his statements."

We finally had unshakable evidence that Fahey was an important witness to a possible conspiracy, having been drawn into it by a woman who had predicted the occasion, time and location of the assassination hours before it happened.

The police and the FBI could hardly ignore such evidence, Faura thought.

The police did not ignore it. They went one better, they tried to destroy it. Three days after Fahey was examined by Gugas, the LAPD contacted Fahey and asked that he submit to their polygraph test. He consented, reluctant and scared. He called Faura and asked if Faura would accompany him to police headquarters. Faura called Bonfante and asked him to come along also. Bonfante agreed.

On Sept. 5, six days after Fahey's original polygraph examination, Bonfante and Faura went to pick him up at his job and deliver him to police headquarters, but he was not there. They called his house. His wife did not know where he might be other than at police headquarters. Bonfante and Faura went to police headquarters and inquired.

"Sorry, but there is no one that can answer your question," was the stock reply.

Where was Fahey? They went to his house and spoke with his wife. She did not know where he would be if he was not at the police station. She was wringing her hands and looking terribly anxious. Faura called his home. No calls from Fahey. Where could he be?

Bonfante and Faura concluded that the police must have picked him up earlier than expected to thwart them. With this in mind they returned to Parker Center, the police headquarters.

More questions. More denials. It was now more than two hours since they had gone to Fahey's workplace. Faura was beginning to lose his temper and Bonfante calmed him down.

"Let's wait and keep trying," he said. They did. Back to the sergeant at the front desk after about an hour's wait. Still he said he could not help after trying the SUS office. "There is no one there," he said, shrugging his shoulders.

This was, of course, a lie. SUS was working 24 hours a day, according to their press releases, Faura wanted to shout at him.

Bonfante had to be conscious and aware not to involve *Life* magazine in any incident with the police. Faura had debated the same thing in his mind before. The day before Faura had accepted a job as press director in Southern California for the presidential campaign of Vice President Hubert Humphrey. If he started something unpleasant with the police it would embarrass a lot of people. Another 30 minutes passed, and he could not take it any longer. He told Bonfante what he intended to do. He could participate, or leave and be clear of it.

Faura explained that he was going to call Sgt. Dan Cooke, LAPD, press relations officer, and threaten to run a story revealing all the details of the Fahey affair and claiming the police were violating Fahey's civil rights. The story would surely make front page.

Bonfante, convinced that he could not calm Faura down any more, put his hand on Faura's shoulder and made his own suggestion.

"Do what you want, but let's call Fahey at home once more."

They did and Fahey answered. After polygraphing him, the police, knowing that Faura and Bonfante were in the front lobby, had taken Fahey out secretly through a back door. Fahey refused to discuss what had happened. He was frightened and upset.

"Everything is resolved. The girl is not involved," he kept repeating, calling Faura "sir."

It was about 11 P.M., and Faura's nerves were frayed. He hung up and went home.

The police version of that polygraph examination claims Fahey failed to pass their test. A first glance at the questions he failed reveals the questions were alien to Fahey's original story and were made deliberately to trip him up.

Typical of the questions that reveal the police ploy were:

1. "Other than pictures of Sirhan, have you ever seen him in person?"

2 "Did any woman tell you of a plan to assassinate Senator Kennedy on June 4th?"

3. "Since Senator Kennedy was assassinated, have you lied to any police officer?"

In their clumsy attempt to discredit Fahey, the police had forgotten that Faura had a copy of the original transcript of Fahey's declarations.

At no time does Fahey say that the girl had told him of a plan to assassinate the senator, nor did he claim to have seen Sirhan.

Had he lied to a police officer since the senator was assassinated? Of course he had! This question is of little value, since the police knew that Fahey was a married man and had from the beginning tried to conceal his original attempt at picking up the girl. He had been the one who suggested taking her along for the ride to Ventura.

Under extreme pressure by the police, Fahey was beginning to get the picture that he had to please them and change his story. He told them that Faura had "romanced" him. It was Faura who had made up the connection between his adventure and the assassination.

He was, of course, lying, as FBI records could prove. Fahey had gone to them and talked to special agents Lloyd Johnson and Eugene B. McCarthy on June 7, two days after the killing and eight days before he sought Faura out.

Another report filed by Johnson dated June 19, clearly establishes that it was Fahey who first contacted Faura. It also shows that he had lied as to when he had told Faura the story.

That report reads as follows: "On June 19th, 1968, John Fahey advised he had told his story concerning his spending the day with one Gilderdine Oppenheimer to reporter Fernando Faura of the *Hollywood Citizens News* newspaper. He said that Faura had a story concerning an unidentified female connected with the Kennedy shooting, and he thought it might be connected with his experience. For this reason, he contacted Faura, after Faura promised he would not publish the story. He stated he does not expect Faura to print the story. Fahey talked to Faura on June 15th, 1968, the same day he told his story to the Los Angeles Police Department."

That report leaves no doubt about Fahey contacting Faura first and the fact he had lied to the FBI about talking to the LAPD the same day. He talked to Faura June 12 and the police June 14. His story was told to Faura and Faura took him to the police afterwards.

It was an unimportant, face-saving lie to avoid incurring the FBI's wrath for having gone to the press before going to the police. It was the kind of face-saving lie that would make him fail a loaded question like, "Have you lied to the police since the senator was assassinated?"

This report and others were available to the LAPD at the time they polygraphed Fahey. They chose to completely ignore them and accept the fabrications planted by SUS members Hernandez and Alexander.

Amazingly, while Fahey tried to please them and get himself out of the jam he was in, he managed to introduce into the tapes of this police interview essentially the same story he had started with.

This is best illustrated by tape No. 29588 of a secret Fahey interview by Alexander and Hernandez on Sept. 9, 1968.

Having been told that his polygraph examination "strongly suggested" that he was not being "completely truthful" he was told – not asked – to change his statements. In Alexander's words: "All we wanted to do is to get this situation straightened out in compliance with the wishes of our superiors, and that is what we feel we have done here by eliciting these truthful statements from you."

The transcript of that secret session has some illuminating passages of Fahey telling the truth and the police refusing to accept it and finally settling for distortion as a way out for both of them.

Page two of that transcript establishes a strong case against the police distortion that was about to occur:

Fahey: "At the time I was excited, and I had this fear in me because of what – of the events that took place that day. I could have done it erroneously, yes, sir!"

Hernandez: "Okay, erroneously now, John, do you remember what you told these people?"

Fahey: "That she could possibly be the girl they were looking for."

In that brief exchange, Fahey had admitted that it was he who made the connection between "the polka-dot girl" and his own adventure. Hernandez and Alexander ignored it. That was not what their superiors wanted out of Fahey. The interrogation continued.

Hernandez set the stage for Fahey before proceeding too far. Instead of asking, he told Fahey: "Okay, as a matter of fact, John, now you know that in your mind all along there was nothing that happened that would lead any reasonable person to form a belief that she was connected with the assassination of Senator Kennedy, was there?"

Obviously for Hernandez, predicting the place, day and time of the killing would not lead any reasonable person to form a belief that she was connected to the assassination.

"Now that I have sat down and thought it all through, you are right, yes, sir!" Fahey answered, telling them what they wanted to hear.

Hernandez, obviously thinking that he had Fahey on the run, attempted to have him deny important parts of his story.

Why did he say he had been followed? Fahey told him the story again. He clung to the same details he had told them before, denying Hernandez his victory.

Not having any room to move, Hernandez tried prompting and some fabrication.

"Did you ever form the idea in your mind that the people that were following, if they were following you, might have been a boyfriend or a husband or someone who knew her?"

"It could have been, yes, sir," Fahey responded.

"Did you think about this?"

"Not at the time, no sir."

"Have you ever thought about it?" Hernandez insisted.

"No, sir," Fahey said.

"Will you think about it now," Hernandez pleaded at the end of the unbelievable exchange.

Ignoring Fahey's prior and truthful declarations of a few minutes before, Alexander brought out his ax to finish the bridges to Fernando Faura and set the stage for the version that was introduced into the skimpy records the public was going to be allowed to examine.

"All right," Alexander said, "has Fernando Faura ever told you, for instance, that – that this woman that you were with had anything to do with the Kennedy assassination?"

Alexander, a tough and unfriendly career man, must have scared Fahey. Fahey, although sticking to his story now, said he had believed that Faura was part of the San Fernando Police Department, and that each step of the way he had heightened his belief that the girl was involved in the assassination.

Alexander knew, or was supposed to know, that Fahey had walked into Faura's office at the newspaper the very first time they had met, but he made no effort to question or correct Fahey. After all, all this was being recorded for posterity, and it would please his superiors.

Hernandez tried again, after Fahey told him about DiPierro identifying the "photo" as the "polka-dot girl."

"But as a matter of fact, John, this girl that you are referring to from the Identa-Kit – you knew all along this girl didn't exist, didn't you?"

"The girl exists," Fahey responded, indicating that the "photo" was of the girl he had been with.

"Is it a good likeness of the girl?" Hernandez was curious.

"Pretty close, yes, sir. Pretty close."

Hernandez could not shake Fahey away from his story. Alexander moved into more productive ground, he hoped.

"Okay, so then he (Faura) did more or less strengthen your mind in these beliefs." Alexander was ignoring the FBI record and Fahey's own admissions that he had taken the initiative in seeking out the FBI and Faura. Faura had to be stopped at all costs.

"Yes, sir, he did," Fahey knew better but he sensed that was what Alexander wanted. Hernandez joined in.

"Fantasy-something that you knew was not true," he said, "he put words in your mouth?"

Not letting Fahey answer, Alexander added what he thought would be the coup de grâce: "In other words, he took the situation as you laid it to him and then he related it back to you and told you how it could possibly have been Senator Kennedy –"

"Yes, sir, Sarge, that's right." Fahey knew what was expected of him.

"That wasn't your idea?"

"No, sir, it was his idea."

Alexander and Hernandez had what they wanted for their superiors.

CHAPTER 45

I t mattered little that the man had contradicted the statements he had made at the beginning of their grilling. It mattered less that the FBI had recorded the truth two days after the assassination and to them on June 14, and that these reports were available to them.

From then on, Hernandez made statements and Fahey agreed to them.

The handful of distilled reports introduced into the public record after the Sirhan trial, reflect this and other distortions and fabrications.

Alexander questioned Fahey again Sept. 19, perhaps to reassure himself that Fahey was now under control. Fahey disappointed him by repeating his story about being with the girl. The original transcripts were kept secret for 20 years, many were destroyed.

This should not be surprising since a complete and honest release of the documents would have shown any competent investigator the unorthodox police methods and procedures and their glaring discrepancies. Considering the third degree Fahey had gone through, it was no wonder his "sir" was coming on strong when Faura called him that night. It was time for the LAPD to go after Faura.

Lt. Manuel (Manny) Pena, in charge of the "day watch" at SUS, called the San Fernando Police Department. He told them Faura had been representing himself as a police officer in order to "stick his nose into LAPD business."

He knew this was not true but what better way to stop a nosy reporter than taking away his base of operations and closing down his police contacts?

Since most police departments in the surrounding communities depend on the LAPD for major services and assistance during disasters or major disturbances, they all look upon the LAPD as their "big brother."

If "big brother" is displeased, everyone bows. Pena's attempt at discrediting Faura and driving a wedge between the *Hollywood Citizen News* and the San Fernando Police Department collapsed under the weight of one question:

"Since what you are accusing Faura of is a felony, why are you not charging him with it," asked the San Fernando Police Department.

LAPD had no answer.

The following year, the LAPD would deny Faura press credentials despite the fact that he had been credentialed by several other police departments and had foreign correspondent credentials from Radio Cadena Nacional, the largest, most influential radio network in Mexico.

The denial of credentials was another clumsy attempt to prevent him from telling the Fahey story.

Soon, Chris Gugas (the polygrapher) and La Scola learned of the LAPD's displeasure at their honest participation in the inquiries.

After ignoring Fahey's story for two months, the LAPD was now moving with deliberate speed – not to confirm but to destroy it!

In spite of the police displeasure, Gugas tried to soothe Fahey on the phone.

"Your words are very kind, sir. Their's were not," Fahey said, giving them a glimpse of what had transpired during his questioning.

He also indicated he had been threatened with jail.

"You want me to go to jail over this," he asked pleadingly, at Gugas' insistence that he tell them what the police had done to him.

Faura remembered that Alexander had stressed the possibility of jail for anybody violating Judge Alarcon's gag order.

Gugas, who had told them Fahey had passed his test, complained to the police about their intimidation of Fahey, only to receive a challenge to "do something about it."

Bonfante and Faura went to Fahey's job to try to talk to him again. When he saw them he became agitated and asked them to leave. When Faura insisted he tell them what they had done or any threats to him. Fahey started screaming.

"Leave me alone! Don't touch me! Don't threaten me," and started to move to the back of the store. They were separated by a display counter at least 30 inches wide. Faura and Bonfante were flabbergasted. They had not done any such things as Fahey was screaming.

They realized he was doing it for the benefit of whomever was in the back, and it might be a police set-up. They left in total shock at the change in Fahey, from eager co-investigator ("let's go get them") to a ranting maniac.

That was to be the end of their contacts with Fahey – the end of the road.

The efforts to bring Sirhan to trial were increasing, The LAPD and the FBI with ample leads that led to a conspiracy steered away from it and settled on the "one killer" theory.

According to police, 10 volumes comprising the total investigation of the killing were being prepared.

In contrast to the protestations of the LAPD that the investigation would be so thorough and open that it could not be subjected to the same criticism of the Warren Commission report, the bulk of the 10 volumes were classified for 20 years. Some still are.

Cashing in as Chief of Detectives, Robert Houghton lent his name to a "quasi-official" version of the assassination, which was then in the works.

By that time all witnesses whose testimony would suggest a conspiracy had been ignored, discredited, or frightened into silence.

A little over three months after the killing the LAPD was to claim that it had concluded the investigation. In their minds only a few loose ends remained, one of which was what to do with *Life* magazine's and Faura's investigation.

On Sept. 13, around 3 P.M., Sgt. Phil Alexander went to Bonfante's office and offered him a deal. If Bonfante would give him the full name and address of Chuck Dirks, the teacher we had hypnotized, Alexander was authorized to give *Life* the police appraisal of Fahey.

Alexander said Capt. Hugh Brown, head of the SUS task force, had given him permission to do so, this in spite of the fact that it would be a violation of Judge Alarcon's court order. The only reason for this offer, Alexander said, was to stop *Life* from "publishing a story and winding up with egg all over its face."

Bonfante deferred his decision for a while, and Alexander went ahead anyway and offered his share of the bargain.

Alexander proceeded to tear Fahey's story apart, saying he had failed their test and his story was full of holes. He said, while admitting that Fahey did not retract his statement that the girl had said "they are going to take care of Kennedy tonight," that Faura had planted things in Fahey's mind.

Alexander did not bother to explain, and Bonfante failed to ask him, why they were worried about a woman they had said, nine weeks earlier, did not exist.

Knowing better, Bonfante let Alexander talk. Six hours later, Alexander was still vehemently and unsuccessfully claiming that it had all been a mistake. That was a lot of egg!

CHAPTER 46

Two days short of a month later, the LAPD finally interviewed Greg Clayton. There is no evidence that the interview was recorded, just document number I-4611 in the Sacramento State Archives of the RFK assassination. The interview was done by Detective Miller and another (name unclear) officer.

Clayton repeats the story he told Faura but since there is no recording there is no way of knowing if he related the incident including the words of the man he stopped – Wayne. "Nor the sickening look of madness in his eyes."

Employing the same tactics used on Sandra Serrano, the police had forced DiPierro to publicly admit that, having been in the same room with Sandra Serrano, he picked up the "polka dot" story from her.

First it was Serrano picking it up from DiPierro; now it was DiPierro picking it up from Serrano! Surely, they could not both be true. In their overzealousness, the police had forced two contradictory confessions of "fabrication."

After the Sirhan trial, KHJ Radio newsman Art Kevin ran a short series in which he raised some questions that had been left unanswered. In that series he brought up the "polka-dot girl," giving DiPierro ample credibility.

Prior to airing the series, Kevin, according to John Christian and William Turner in their book *The Assassination of Robert F. Kennedy*, "Inspector John Powers of the LAPD had visited Art Kevin … and put pressure on him not to raise the question of the 'polka-dot dress girl.' Kevin declined."

Now, provided the story is true, and there is no reason to doubt these three top-notch investigators (Turner was ex-FBI), why would Inspector Powers do this if the LAPD had denied the existence of the woman a year earlier, and discredited every witness who claimed to have seen her?

A few days after airing the series, Kevin received a letter from DiPierro in which the young man expressed his real feelings about what the police had done.

Again from *The Assassination of Robert F. Kennedy*: "On Sunday, April 20th, 1969," DiPierro wrote, "I listened to your special report concerning the 'girl in the polka-dot dress.' Since the question of the 'polka-dot dress girl' concerns my character personally I was deeply interested in hearing the facts straight for a change.… I felt it necessary to congratulate you on the extensive research and brilliant job of reporting a factual story," DiPierro wrote, offering his assistance "in this controversial issue."

A few days later, Kevin drove out to the DiPierro residence. Vincent's father, opened the door while Vincent stayed in the background; both looked "shook up." Mr. DiPierro (father) told him that the FBI had been by, and pleadingly asked Kevin to forget it, that his son's life might be in danger. Pressed on by Kevin the father blurted out that he knew who Kevin was and accused him of "running around with those kooks Turner (*The Assassination of Robert F. Kennedy*) and Mark Lane (*Rush to Judgment*)" and shut the door in his face.

These actions by the FBI a year after the trial and their denial of the existence of the "girl in the polka-dot dress," begs the questions: Why were they interested in suppressing the story? If Sirhan was a convicted lone assassin and was in jail, why would Vincent DiPierro's life be in danger? Just as important, how did they know Kevin was going to see DiPierro and get there before he did?

All this effort to silence the man the police had forced to "admit" that he had learned of the "polka-dot girl" from Sandra Serrano. Weird indeed!

Faura and Bonfante were making arrangements to go to Guam where they hoped to track down "Oppenheimer Guam lead." They felt they might need protection in Guam and Bonfante talked to some Palm Springs hoods that were willing to provide the protection. Faura was surprised that *Life* would do such a thing, but beggars can't be choosers so he went along with it. Before the trip took place Bonfante informed Faura that *Life* had withdrawn support for any further search.

Why? asked Faura.

"They just won't," Bonfante replied, not pleased with the decision of his superiors.

Frustrated, Faura asked Bonfante to check with his sources at the "Skunk Works," The "Skunk Works" was an elite team of investigators *Life* had put together that had published a serious of explosive exposés on organized crime. They were anonymous and their expense accounts and credit card charges handled by a special person in accounting so their movements could not be traced and put them in danger.

Bonfante said he would. A few days later he told Faura, "There is no chance of pursuing that woman. The decision was made by somebody high up after a call to the publisher from a very high-up person in Washington," Bonfante said.

National security? Again? Faura was aghast. He had read about such rumors before – regarding President Kennedy's assassination.

"It's over, Fernando, let it go," were Bonfante's final words.

The search for the "polka-dot girl" was abandoned by *Life* magazine four weeks after the assassination. Supposedly so it was by the FBI and the LAPD. But they all knew she existed and had slipped through their fingers.

Life had also asked that Faura and Bonfante produce the girl before they would publish the findings of their investigation, even though their own representative, Bonfante, could vouch for their legitimacy. They might as well have asked that they bring the senator back to life.

Chief Houghton had privately said, "That woman will haunt me the rest of my life." Faura felt the same way. She was the only real lead they had. She was also the weak link in the conspiracy, having expressed the desire to get away from it, by telling Fahey about their plans.

By this time Faura had developed his own theory. The woman had looked worried, desperate, sweaty hands, conflicted, when she was with Fahey and tried to recruit him to help her. It would have been insane to just casually invite him to see the killing, as she did. She was alternatively composed, silent, worried and forthcoming, telling him at different times small pieces of the puzzle but holding back, as she caught herself talking to a stranger: "They will take care of him tonight"; "I belong to an organization"; "They will take care of me"; "They will take care of you"; "They are following us" (she was the first to notice); "They have radios and will find us."

The easiest road would have been for her to go to the police, but what if she knew she could not trust the police?

What if she knew she had become involved with people of such power that they had resources in the investigating agencies? In that case she would be walking into the lion's mouth. She may have been a pro but only at the operational level. She knew that real power was well above her. What to do?

Warn somebody of what was going to happen and get out of the country into safe territory and the safety of friends or family.

Fahey was her unfortunate choice. A married man on the make who did not go to the police, because he was not about to walk into the police station and tell them, "I just picked up a woman who says her friends are going to kill Senator Kennedy tonight."

It was too late anyway. She had told Fahey the night the killing occurred. He had dropped her around 7 P.M. at the Ambassador Hotel that night and gone home. The next day he heard by radio and TV that her prediction had come true and fearing he may be involved in it, and in danger, he went to the FBI first, then to the press (Faura), then to the LAPD after arranging it with Faura. The reporter felt the polka-dot girl was on the run pursued by the police and her co-conspirators. She had told Fahey that she had a "lot of clothes" and he had seen her with a lot of money in her purse. Maybe she could manage to elude her pursuers for a while.

In the meantime, it was necessary to prove that she was a real person and keep her alive.

The substance of Serrano and DiPierro's testimony had to be shored up since, having attracted public attention, their stories were being destroyed by police. In Faura's mind they could not have been the only ones to witness the events they related. There had to be others.

Faura's search continued, hampered by lack of resources.

Informants, hoods, friendly cops and federal agents, secretaries, newsmen and politicians were interviewed.

CHAPTER 47

An airline pilot told him that he had just returned from Guam where the newspapers reported the police were investigating the death of a woman in an unusual car accident in the mountains. She was the wife of an FAA official in Guam. He promised to check the story out for Faura. The pilot was just an acquaintance, and Faura never saw him again. And Faura was lacking the resources to go to Guam himself.

In the process, numerous other cases of corruption and political skulduggery helped clarify in Faura's mind how such a crime could be committed and how so many people could act in apparent concert. One such story came from another newsman.

Joel Garcia was a young, personable newsman for the *Van Nuys News*, also known as the "Green Sheet" because of the color of its front page. Faura and Garcia had met while they were both covering the meetings of the San Fernando City Council. They had become good friends and shared the same barber near the Van Nuys county courts. As the Sirhan trial was about to start, they ran into each other at the barber shop. After the usual greetings and Garcia congratulating Faura on his stories about the assassination, Garcia surprised Faura.

"I am going to give you the heads up on a story about the trial," Garcia said. Faura knew the courts were not Garcia's beat so it was no big deal for Garcia to pass up on the story.

"Okay," Faura said expectantly.

"Tom and I are good friends and –"

"Who is Tom?" Faura interrupted.

"Noguchi, Thomas Noguchi, the coroner, you know him."

"No, I don't know him, but I know who he is," Faura corrected him. "What about Noguchi?"

"He told me a story but asked me not to publish or pass it on yet, because the trial is about to start, and he is in a pile of trouble. You must promise me that you won't publish until Noguchi is ready to go public, at that time I will arrange for you two to meet and he can give it to you directly. I don't want to be part of it."

"Okay, I won't publish until you or him give me the okay," Faura agreed.

"Tom says that during the autopsy he was busy and nervous trying not to make any mistakes. He did not like that there were a lot of people in the operating room."

"Who was? Why were they there? An operating room is supposed to be sterile, were they cops?" Faura asked.

"He assumed some were cops, but he did not know who was there."

"Okay, so what happened?" Faura urged him on.

"Tom says he extracted a bullet, put it on a tray and continued on. Shortly afterwards, one of the men in the room came and picked it up and walked out of the room. Tom was alarmed and wondered who the man was, but could not stop what he was doing. A few minutes later the same man came back and put the bullet back on the tray. Again, Tom looked at him but said nothing, but wondered what was going on."

"Joel," Faura interrupted, "You are pulling my leg, you just described what they say happened in the autopsy room in Dallas with President Kennedy; come on!" Faura said, taking it as a joke.

"I am serious, and Tom is not joking either. It happened. I don't know about Dallas, but this happened here, and I believe Tom. Why would he lie to me?" Garcia was quite serious. Garcia's turn with the barber came, and Faura waited for him, pondering the story.

A repetition of Dallas? Identical? No way! The trial was just starting, so he assumed Noguchi would testify about the interference in the operating room. He made a mental note to find out when Noguchi was testifying so he could make arrangements with Garcia for a meeting with Noguchi to verify the story and find out if he was going to drop that bomb during the trial. That would be a hell of a scoop. Little did he know that the bullets would become a big issue at the trial, and he waited for Noguchi to drop his bomb. It never happened.

Noguchi had been accused of very serious ethical violations and resigned on Feb. 26, 1969. He testified the next day. DeWayne Wolfer, LAPD ballistics expert, came under fire for mishandling evidence and shoddy procedures with gun testing. A ridiculous and pitiful circus of finger pointing developed about the bullets.

According to Shane O'Sullivan in his book, *Who Killed Bobby?* Noguchi met with Dr. Robert Joling, former president of the American Academy of Forensic Sciences, at the Drake Hotel in Chicago on February 1969 to hand him a micro-photograph of a bullet comparison made by DeWayne Wolfer on June 6, 1968, between the Kennedy neck bullet and ostensibly a test bullet.

O'Sullivan quotes Noguchi as telling Joling: "Hold on to this for safe-keeping. We may need it in the future" – presumably because he doubted the micro-photograph as proof that the test bullet matched the bullet from Kennedy's neck.

Noguchi had withdrawn his resignation before the supervisors could act on it, and Lin Hollinger, county chief administrative officer, fired him. Noguchi courageously fought back and was cleared of all charges on July

31, He could have sued his detractors but didn't. He later wrote in his book *Coroner* that it would have been "hopeless-suicidal."

Three years later Donald A. Stewart, an Englishman hired by the County Coroner's Office just three weeks after the assassination and one of the most damaging witnesses against Noguchi, was found to be an impostor who had practiced using fake credentials in Chicago, the Bahamas, the Florida Keys and other places.

He was not charged with any crimes so the D.A.'s office refused to prosecute.

Faura obtained some of the records he was looking for. The records are a study in FBI and police manipulation.

Unknown to Faura and Bonfante, since the investigation was secret and nothing was leaking out of it, the observations of Serrano, DiPierro and the others, had been confirmed by other witnesses whose accounts and descriptions of the principals were so close that no doubt could remain as to the existence of the "polka-dot girl" and her companions.

Other sources provided further evidence of police falsification of records, in areas other than the "polka-dot girl" part of the investigation.

In respect to the "polka-dot girl," George Green, co-chairman of Images, an organization working within the Los Angeles black community, told the FBI of seeing Sirhan Sirhan at the edge of a crowd of newsmen who were conducting an interview.

According to an FBI report, Green saw Sirhan "near a tall, thin person and a female Caucasian,"

"The female Caucasian was in her early 20s and she wore a polka-dot dress with white and black dots. She had a good figure, but he cannot further describe her," the FBI report prepared by Special Agent David H. Cook says.

This report, dated July 16, 1968, is significant not only in that it provides another witness who saw the "polka-dot girl," in the kitchen but also for what it omits.

An earlier report made by Special Agent George F. Benz on June 7, two days after the assassination, contains crucial information that was censored in the later report.

The June 7 report reads: "Green stated that once inside the kitchen door he notice a woman in her 20 with long, blond free flowing hair in a "polka-dot dress" and a light colored sweater running with their backs towards him, and they were attempting to get out of the kitchen area. Green stated that the reason he noticed them was that they were trying to get out of the kitchen area while everyone else seemed to be trying to get into the kitchen area," the FBI report concluded.

An LAPD's SUS report dated Aug. 1 fails to note the proximity of the "polka-dot girl" and her companion to Sirhan and states that Green had said that the girl was wearing "a dark dress," which may have had some sort of dots."

In spite of the fact that Green had repeatedly told newsmen and the FBI essentially the same story, the police were now clouding the story by claiming that he "could not be sure of the clothing!"

Green's testimony is further confirmed by that of Evan Phillip Freed, a Cal State college student and part-time photographer for the *Evening Star News* in Culver City.

Freed was interviewed by police on June 14. He told them of his movements and of being in the kitchen when the shooting began. After the first shot, he was shoved against the wall. The police report tells the story best: "A few seconds after being pinned against the east wall of the kitchen, Mr. Freed stated he saw three people running in his direction. One was a woman, the others two men. The woman ran out the door to his right and a man wearing bright blue sports coat ran out the door to his left. The third man was yelling at him 'get him, get it.' He ran out apparently chasing the man in the blue coat."

Freed described the man being pursued as "a male, Caucasian, 24 years old, 6'1," 150 to 160 pounds, black hair, medium length, dark complexion."

According to the report, Freed had no other description of the woman "except that she was a female Caucasian, possibly wearing a polka-dot dress."

The reporting investigator added his appraisal of Freed's account. "There seems to be some credibility to Mr. Freed's story," and proceeded to question his character by adding, "however, it is believed that Mr. Freed is a name dropper."

The relevancy of the gratuitous slap was not explained, nor was it mentioned whose names he had "dropped."

Booker Griffin, director of the Los Angeles Chapter of the Negro Industrial and Economic Union, was in the kitchen when the shooting started. He was interviewed by FBI agents Leroy W. Sheets and Vincent J. Horn Jr. on June 11, six days after the shooting.

The report records that Griffin arrived at the Ambassador at approximately 10:15 P.M. and continues: "about 20 minutes later, Griffin stated that he saw an individual in the Embassy Room whom he later saw shoot Senator Kennedy."

"Griffin looked this individual in the eye," the report continues, "At which time the individual stared back. Griffin stated he noticed a girl whose description he does not recall standing in close proximity to Sirhan. He never noticed them converse with each other, but he had the feeling that they were there together."

The police report goes on to say that Griffin saw Sirhan twice again in the corridor where the senator was shot. One of those times, the report claims, Griffin saw Sirhan in the corridor and also saw a white male about 6'2," further description of which he does not recall, and a white female, 5'5," with bouffant hair, dressed in a white flowing dress with colorations, standing in close proximity with Sirhan. Neither of these individuals had press passes nor Kennedy buttons. He saw these three individuals at least two or three times in the corridor among numerous other individuals who were in the area.

The interviewer noted that Griffin saw Sirhan shoot Kennedy.

"Immediately after the shot, Griffin went over to where Kennedy was lying and spoke with him for a few moments. He then stood up and noticed the male and female who he had seen in the corridor leave the area through the kitchen. He tried to follow these two individuals in the corridor but was unable to do so."

And so, Griffin, like Sandra Serrano and Greg Clayton lost the opportunity to apprehend the "polka-dot girl" or her companion.

On July 25, 1968, SUS Sgts. C.E. Collins and F.J. Patchett, and J.R. MacArthur grilled and verbally pushed Griffin around.

The verbal jousting between them is a credit to Griffin:

"It was that time you think, you saw –"

"I know there were three people I know that I saw –"

"And in that group?"

"Was the short guy, the suspect, a tall lady, and a tall gentleman."

And so it went, the police trying to trip Griffin and he resisting. One can only wonder what would have happened if Serrano and DiPierro had withstood the police onslaught as Griffin did.

CHAPTER 48

S errano might have done just that had she known what was happening with Albert Victor Ellis, a friend of John Shamel, convention manager at the Ambassador Hotel.

Ellis told police he was just outside the Embassy Room with Shamel when a man name "Uno" asked Shamel to call for an ambulance. Ellis then went to the exit by the kitchen and assisted in holding back the crowd.

"Ellis stated that when Uno called out for an ambulance, he heard a female yell 'we killed Kennedy.' Ellis cannot remember anything about this female other than that statement," the report says.

This report launches into a lengthy explanation of discrepancies between FBI reports and Ellis declarations and the LAPD's own findings.

Two statements by Ellis to police are most significant: "Ellis is absolutely positive that the remark he heard was "we shot him," and that he was not confusing it with any other phrase," the report clearly states.

The second denies that Ellis was ever shown a photo of Sirhan for identification. This is in contradiction with the FBI report submitted by Special Agent Robert F. Pickard, which says: "He was shown a photograph of Sirhan Bishara Sirhan, and he advised that Sirhan is the individual he observed in the Embassy Room at approximately 10 P.M. on June 4, 1968." If Pickard lied in his report, the FBI is not saying.

The police-Ellis-FBI report triangle, as with Sandra Serrano, got confusing. In the end, the police recorded that Ellis interpreted the "we" as referring to the people in general.

Fahey might also have braced his backbone had he known what Susan Locke was telling the FBI just about the same time he was telling them his story.

Special Agent Phillip B. Deily dutifully recorded for his superiors the Locke account. The second page of his report dated June 7, 1968, tells why.

"She recalls seeing a girl in the Embassy Room, just before Senator Kennedy entered the room to speak, stationed near her immediate vicinity wearing a white shift with blue polka dots. She observed that the girl was not wearing a yellow press badge and thought that this was unusual since it was necessary to have such a badge to gain entry into the Embassy Room. She mentioned this to Carol Breshears who is in charge of the Kennedy Girls and Mrs. Breshears pointed her (the girl) to a guard nearby.

"The girl was expressionless and seemed somewhat out of place where she was standing. She was Caucasian, in her early 20s, well-proportioned with long brown hair pulled back and tied behind her head. Her hair appeared to be dried and similar in appearance to hair of a girl who does a lot of swimming."

Twenty-eight days later, SUS member Patchett, McArthur and Collins, the same team who attempted to browbeat Griffin, interviewed Locke.

They duly recorded her presence in the kitchen at the time of the shooting. The official police version of this interview does not have a word about the "girl in the polka-dot dress"

Locke's description of the girl was a carbon copy of that given by Fahey.

Having said that the "polka-dot girl" was a figment of Serrano's imagination, the police ignored this witness as well as an insurance executive who claimed to have seen Sirhan at target practice with an attractive girl at Rancho California.

A Pomona, Calif., bartender who reported Sirhan and a pretty girl stalking Senator Kennedy, was also discarded. The police chose instead to plunge into the Sirhan trial preparation.

In blatant contradiction of the facts, and knowing full well they were lying, police claimed to have uncovered no leads to justify the pursuit of a conspiracy investigation.

Sirhan Sirhan was tried as a "lone assassin."

For a well-researched and full documentation of that farce, the reader is referred to *The Robert F. Kennedy Assassination: New Revelations on the Conspiracy and Cover-Up, 1968-1991* by Phillip H. Melanson, Ph.D.

Once more with another Kennedy killing, the American people and justice had been had.

For a while it looked as if the FBI and LAPD would get away with it. But the truth dies hard, if at all. Too many questions remained unresolved. There was a legitimate reason to suspect a conspiracy. The FBI, with its vaunted image and untold resources, failed to solve the crimes of most political importance in the United States. Why wasn't the American public told?

National security. Or so the players say.

Of great import to the traditional American concept of peaceful change of political philosophies, was the need to find the reason why the FBI and the LAPD, as well as other investigating agencies involved with national security, had deliberately and methodically misled and defrauded the American populace at large.

Mark Lane and others had already thoroughly discredited the investigation of the President John F. Kennedy assassination, to the point where 80 percent of the population do not believe the official findings. The conspiracy syndrome, hitherto described derisively as a South American and European phenomenon, had caught up with the United States, and with good reason. The carbon copies of the Robert and John Kennedy investigations are headed in the same direction.

The FBI and the LAPD, in a reflection of the Dallas investigation, made "mistakes" in Los Angeles that clearly point to a dispassionate conclusion that both agencies were interested in hiding the truth from the public – and clearly some agents of both organizations participated in scuttling any lead in the investigation that pointed to a conspiracy.

In the case of the Robert Kennedy killing, the "national security ploy" may very well have been the reason. If the White House says so all branches of government will stumble over each other to toe the line.

CHAPTER 49

Fahey's information about the woman he spent the day with having known Anna Chennault would have surely opened up a feverish line of investigation, had Chennault's treasonous activities been known at the time.

It tied up with the woman's desire to get to Australia because "the Chinese" could not get her there. She would be safe in Australia.

At the time no one knew (other than President Johnson, his advisors, NSA and FBI and the conspirators), that Anna Chennault was a principal in a conspiracy to scuttle the Paris Peace Talks to help candidate Nixon win the election.

No one knew that "the girl in the polka-dot dress" had met with Anna Chennault the week of the assassination.

Not the LAPD, not the FBI. Only Fahey, Faura and the "girl in the polka-dot dress."

None of the investigators, and over time the researchers and historians of the killing, made the connection between the two conspiracies since the "peace talks" conspiracy was top secret, and neither Faura nor Life magazine had revealed that the "polka-dot girl" had met with Anna Chennault three days before the killing.

Did "National security" trump Faura and *Life* magazine's investigation because it was headed towards Anna Chennault, presidential candidate Richard Nixon, future Vice President Spiro Agnew and an influential and powerful senator from Texas, John Tower?

But who was Anna Chennault?

Anna Chennault, also known as Anna Chan and Anna Chen, was born (Chen Xiangmei) in Beijing, China, on June 23, 1925. She married Gen. Claire Chennault, the legendary founder of the famed Flying Tigers during the Sino-Japanese war, on Dec. 21, 1947. The Flying Tigers were a group of American mercenary pilots flying for the Chinese during that war.

Their storybook love story and years of marriage is well documented and the subject of several TV productions in Taiwan.

Claire Chennault was a daring pilot who attained the rank of general before he died. He had an avocation for intrigue and intelligence work. He was also a close friend and confidant of Gen. Chiang Kai-shek, who ruled China and fought the communists under Mao Tse Tung, until Mao's forces overwhelmed him and forced him to retreat to Taiwan.

Among Gen. Chennault's many accomplishments and cloak-and-dagger work for the United States during the clandestine war for China against Japan, before Japan attacked Pearl Harbor, was the organizing of the Flying Tigers, and founding Flying Tiger Airlines and Civil Air Transport (CAT), which later morphed into Air America – both of them CIA proprietaries. By the time he died, in 1958, he had a long list of intelligence associations with the U.S. government.

CAT operated until June of 1968, the same month Senator Kennedy died – coincidentally?

Anna Chennault, a very rich and enterprising woman became a powerhouse in Republican politics in Washington, D.C., and a member of the Republican National Committee after her husband's death. Being very wealthy and seeking influence, she became known as "Washington's hostess." Her detractors called her "The Dragon Lady."

A woman of many talents and unending energy, she was, at various times, the publicist for CAT airlines, vice president for Flying Tigers Airline, correspondent for Central News Agency, and a broadcaster for the Voice of America, another CIA front.

Her status and influence was such that she accompanied Richard Nixon on one of his trips to the Far East. She also played a crucial role on behalf of the Nixon campaign during the war in Vietnam.

Allegedly she arranged a contact between South Vietnamese Ambassador Bui Diem and Richard Nixon. Diem and Nixon met secretly in New York.

Republicans at the time were secretly urging Diem to refuse participation in the Paris Peace Talks and it was Anna Chennault who arranged the contacts with him.

All this was going on while Senator Kennedy was within sight of the White House in his campaign. He was a clear threat to Nixon's manipulations because of his declared opposition to the Vietnam War. He was the only real obstacle between Richard Nixon and the White House. Had he won the election, Nixon and his cohorts might have been charged with treason.

The National Security Agency intercepted a cable from the South Vietnamese Embassy to Saigon explicitly urging South Vietnamese President Nguyen Van Thieu to stand fast against an agreement until after the elections. President Johnson learned of this and ordered phone wiretaps on the embassy and the FBI to place Anna Chennault under surveillance.

On Nov. 2, FBI wiretaps recorded Mrs. Chennault on a call to Diem saying, "Hold on. We are gonna win."

President Johnson considered her and Nixon's action as "treason."

He was probably thinking of the Logan Act. But he must have come to realize that the Logan Act is a useless statute, considered unconstitutional by some experts.

The statute was passed in 1799 and is still on the books but constantly violated by both parties. It prohibits citizens from conferring with foreign governments against the interest of the United States. Specifically it prohibits citizens from negotiating with other nations on behalf of the United States without authorization. The violations of the Logan Act are many, and some very recent.

Barack Obama, as a candidate for president, was accused of violating it when it was reported that Iraqi Foreign Minister Hosyar Zebari, alleged that Obama had advised "that rather than reach an accord with the 'weakened Bush Administration' Iraq should seek an extension of the UN mandate." The exact card Nixon had played against President Johnson.

Rev. Jesse Jackson went to Nicaragua and Cuba, where he met with President Fidel Castro, and returned with Cuban prisoners and a 10-point agreement.

Jimmy Carter did it with Syria. The Ronald Reagan campaign with Iran. The Richard Nixon campaign with North Vietnam, and in 2015 a group of Republican members of Congress wrote to the Iranian government trying to scuttle the Iran nuclear negotiations being conducted by Secretary of State John Kerry.

Impotent to prosecute, President Johnson and his advisors decided to document and create a record of the "treasonous" act for posterity.

Walt W. Rostow, National Security Advisor to President Johnson, compiled a dossier of documents from FBI, NSA and other agencies recording the details of the treasonous conspiracy. He called it "The X-Envelope."

In 1973, after the Watergate Scandal was developing, he delivered it to the LBJ Library with instructions that it not be opened for fifty years, and then another fifty if found necessary. Rostow believed the Watergate scandal was an offshoot of the 1968 treachery of the Nixon-Chennault campaign conspiracy. The envelope was opened just over two decades later.

"The file concerns the activities of Mrs. Anna Chennault and others before and immediately after the election of 1968. At the time President Johnson decided to handle the matter strictly as a question of National Security; and in retrospect he felt that decision was correct," Rostow wrote to the LBJ Library.

Undersecretary of State Eugene Rostow wrote to his brother Walt that a source close to Nixon had a meeting with other Wall Street bankers to discuss "the future of financial markets in the short term." The speaker (Alexander Sachs) thought the "market would be adversely affected."

In a separate memo Eugene Rostow said Alexander Sachs had said that Nixon was "letting Hanoi know" that if elected it would benefit them and inciting Saigon to increase their demands to sabotage the peace talks. In short, the bankers were placing their bets based on inside information that the peace talks would fail.

President Johnson was adamant about ending the war. He wanted to "stop the killing" and tried calling several influential Republicans. According to Robert Parry, in his outstanding ConsortiumNews.com, Johnson told Senator Everett Dirksen, a Republican powerhouse, "He better keep Mrs. Chennault and all this crowd tied up for a few days."

It did not happen.

Nov. 2, 1968, an FBI intercept recorded Anna Chennault calling Ambassador Bui Diem to relay a message from "the boss" asking Diem to "hold on we are going to win."

Johnson consulted with Secretary of State Dean Rusk, Rostow and Secretary of Defense Clark Clifford. They decided not to go public with information in the interest of "national security," for the "good of the country."

It turns out Bonfante's source at *Life* magazine had been correct.

It is no wonder the White House did not want the "polka dot girl" pursued, it would have led to Anna Chennault and the Richard Nixon campaign. Lacking sufficient credible proof, how do you tell the American public of a link between the assassination of Senator Kennedy and the Nixon campaign?

It could have been interpreted as a crude below-the-belt blow to gain political advantage. Five months later NSA learned of Anna Chennault's alleged "treasonous" activities with Richard Nixon and his other co-conspirators and informed Pres. Johnson.

"National Security" still trumped the American public right to know.

This sordid affair is best understood by reading a Memo dated 2/25/70 in White House stationary from Tom Charles Huston, a national security aide to President Nixon.

Huston is best known for this proposed controversial plan to expand spying on the Anti-Vietnam war movement.

The memo dated is indexed in this book in its entirety.

Robert Parry in Consortiumnews.Com (7/5/14) in talking about the Paris Peace talks sabotage quotes Huston as saying: "Over the years as I have studied it, I have concluded that there was no doubt that Nixon was- would have been directly involved, that it's not something that anybody would have undertaken on their own".

Later Anna Chennault in her biography *The Education of Anna* (1980) validated that thought.

The sabotage of the Paris Peace talks led to four more years of war costing 20,000 more American youths' deaths, more than 100,000 wounded and billions of dollars to the American tax payer.

Richard Nixon's obsession with learning how much the democrats knew about his discovered conspiracy with Anna Chennault led to the Watergate scandal. Which leads us to ask, was he aware and did he fear discovery of the Chennault-Kennedy-killing link?

CHAPTER 50

But what role did Anna Chennault play in the assassination of Senator Kennedy, if any?

Faura as a responsible investigator knew it was a great leap of faith to allege that Anna Chennault was involved in the Robert F. Kennedy killing just because she knew and met with one of the conspirators three days before the assassination took place.

But he knew also that it was true she would have become a primary suspect and subject of investigation. She had the motive, opportunity and means to commit the crime.

A fountain of questions sprang forth in Faura's mind:

1. How does "the woman in the polka-dot dress" get to know such a high-powered, highly placed personage as Anna Chennault?

2. What was their relationship?

3. What was the purpose of their meeting three days before the assassination of Senator Robert Kennedy?

4. Why does the "woman in the polka-dot dress" think she could get passage to Australia (or points beyond) in a CIA proprietary (CAT) with which Mrs. Chennault had a long association and ended operations the same month of June?

5. Who were "the Chinese" she was afraid of?

6. Why is the CIA shadow all over this?

Richard Nixon's chances were much better against Vice President Hubert Humphrey, who was saddled with the Johnson legacy, than against Robert Kennedy, who was a real threat to the conspirators. After all, on the table was the biggest prize in the history of the world: the US government. What better motive?

Murder is not usually in the United States political environment, but these were extraordinary times. The country was in turmoil over the Vietnam War, President Johnson was trying to stop it, and Wall Street was gambling billions of dollars. If the Democrats won (Robert F. Kennedy) the conspirators faced opprobrium and prison. The players in the treasonous conspiracy were not of sterling quality, as we were to learn later.

Anna Chennault had suggested at one time that she "eliminated" her opposition. With the stakes so high, it is not beyond credibility that the "peace talks" conspiracy was the genesis of the Kennedy killing.

The questions posed before are all legitimate on the assumption that "the girl in the polka-dot dress" was telling the truth about meeting with Mrs. Chennault. She did have some credibility. After all she had predicted the killing on the date, time and place it occurred.

The "woman in the polka-dot dress" had also mentioned a man named "Oppenheimer" (same as the last name she gave herself) in Guam or Taiwan; that was her destination if she could get on CAT Airlines. So her connections and safety were in the Far East, not the Middle East.

Her trail was leading Faura and Bonfante to the Far East, but they did not know, nor did anyone else, of a domestic political conspiracy with Chinese and Vietnamese conspirators, associated with the Republican party.

Their interest?

The outcome of the Paris Peace Talks for domestic political reasons – with the brass ring being the White House.

It is difficult to accept Richard Nixon, Sen. John Tower, Spiro Agnew and John Mitchell in a conspiracy to commit murder until you bring into the equation the very high stakes game they were playing: the White House, billions of dollars more for four more years of war (don't forget the bankers; Nixon had been a lawyer in a Wall Street law firm), and the future of Vietnam.

It becomes easier to accept once you learn the fact that years later Nixon had to resign the White House; Agnew went to prison for tax fraud after being accused of extortion, bribery and conspiracy; Mitchell went to jail over the Watergate scandal; Tower had a reputation for being a womanizing heavy drinker and rumored to be Anna Chennault's lover – making it all quite believable.

A true-to-life cast for the Usual Suspects.

With Nixon in the White House, they all knew there would be no prosecution for treason or any other offense.

Plausible denial requires that you distance yourself from illegal or questionable actions. Enter Anna Chennault, an extremely rich, powerhouse in Republican politics who entertained and was friendly with the secretary of Defense, the attorney general, Nixon and other powerful political figures.

An aggressive adventurous woman and risk-taker, Anna Chennault had extensive experience in Far East politics as well as close contact with clandestine operations. Her husband Gen. Claire Chennault, an adventurous pilot, had a long history of association with U.S. clandestine operations in the Far East.

Anna Chennault was once asked how did she handle her opposition. She just made a slicing motion across her throat. The questioner was so stunned he changed the subject.

Decades later when the treasonous conspiracy to scuttle the Paris Peace Talks came to light, she admitted her role and said she had been acting "under orders" since she could not engage in such activities on her own.

As the Watergate scandal developed, Johnson and his aides suspected that the Watergate burglary occurred because Nixon was worried about how much more ex-President Johnson knew of his treasonable acts.

Faura believes it is important that all those records, especially anything on Anna Chennault, be re-evaluated to determine if she was involved in a conspiracy with the "woman in the polka-dot dress."

How do you tell the American people about such political intrigues at a time when the country was so polarized? President Johnson and his advisers decided they could not be told.

William Turner and John Christian – authors of *The Assassination of Robert F. Kennedy* – and Sirhan's biographer and late convert to the theory of Robert Kaiser, author of *RFK Must Die*, believe Sirhan was a Manchurian Candidate. They would have been delighted had they picked up on the reference to "Mrs. Chennault" by Fahey. Of course this was not on the original Fahey tape. He had said it to Faura on their trip to Ventura.

CHAPTER 51

Could Sirhan Sirhan be, truly, a "Manchurian Candidate"?
While inclined towards the theory, Faura was always hesitant to endorse it for lack of proven, competent evidence. Such evidence may have come into his possession with an email message from Shane O'Sullivan, the author of *Who Killed Bobby?*

That mail included the Declaration of Dr. Daniel P. Brown PhD to the Parole Board of California prior to a Parole hearing for Sirhan.

Dr. Brown is an Associate Clinical Professor of Psychology at Harvard Medical School at Beth Israel Deaconess Medical Center (BIDMC).

Dr. Brown is the author of *Memory, Trauma Treatment and the Law*, a textbook for which he received awards from seven professional societies for "outstanding contribution to forensic psychiatry and the law."

He also served as an expert witness and consultant for the prosecution at the The International War Crimes Tribunal, The Hague, Netherlands where his expert testimony has been adopted as the standard of evidence by the tribunal.

Dr. Brown has also written four books on hypnosis – among them a standard textbook, *Hypnosis and Hypnotherapy* (Erlbaum, 1986-coauthored with Erika Fromm). He also wrote the current guidelines on forensic interviewing for *The Comprehensive Textbook on Psychiatry*.

Dr. Brown, at the request of the Sirhan defense team, conducted a forensic assessment in six different two-day sessions over a three-year span spending over sixty hours interviewing and testing Sirhan at Corona Penitentiary and Pleasant Valley in California.

Dr. Brown's "Declaration" to the Parole Board convinced Faura that Sirhan is in fact a "Manchurian Candidate."

The relevant excerpts from Dr. Brown's declaration regarding the girl in the polka dot dress follow:

Paragraph 10.3
"... After arriving at the Ambassador Mr. Sirhan recalled ' I felt out of place there ... it was very hot ... sweltering hot. I wanted to cool down ... I had the idea to get some lemonade. There was a bar there." Mr. Sirhan's memory of the bartender suggests a strange feeling of familiarity, between them as if even though Mr. Sirhan, didn't know who the bartender was, he felt as if some previous relationship had been established. Mr. Sirhan ad-

ditionally recalls that the bartender communicated by nonverbal signals like making unusual eye contact and nodding, and through this processes of handling Mr. Sirhan alcoholic drinks and nonverbal gesturing to him, Mr. Sirhan got very "tired."

"…he looked Latin … It's like I have a relationship with this guy … he looks like an Abbot and Costello … the short one … this bartender … he was not looking for a sale … he wasn't talkative. It's as if he was communicating with gestures … a nod after I paid for it … I am still looking around … he did not make the drink in front of me … he made it and brought it over … after that I came back again … it was like a routine between us.…"

"At this point, the declaration continues, Sirhan can only think about going home."

Sirhan went to his car and realizing that he could not drive in his inebriated condition he re-traced his steps back to the bar to get some coffee.

Paragraph 10.6 continues:

"Mr. Sirhan recalls retracing his steps to the same bar. When Mr. Sirhan arrived at the bar he asked the same bartender for coffee. The bartender told him that there was no coffee at the bar. An attractive woman with a polka dot dress was sitting at the bar talking to the bartender. She overheard Mr. Sirhan asking for coffee and she said she knew where the coffee was.

The woman in the polka dot dress then took Mr. Sirhan by the hand and led him to the ante-room behind the stage where Senator Kennedy was speaking. There they discovered a large coffee urn and cups."

The next paragraph of 10.6 goes on to describe Sirhan's sexual thoughts about the girl and his desire to be with her but she behaved like a "lady."

Paragraph 10.7 gives us some important clues about how Sirhan was placed into position to play out his role:

"While Mr. Sirhan is flirting with this girl (Mr. Sirhan had gone to the party to pick up a girl), they are interrupted by an official with a suit and clip board. This official tells them that they cannot stay in the anteroom for security reasons, and the official then tells the girl in the polka dot dress to go to the kitchen.

"Mr. Sirhan recalls. 'All of a sudden they tell us we have to move. This guy comes by wearing a suit … darkish hair … a big, big full face … seems like he was in charge.… He wasn't wearing any uniform … wearing a suit.… She acknowledges his instructions.… He motions towards the pantry The man said you guys can go back in this room." I followed her. She led … I was like a puppy after her. I wanted to go back to the Mariachi band … but she went straight to the pantry area with my being so attracted to her I was just glued to her.

Paragraph 10.8 says:

"According to what Mr. Sirhan freely recalls, his memory suggests that Mr. Sirhan was led directly to the kitchen by the girl in the polka dot dress, immediately after she had been given this information by an "official.""

In the second paragraph of this section Sirhan goes on to describe his fascination with the girl and his sexual thoughts about her, his desire to "hit" on her and how he was fascinated by her looks.

He describes how he was "consumed by her" and describes the moment as "erotic" and her as a "seductress with an unspoken unavailability."

In paragraph 10.10 Dr. Brown notes: " The next part of Mr. Sirhan's recall is strongly suggestive of an automatic behavioral response to a specific post-hypnotic cue, namely when Mr. Sirhan was tapped on the shoulder Mr. Sirhan automatically took his weapon stance and began experiencing a "flash back" that he was firing at a target at a firing range. Mr. Sirhan specifically recalled taking his stance and specifically recalled seeing circular targets in his field of vision. The next thing that Mr. Sirhan remembered after that is that he was being choked, partially wakes up and had the thought, "I am not at a firing range I just shot somebody.""

Dr. Brown recorded Sirhan's exact words: " I am trying to figure out how I am going to have her.... All of a sudden she is looking over my head toward an area.... Then she taps or pinches me .... It is startling.... It was like a wake up ... the contact with my body ... this is too abnormal for people to pinch like that for no given reason It was like when you are stuck with a pin or pinched ... a very sharp pinch.... I thought she did it with her fingernails ... like a wake up ... it snapped me out of my doldrums ... yet I am still sleepy ... she points back over my head ... "look, look, look."... I turn around ... she was turning my attention to the rear ... way back ... there are people coming back through the doors.... I am still puzzled about what she is directing me to ... it did not seem relevant to me ... some people started streaming in ... She kept motioning towards the back ... then all of a sudden she gets more animated ... she put her arm on my shoulder.

In paragraph 10.11 Dr. Brown observes that "When the girl put hand on Mr. Sirhan he said 'I thought it was romantic.' However he noted that she was not at all looking at him but "looking way above my head."

In this part of the Declaration Dr. Brown describes how Sirhan reacts after the pinch on the shoulder. He records Sirhan's words thus: "Then I was at the target range ... a flash back to the shooting range...

I didn't know I had a gun ... there was this target like a flashback to the target range ... I thought I was at the range more than I actually was shooting, at a person let alone Bobby Kennedy.... I think I shot one or two shots ... then I snapped out it and thought 'I am not at the range' ... then 'what is going on' ... then they started grabbing me ... I'm thinking the range, the range, the range ... then everything gets blurry...

I think that's when Uecker grabbed me." According to Dr. Brown in paragraph 10.15 of his Declaration "Mr. Sirhan's memory report is consistent with hypnotic programing hypothesis. He goes on to explain that "at least some aspects of covert mind control research conducted by intelligence agencies concurrent with the RFK assassination was documented in J. Marks' *The Search for the Manchurian Candidate: The CIA and Mind Control: The Secret History of the behavioral Sciences* (1979) published as a reparation agreement by the American Psychiatric Association because one of the main "programmers" Dr. Erwin Cameron served as president of the American Psychiatric Association while conducting illegal mind control on unsuspecting citizens without their consent." Dr. Brown goes on to say that "these experiments were conducted within the same time frame as the RFK assassination and at least three of the redacted documents describe successful assassinations in other countries using the unconscious assassination method."

Dr. Brown, in paragraph 10.16 categorically states that "Sirhan has a rare combination of personality characteristics that make him highly vulnerable to coercive persuasion and mind control methods."

Amazingly Sirhan strengthens the second gun theory on paragraph 10.20 when under hypnosis he says "Steadily in front of me … then a flashing streaking in front of my eyes … very bright spots … then dark, blank." Dr. Brown clarifies Sirhan's words (paragraph10.21) "In a follow up interview I asked Mr. Sirhan whether the "gun flash" he reported seeing came from his own gun or from somewhere else. "He said my gun does not flash." In this passage Mr. Sirhan clearly concedes indirectly that without knowing it Mr. Sirhan actually saw the flash from another gun at the time of the assassination."

Dr. Brown explored deeper into the "range mode" aspects of Sirhan's recollections (paragraph10.23): "Since Mr. Sirhan seemed to respond immediately and compulsively with "range mode" behavior to the touch cue by the girl with the polka dot dress, I subsequently asked Mr. Sirhan 'Did anybody ever touch you like that before?" Mr. Sirhan replied, "I don't remember. It could have been at the range. With her I was more elated."

Dr. Brown asked Sirhan if "anyone, at any time ever give you such a cue?"

"It might have happened at the range," Sirhan responded.

According to Dr. Brown "the range" does not refer to Fish Canyon (which Sirhan visited the day of the assassination.) but to a police and military firing range, where Mr. Sirhan recalls he was trained to shoot at human targets. This assertion is underscored by Dr. Brown in paragraph 12.1.5 by declaring: "Even where elements of his recall appear unusual, there is some corroboration for his recall, like the LAPD documentation regarding his presence at the police and military firing range."

In effect paragraph 10.13 summarizes the events of that night. Dr. Brown declares: "According to his memory, the bartender, the girl in the polka dot dress, and an unknown official, all play a central role in leading Mr. Sirhan to the scene of the crime, whereupon the girl taps him on the shoulder and Mr. Sirhan responds upon cue with automatic and compulsive behavior – what Mr. Sirhan eventually described as "range mode" – wherein Mr. Sirhan takes his firing stance and experiences a "flashback" at a target at a firing range in a way that has been well practiced While interviewing Mr. Sirhan, I along with Attorney Dusek, directly observed Mr. Sirhan spontaneously switch into "range mode" on several occasions, whereupon Mr. Sirhan automatically took his firing stance, and in uncharacteristic robot like voice described shooting at vital organs. Following brief reenactments or range mode Mr. Sirhan remained completely amnesic of the behavior.

The conclusion of Dr. Brown is that: "The evidence revealed by my extensive interviews substantiates the less refined allegations that he engaged in this activity in response to a cue given by another party, and thus compels the conclusion that his action of firing the gun was neither under his voluntary control or done with conscious knowledge but is likely the product of automatic hypnotic behavior and coercive control. I am convinced that Mr. Sirhan legitimately recalled a "flashback" to shoot target circles at a firing range in response to the post hypnotic touch cue and did not have the knowledge, or intention, to shoot a human being, let alone Senator Kennedy. Even after 40 years Mr. Sirhan still is confused when told by others that he shot Senator Kennedy. ' And "further that the system of mind control which was imposed upon him has also made it impossible for him to recall under hypnosis or consciously, many critical details of actions and events leading up to and at the time of the shooting in the pantry of the Ambassador Hotel."

The Declaration is signed by Dr. Brown under penalty of perjury.

LAPD document I-4565 talks about an interview with Merla Stevens and "acquaintances" of Sirhan Sirhan in a group interview.

According to that document the women described the interaction between Sirhan and Ali, another acquaintance. They state that Ali would say something to make Sirhan crazy, and then say something to stop him. The women also state that Sirhan was going to kill Senator Kennedy and that the group of Arabs Sirhan and Ali were part of had plans to kill many politicians.

It is a proven fact that Sirhan was into hypnosis and his behavior with Ali, typical of hypnotic behavior as described, showed he was under Ali's control at those times.

Faura found no record of a follow-up on this information.

Inevitably the Robert Kennedy investigation led to and overlapped his brother's investigation. It was not intended that way. It happened.

It is difficult, after years of investigation and analysis to separate one from the other. Keeping in mind and sympathizing with the universal desire to discard difficult and complicated problems, an effort has been made in this book to address the Robert Kennedy killing investigation only. By doing this, public opinion, if sufficiently aroused can force a clean, factual, court showdown between independent investigators and the authorities.

The charges that the authorities wanted to hide the truth of the assassination of Robert Kennedy are not without basis of fact and can stand the scrutiny of the American public.

What is more difficult to prove is the actual involvement of police forces in the execution of the conspiracy.

This is only difficult in the legal requirements of the law and the involved procedures of present American justice.

Fortunately the public is still free to look at the facts and make up their own minds. Faura listed the facts as known to him.

Fact: Sandra Serrano, shortly after the shooting, saw a man and a woman run by her, the woman crying, "We shot him, we shot him." Asked who they shot, she replied, "Senator Kennedy," whereupon she and her companion disappeared into the night. The woman wore a "polka-dot dress."

Fact: Minutes earlier, before the shooting, Sandra Serrano had seen the same woman, accompanied by two men, as they excused themselves and walked past her towards the kitchen where Senator Kennedy was shot.

Fact: More than a dozen witnesses placed Sirhan Sirhan, the assassin at the Ambassador Hotel accompanied by a man and a girl. The girl wore a "polka-dot dress." The man fit the description of the man who ran past Serrano with a woman in a "polka-dot dress" screaming, "We shot him, we shot him." In spite of police bullying Serrano still sticks to her story.

Fact: Mrs. Carlos Gallegos, a South American émigré with little taste for intrigue and a deep sense of loyalty towards the USA, placed Sirhan, in kitchen garb, at the Ambassador kitchen five hours before the killing, in the company of two other men in similar attire. The description of one of them fits perfectly that of the man seen by Serrano and John Fahey.

Fact: John Fahey spent the day with a woman who fit the description of the "girl in the polka-dot dress," and who predicted Senator's Kennedy's killing not only to the exact date, but also to the place and time.

Fact: The woman told Fahey that she had to go to the Rosicrucian Temple in San Jose, Calif. Sirhan was a Rosicrucian and expressed concern that his dues be paid after he was arrested. His notebooks prove his self hypnotic trances taught by the Rosicrucians.

Fact: Fahey saw and was watched by a man whose description was the same as that given by Serrano and Gallegos.

Fact: Not one of these citizens knew the others or was aware of what the others were telling the police.

Fact: Vincent DiPierro, an important witness and hotel employee, identified the "girl in the polka-dot dress" as the girl he had seen "whispering" to Sirhan before Sirhan opened fire on Senator Kennedy. The girl identified by DiPierro was the same girl who had predicted the killing to John Fahey.

Fact: Hotel workers admitted to having seen the girl prior to the shooting and, after the shooting running to escape.

Fact: Fahey was independently polygraphed and found to be telling the truth.

Fact: The police bullied Fahey to change his story, which he modified, only to later come back to it and stay with it.

Fact: Greg Clayton, a Rafferty campaign worker, saw Sirhan in the company of four other men and a girl in a "polka-dot dress." The men fit the descriptions of men seen with Sirhan by other witnesses. Clayton also saw at least one of the men he had seen with Sirhan earlier running away from the kitchen area immediately after the shooting. A month after the killing, he had not been interviewed by the police in spite of his immediate offer to help right after the shooting and the police were already denying the existence of the "polka-dot dress girl."

Fact: Dean Pack, an insurance salesman, saw Sirhan and another man in the company of an attractive girl practicing shooting in the mountains near Los Angeles. His declarations were not investigated by the police.

Fact: Booker Griffin, a local newsman, saw Sirhan with a girl wearing a "polka-dot dress" earlier in the evening. He saw the same girl running away from the kitchen in the company of a man right after the shooting. The man fits the description of one of the men seen by Serrano, Gallegos and others.

Fact: Albert V. Ellis, also heard a woman crying, "We shot him," confirming Serrano's story. So did several kitchen employees who were, and still are, afraid to talk.

Fact: "The girl in the polka-dot dress" said she met with Anna Chennault three days before the assassination.

These facts, thoroughly investigated or obtained from the official police and FBI record, are sufficient to establish that there was ample reason to suspect a conspiracy.

There are others.

Hours after the killing the authorities were claiming there was no conspiracy. They also set out to discredit and bully witnesses whose testimony pointed in the direction of a conspiracy.

Fact: The LAPD, less than a month after the "girl in the polka-dot dress" had gone worldwide, denied her existence, this in spite of the numerous witnesses who had seen her.

Fact: The LAPD, instead of trying to confirm Serrano's story, set out to discredit her.

Fact: The LAPD claimed that DiPierro had been influenced by Serrano and had not, in fact, seen the girl in the "polka-dot dress." They also said the reverse: that DiPierro had influenced Serrano. Obviously, both statements could not be correct, yet after supposedly extracting their admissions, the statements were allowed to stand.

Fact: The police completely ignored the Fahey story for two months (giving "the polka-dot girl" ample time to disappear) in spite of its seriousness and importance. After two months the main effort was not to confirm the story but to discredit it. In spite of their efforts they never really shook Fahey from his story and never succeeded in making him retract that the girl had predicted the killing.

Fact: Members of SUS scared and/or embarrassed Jan Page, a waitress, into silence. She had confirmed the Fahey story and identified the woman with him at Trancas Restaurant as the one in the "photo," in effect "the polka-dot girl" and her companion.

Fact: After her initial interview the LAPD never investigated Gallegos' story of Sirhan in kitchen garb in the company of two men two days before the killing.

Fact: The police did not learn of Greg Clayton's polka-dot girl story, in spite of its serious implications, till after they had said the "girl in the polka-dot dress" did not exist. They did not record the interview so there is no way of knowing if they learned of the "polka-dot girl" with Sirhan from him also.

Fact: The presence of Sirhan in a bar in Pomona, Calif., with a man and a woman was never fully explained by the police, and they will so admit.

Fact: Robert Kaiser (*RFK Must Die*) in a declaration claims, "Suppression of Evidence of Impostor/Handler at the Corona Police Gun Range:

According to Kaiser, "An impostor signed Sirhan's name at the Pomona Police Target Range on June 2, 1968, three days before the Robert

Kennedy assassination. DSA (daily summary of activities) 12-11-68, DSA 12-12-1968. The report of this outstanding incident was NEVER shared with the defense.

"The report states, "The Rangemaster is a regular Corona policeman, and he is still positive that the person who signed Sirhan Sirhan on the roster is over six feet and over 200 pounds with a face similar to Sirhan's.

Sirhan himself was about five feet six and weighed approximately 120 lbs.

Kaiser continues: "The impostor was thus a shadow figure, who may have led Sirhan in the same way as the "girl" described above. He certainly "set up" Sirhan by creating a paper trail linking Sirhan to the gun range within less than three days of the assassination."

Fact: Police deliberately caused false information to be entered into the record by claiming that Mr. Woo had seen Fahey and Faura together prior to June 4.

The LAPD and FBI's own records prove that this is false information. Yet it is allowed to stand. There are many others.

Other ominous occurrences took place.

Preacher Jerry Owen, the man who claimed that he was almost duped into selling a horse to Sirhan and possibly used as a patsy for Sirhan's attempted escape was polygraphed in San Francisco. He is a well-known right-winger with a healthy dossier in the Criminal Investigations and Investigation files.

LAPD sent two men to San Francisco to polygraph him and claimed he failed the test and was just looking for publicity. And so his involvement was set aside and died publicly.

Shortly afterwards, two attempts were made on his life, according to him, and the police refused to investigate.

The problem with that is he had a witness to the second attempt, made in Hollywood after his house was ransacked. An associate of Owen was driving Owen's car near Griffith Park Observatory when another car zipped past and shot at them.

Shaken, they went to the police department in Hollywood and filed a report. A newsman heard about it, called the police station and the officer in charge read him the report filed by Owen and his companion.

The same day the report disappeared from the police station and the police will not admit to its existence or to know about the shooting.

The LAPD is not talking about the investigation, if any, of other strange occurrences surrounding Owen.

SUS investigators became aware of a sheriff's report that Owen had been seen riding horses with Sirhan at the Shamel Ranch, a few days prior to the Kennedy shooting.

There is a man by the same name, "Shamel," working at the Ambassador Hotel, who was one of the first persons at the scene of the killing. While this does not suggest his involvement in a conspiracy, it is ample grounds to warrant an investigation of his relationship to Owen, if any, and the presence of Sirhan at the Shamel Ranch.

If the Shamel Ranch is his property then a Sirhan-Owen-Shamel connection would be established. There is no evidence any investigation was made.

Noteworthy is the fact that Sirhan had been receiving money from another right-wing horseman in Northern California. This was known to the police as it appeared in Sirhan's own notebook. For some undisclosed reason the U.S. Marshal's office had been asked to help and they had the same information.

Faura had confirmed this fact by walking into the marshal's office with a "friend" that worked out of that office, as if he belonged there. His "friend" took the file out, and Faura nervously and hurriedly read the report.

The information in the marshal's report raised some serious questions, but not to the LAPD. The person who gave the information to the marshal's department was questioned once and the matter dropped.

In June 1971, Baxter Ward, news director and anchor for KHJ-TV, and a man of impeccable credentials and integrity, learned that Robert Weatherly, the young man who had given the information to the sheriff's department was shot at. Ward investigated.

Weatherly refused to make a police report, claiming that he suspected the attempt on his life stemmed from his declarations to the sheriff's department connecting Owen to Sirhan. He was understandably scared, but reluctantly told of driving home in the early hours of the morning with two friends, one in the back seat and the other beside him. Both of his companions were half asleep and not visible from the outside of the car. It appeared that Weatherly was alone.

Before turning into his driveway, Weatherly noticed another car cruising slowly in the same block with the lights off. Upon turning into his driveway, Weatherly claimed, the mystery car cruised in front of his house, and it was then he heard the shot.

His car lurched out of control, the back window shattering, abruptly awakening his friends.

He pushed the head of one of his companions down to keep him out of the line of fire, and then the three sought protection in the house by running in the dark, half crouched, to the door.

The LAPD is aware of the shooting but is unable or unwilling to investigate it, much less talk about it.

Four known attempts at assassinations in the aftermath of the senator's killing: one each on Said Sirhan and Robert Weatherly, and two on Reverend Owen.

Twenty years after the assassination, the conspiracy ghost came back to haunt the LAPD.

Jamie Scott Enyart sued the police department to recover film and photos he had taken during the very act of the killing. Not one of the early researchers knew about Enyard (15 years old at the time of the killing) because his film and pictures where never mentioned by the police before or during Sirhan's trial. According to William Turner, co-author of *The Assassination of Robert F. Kennedy,* reports in his book, *Rearview Mirror* that Enyart believes his photos contain "the only record of the assassination."

Enyart was a high school student trailing his hero, Senator Kennedy, snapping pictures. He was slightly behind the senator and to his left when the shooting began and he shot pictures as fast as he could. According to Al Benson (*Los Angeles Free Press,* 1996) Enyart saw Eugene Cesar (a security guard) get up with his gun drawn. (There is no record that the LAPD gave Cesar a paraffin test to determine if he had fired the gun). As Enyart left the pantry two LAPD officers detained him at gunpoint and seized his film.

According to an article by Al Benson (*Los Angeles Free Press,* 1996) "somewhere in the neighborhood of 17 people also saw a woman in a polka-dot dress with Sirhan in the kitchen." After Enyart's film was confiscated, Detective Dudley Varney of the Special Unit Senator told him that his film would be developed and was needed in the Sirhan trial. The photos were not used in the Sirhan trial and Varney told Enyart that the court had ordered that all evidential material be sealed for 20 years. The 20 years passed and Enyart politely requested that his photos be returned. First he was told that the state archives could not find them. Then they told him that they had been burned. Enyart sued, his lawyer charging "improper handling of Enyart's property; failure of the LAPD to perform a proper investigation; deliberate misuse of Enyart's film; willful misidentification and mislabeling of his property; willful and deliberate failure to provide Enyart with a receipt for his property even when one was requested; failure to properly and safely preserve property (the film); the transfer of title to his property without Enyart's express permission or authority and even without his knowledge; false assertion by the City of Los Angeles that Enyart's property, in its entirety, had been returned to him."

The lawsuit came to trial in 1996, and the jury awarded Enyart $450,000. However, during the trial the city attorney trying the case announced that the photos had been found misfiled, in Sacramento.

Enyart, and attorney Christine Harwell, traveled to Sacramento only to have Enyart declare that the film found in the archives was a different brand and ASA 125, while his was Kodak Tri-X 400 ASA. He also suggested that some sort of forgery had taken place. He testified under oath that he noticed "enhanced contrast in the images suggesting a generational copying from the original negatives." He also noticed that the single role of film in the archives appeared to include photos from all three of the rolls he had shot that night; and that some of the photos appeared to be out of sequence, and most importantly there were no photos from inside the pantry.

With the authenticity of the film found in Sacramento now challenged, Superior Court Judge Emile Ellas ordered the evidence delivered to Los Angeles.

Professor Philip H. Melanson and William Klaber – authors of *Shadow Play: the Murder of Robert F. Kennedy* – picked up the developing drama this way: "On Jan. 12, 1996, just a month before the scheduled start of the trial, courier George Phillip Gephardt flew from Sacramento to Los Angeles. In his briefcase was a folder containing the negatives. When he arrived in Los Angeles he went to the Midway Rent-a-Car agency where he picked up a white Mazda sedan. Just outside the airport, the courier stopped for a red light.

"According to his videotaped testimony in court (Gephardt had suffered a heart attack shortly after this incident and testified from his hospital bed), a red car pulled up next to him and a Hispanic man got out and started banging on his own car for no apparent reason. A block later the white Mazda was making a dull thumping noise. Gephardt pulled over, got out to inspect, and found out that his right rear tire was slashed. When he got back into his car, the briefcase with the negatives was gone."

William Turner, co-author of *The Assassination of Robert F. Kennedy*, says in his book, *Rearview Mirror*: "Thus vanished the RFK version of the Zapruder Film, which might have shown who shot him from behind."

Alvin Greenwald, an Enyart lawyer, hinted at conspiracy: "Somebody, for some reason," he said, "is making sure those photos do not reach public view."

Skip Miller, attorney representing the city, called the incident, "a simple petty theft, a run of bad luck." He called the string of lies and missteps of the LAPD and the city simple "clerical errors."

The State Bar of California later "admonished" Miller for jury tampering in another case. The LAPD makes nothing of it.

Jim Garrison, Louisiana's D.A. – a man carefully avoided by some of the investigators of the Robert Kennedy killing – charged that the CIA was involved in the killing of President John Kennedy.

After attempts to discredit Garrison were well underway, some investigators of the Robert Kennedy killing avoided contact with him, not because they did not believe what he was saying, but because they wanted to operate unhampered by the troubles that were already besieging Jim Garrison.

However, there was no forgetting Garrison's charge of CIA involvement in the light of information that was surfacing in the Robert Kennedy killing.

In order to understand fully the possible presence of the CIA in the killing of Senator Kennedy it is necessary to provide some background.

CHAPTER 52

Although the evidence is purely circumstantial and likely to remain so because of the secrecy that surrounds the CIA and the collusion of the local police departments and the FBI, the information presented is factual and a matter of public record.

In 1970, Dan Mitrione, an American advisor to the police forces in Nicaragua, was kidnapped and held captive by an organization of revolutionaries called the Tupamaros. He was one of several people kidnapped by the Tupamaros and received extensive press coverage in the United States.

A few weeks after his capture Mitrione was returned dead by his captors, who charged that he was one of several CIA agents working under the cover of the Agency for International Development (AID).

The AID has for years recruited policemen from U.S. police departments, sent them to McClean, Va., home of the CIA, for training and then assigned them to tours of duty with foreign police forces.

Mitrione was one of them. Whether the Tupamaros were correct in their charge that Mitrione was a CIA agent, was of course, never admitted by the CIA or the State Department. Ironically, Senator Edward Kennedy, unknowingly, partly substantiated the Tupamaros charges. During Senate hearings Edward Kennedy got the Director of AID to admit that the CIA had been using AID. The AID director declared that he was "unhappy with the arrangement," but that it was "a fact of life."

Without any doubt, in the records of the United States Senate the CIA-AID link has been established for years.

Back in Los Angeles in 1967, Lt. Manuel "Manny" Pena had been retired from the LAPD and gone to work, according to the story, for the State Department.

Covering his retirement dinner, which was attended by Chief of Police Thomas Reddin and many other dignitaries, Faura learned that Pena was going to work for AID in Washington, D.C.

Pena had said that he had on other occasions gone overseas as an "advisor" to foreign police forces primarily in Spanish-speaking countries and Hawaii.

He was then working in the same capacity as Mitrione.

A few weeks after the LAPD had confiscated Faura's tape, for which he had to sue, Faura ran into Manny Pena. Making an inquiry into the whereabouts of the tape, Faura was told to talk to the man in charge of the "day watch" of the investigation.

The day watch was the most important watch of three shifts the police were working at the time. The man in charge turned out to be "Manny" Pena. He had grown a thick mustache and looked as fit as ever.

Finding him working back at the LAPD was a shock to Faura, since he was supposed to be working back in Washington for AID.

"What happened?" Faura asked.

"They tried to give me a desk job, and I didn't like it. So I came back." He said no more. Queried about the tape, he claimed to know nothing about it. This of course was a lie. Pena had personally undertaken to call the San Fernando Police Department to complain about Faura having taken Fahey there for questioning.

Pena was also the man who signed the report that states that Mr. Woo had seen Fahey and Faura together in his office, the week prior to the Kennedy killing. Another fabrication.

Pena came to be known as the second in command of the complex SUS investigation team. He made assignments, read reports, and caused to be entered into the record information which can and will ultimately be discredited – for instance, the Woo report.

His boss Capt. Hugh Brown was the nominal head of the SUS investigating team. He is a member of the Amapola Horse Association, a known right-wing leaning organization.

There are other reports of Manny Pena being involved in portions of the investigation that were carelessly disregarded. This Faura himself disregarded as unsubstantiated and lacking adequate proof.

Hank Hernandez, the polygraph expert used by SUS to supposedly discredit witnesses, is reportedly another AID trained policeman. This information relating to the CIA-AID is factual and on the record.

Whether these men, as well as countless others returned by AID to their police departments are still working for the CIA is an issue of major importance to the country at large and should be investigated.

If there is still, in fact, any connection between these men and AID or the CIA placing them in key positions in the investigation of Senator Kennedy's killing has ominous overtones in the light of Jim Garrison's charges.

Motive and circumstantial evidence has placed many a man on death row and should not be discarded. With the seriousness of the crime in this instance – a political assassination – they should be investigated.

It is no secret that there was a lot of animosity between the Kennedys and the CIA. It is also a recorded fact that Robert Kennedy had a bitter feud with AID for its failure to follow presidential directives.

Police informants and other "defectors" have come forward with information which helps fill in gaps in the narrative and voluminous files of independent investigators.

The information has to be checked out, confirmed and must stand court examination if it is to be published. It is a difficult task, but the story, in the long run, will be told.

Regardless of any wrong doing by Jim Garrison in the performance of his duties, much of what he claimed has already been confirmed by independent investigators.

The Agency for International Development, with a huge budget, has been referred to as a "second CIA" or a "parallel CIA." Some Latin American countries have asked the agency to leave. They can't do that to the CIA because it is entirely covert.

For the time being, and until the full story is in, it would be well for everyone to remember Jim Garrison's words: "There was a coup in the United States on Nov. 22, 1963."

Faura, for one, is not forgetting them.

THE WHITE HOUSE
WASHINGTON

~~TOP SECRET~~/NODIS/HARVAN/DOUBLE PLUS ▮▮▮▮ **SANITIZED**

per sec 1.4(c)

February 25, 1970

MEMORANDUM FOR THE PRESIDENT

FROM: Tom Charles Huston

SUBJECT: Vietnam Bombing Halt -- The Chennault Affair

        Attached is a report on the contacts between Mrs. Clare Chennault
and South Vietnamese Ambassador Bui Diem during October and November 1968
as they related to the bombing halt negotiations and as seen from the per-
spective of the Johnson White House.

        The Chennault Affair strikes me as important for three reasons:
(1) for the light it sheds on the state of relations between Saigon and
Washington during this critical period; (2) for the insight it provides
into the seriousness with which President Johnson viewed the situation; and
(3) for the questions it raises about the methods which LBJ employed to
gather information of a sensitive political nature.

        While there are a few gaps in the record, I believe I have been
able to dig up nearly all the relevant information. My sources in the FBI
were very cooperative, perhaps because they resented the way President
Johnson used the Bureau without regard to the propriety of the actions which
he directed be undertaken. Other Federal agencies having information were
less cooperative, perhaps because they have a vested interest in maintaining
the iron curtain which has descended over all pre-January 20, 1969 activities
of the Federal Government.

        I am continuing my efforts to dig out the facts surrounding the
negotiations for a bombing halt. Unfortunately, it is likely that there will
be many more gaps in that report since the resistance within the bureaucracy
to divulging information on the subject is rather great. I hope to have a
interim report on the Sovietphilia of Ambassador Harriman ready for you shortly.

                               Tom
                          Tom Charles Huston

~~TOP SECRET~~/NODIS/HARVAN/DOUBLE PLUS ▮▮▮▮

~~TOP SECRET~~/NODIS/HARVAN/DOUBLE PLUS ███ **SANITIZED**

per sec 1.4(c)

THE CHENNAULT AFFAIR

I. Summary

In late October, 1968, when negotiations with Hanoi for a bombing halt had reached a crucial stage and intensive efforts were underway to enlist the cooperation of President Thieu, the White House learned that individuals purporting to represent candidate Nixon were involved in contacts with the South Vietnamese Government. The details were difficult to piece together, but available evidence suggested that an overt Republican attempt was being made to convince GVN to hold out against a bombing halt until after the elections.

The existence of GOP contacts with GVN aroused great concern among high level Administration officials and angered President Johnson. He personally directed the effort to determine who was involved and what they were attempting to accomplish. The full resources of the intelligence community were employed to ascertain this information. Mrs. Clare Chennault became the focus of attention, but the activities of Ambassador Bui Diem in Washington and Vice President Ky in Saigon were also scrutinized in an effort to determine the role they were playing in the affair.

In terms of policy formulation, the existence of such contacts added an additional strain to Washington-Saigon relations. President Johnson appeared to believe that double-dealing was involved and he was insensed.

~~TOP SECRET~~/NODIS/HARVAN/DOUBLE PLUS ███

He regarded himself as "the best friend" which Saigon had, and he could not understand why President Thieu and his colleagues hesitated to go along with him when his feet were to the fire in Paris.

II.   Early Signs of GOP-Saigon Contacts

When the anticipated bombing halt agreement failed to be realized on October 15, a two-front negotiating effort was launched: in Paris to bring the DRV around on largely procedural questions and in Saigon to ameliorate GVN fears over the implications of NLF participation in post-bombing talks.

Unlike Secretary Stimson, President Johnson did not hesitate to read other people's mail and technical surveillance of the South Vietnamese Embassy was intensified in order to keep him posted on Saigon's attitude toward developments in Paris.

On October 26, Vice President Ky had met with the Korean Chief of
Staff in Saigon. A few days later, the White House learned that Ky expressed
the opinion to his Korean guest that "although the US wants a bombing halt in
the interest of the number of votes of Vice President Humphrey, it is impossible
without the concurrence of the Vietnamese Government, and there cannot be
the ruination of (numerous) persons for the sake of one person, Vice President
Humphrey."

By the end of October several facts were obvious to the White House:
(1) Bui Diem was in contact with representatives of the Nixon campaign; (2)
these representatives were anxious to have Saigon hold out against a bombing

cessation prior to the elections; and (3) Vice President Ky was not favorably disposed toward a pre-election bombing halt which, he thought, was designed to enhance the election prospects of Vice President Humphrey.

III. LBJ Orders Surveillance of Mrs. Chennault

That these activities were causing concern at the top level of the Government is clear from a cable Secretary Rusk sent Ambassador Bunker on October 29. The Secretary of State reported that he had "disturbing information" that "certain political elements" in the United States had attempted to intervene in Saigon. He also added cryptically that he had information that the same political circles had given indications to Hanoi that would be disasterous for South Vietnam. The Secretary concluded that if these facts became known, the American people "would react furiously and our joint effort with South Vietnam would be completely undermined." Rusk reminded Bunker that President Johnson was the best friend GVN had in the world and the President expected Thieu's "understanding and full cooperation in the present situation." At this point, Thieu was balking and LBJ was determined to halt the bombing, hopefully with the South Vietnamese President's blessing, but without it if necessary.

> Comment: I have been unable to turn up any information which sheds light on what Rusk had in mind when he referred to overtures to Hanoi by the same political circles which had been in contact with Saigon.

On October 29, a concerted effort began to determine more precisely what Bui Diem and his GOP contacts were about. On that date, Attorney General

Clark approved a phone tap on the SVN Embassy and the following day a tap on the residence of Bui Diem. On October 30, President Johnson ordered the FBI to initiate physical and technical surveillance on Mrs. Chennault. A 24-hour physical surveillance was immediately established, but the wiretap was not installed. Her residence phone at the Watergate was routed through a switchboard, and the FBI determined that it would be too risky to attempt to install a tap in view of the political sensitivity of the coverage effort. Physical surveillance of the SVN Embassy was also initiated on October 30, so that by that date full coverage of visitors and phone calls into and out of the Embassy was established.

For the week prior to the elections, Mrs. Chennault was a frequent visitor to the SVN Embassy and placed periodic phone calls to Bui Diem.

On November 2, she placed a particularly important call. She told Ambassador Diem that she had received a message from her "boss" (not further identified) which he wanted her to give personally to Diem. She said the

message was that he was to "hold on, we're going to win" and that her boss
had also said, "hold on, he understands all of it."

She repeated that this was the only message, "he said please tell
your boss (apparently President Thieu) to hold on." Mrs. Chennault advised
that her boss had just called from New Mexico.

> Comment: This message prompted an interesting response
> from President Johnson. On November 11, the
> White House asked the FBI for the exact arrival
> and departure times for then Vice Presidential
> candidate Agnew's visit to Albuquerque on November 2.
> This information was promptly provided and the
> next day President Johnson requested the FBI to
> make a careful check of all out-going phone calls
> made by Agnew and his staff from Albuquerque.
>
> The FBI checked out all calls placed from the
> phones aboard Agnew's plane and from pay phones
> at the airport. Six long distance calls turned
> up: one from Agnew to Dean Rusk and five calls
> placed by Kent Crane, two of which were to Bob
> Hitt at the Nixon-Agnew Headquarters in Washington
> while the others were to individuals apparently
> not associated with the campaign.
>
> On November 13, President Johnson personally called
> C. D. DeLoach at the FBI (the LBJ-DeLoach relation-
> ship would make an interesting study in itself).
> He requested the results of the investigation and
> was given the information about the phone calls.
> LBJ instructed that the calls from Crane to Bob Hitt
> be checked to determine if Mrs. Chennault could
> have been reached at the Nixon-Agnew Hdqrs. He also
> requested that a check be made to determine if any
> phone calls were placed on November 2nd by Mrs.
> Chennault or the SNV Embassy to New Mexico, Texas,
> or Los Angeles. The FBI made a check and determined
> that there was no record of any such calls having
> been made; moreover, Mrs. Chennault had been at home
> until late afternoon when she departed for Baltimore
> and could not have been reached at the Nixon-Agnew
> Headquarters. Of course, there was no way to determine
> if Bob Hitt had served as a conduit for the transmission
> of a message from Albuquerque.

After this intensive investigation into the
activities of the Vice President-Elect, LBJ
had to conclude that there was no hard information available to identify Agnew as Mrs.
Chennault's "boss".

IV. The Chennault Affair Threatens to Blow the Roof Off

On November 4, Saville Davis called the SVN Embassy and asked for
an appointment with Bui Diem. He said he wanted to check out a report received
from a correspondent in Saigon. When told that the Ambassador was not available,
Davis replied that the story he was checking out contained the elements of
a major scandal which involved the South Vietnamese Ambassador and which
would affect Nixon if the Monitor published it. He speculated that if the
story were printed, it would create a great deal of excitement.

Davis went to the Embassy where he remained for 45 minutes before
leaving for the White House. It is not known whether he saw Diem and it is
not clear that he had wind of the Chennault affair, although it appears likely
that he did.

Later in the day, Bromley Smith of the White House staff called
DeLoach and stated that LBJ had instructed him to request that all copies
of messages being forwarded to the White House in connection with the coverage
of the SVN Embassy and Mrs. Chennault be treated in the strictest confidence
and that all precautions be taken to protect these communications. Smith said
that the situation might very well "blow the roof off of the political race yet."

Comment: Another unanswered question is why Davis did
not write the story of the Chennault affair

TOP SECRET/NODIS/HARVAN/DOUBLE PLUS ███ **SANITIZED** 10.

per sec 1.4(c)

the talks was made "to help Nixon, and had Saigon gone to the conference table, Humphrey would probably have won." There is some evidence to suggest that within Saigon political circles opposition to participation in the expanded talks by GVN was clearly linked to US political factors, but that is beyond the scope of this report and will be covered in detail in another paper. It is sufficient to say, however, that the foreign policy implications of the Chennault affair are directly related to Saigon's refusal to go to Paris and President Johnson had good reason to be concerned about the ramifications of the efforts which he thought Mrs. Chennault and Bui Diem were undertaking.

The most sensitive -- and perhaps most troubling -- aspect of the Chennault affair was the use of Federal investigatory and intelligence agencies in an operation which had highly political domestic implications. While technical and physical surveillance of a foreign embassy is a legitimate action, it may be that a fine line was crossed when the full investigatory powers of the Federal Government were brought to bear on the private activities of a private citizen. At no point was there any evidence that Mrs. Chennault was engaged in illegal or subversive activities. While her contacts were undoubtedly related to the conduct of foreign affairs, they were essentially political in nature. Civil libertarians -- and many less sensitive people -- might correctly believe that private contacts between a private citizen and an ambassador of an allied government do not merit 24-hour physical surveillance and wiretapping (which would have been initiated if it could have been done discretely).

TOP SECRET/NODIS/HARVAN/DOUBLE PLUS ███

TOP SECRET/NODIS/HARVAN/DOUBLE PLUS ███ **SANITIZED**   11.

per sec 1.4(c)

The most interesting aspect of the affair, however, was the personal
interest of President Johnson in whether Agnew was involved. At the time LBJ
ordered the FBI to check on all phone calls placed by Agnew in Albuquerque,
Angew was Vice President-Elect of the United States. One might ask what
possible purpose could have been served at this late date by such an investigation,
assuming even that some substantial evidence had been turned up. More important,
if such an investigation can be ordered into the activities of the Vice President-
Elect, what protection does a private citizen have against governmental surveillance
However, those familiar with LBJ's use of the FBI as a personal Pinkerton agency
during the 1964 campaign can't really be surprised at anything the former
President did: he was not a man to leave stones unturned when some tool was
available to do the digging.

                              TCH